The Scandal of
EMPIRE

The Scandal of
EMPIRE

 *India and the Creation
of Imperial Britain*

NICHOLAS B. DIRKS

THE BELKNAP PRESS OF HARVARD UNIVERSITY PRESS
Cambridge, Massachusetts · London, England
2006

Library of Congress Cataloging-in-Publication Data

Dirks, Nicholas B., 1950–
The scandal of empire : India and the creation of imperial Britain /
Nicholas B. Dirks.
p. cm.
Includes bibliographical references and index.
ISBN 0-674-02166-5 (alk. paper)
1. Hastings, Warren, 1732–1818—Trials, litigations, etc.
2. Burke, Edmund, 1729–1797.
3. East India Company—History—18th century.
4. Political corruption—India—History—18th century.
5. India—Colonization—History—18th century. I. Title.

DS473.D57 2006
954.02'98092—dc22   2005057042

⇥ *Contents* ⇤

✎ *Illustrations* ✎

⇥ *Preface* ⇤

As a historian of India, principally southern India, with interests in matters ranging from political sovereignty to caste society, and from precolonial state processes to the British colonial state, how did I come to write a book about Edmund Burke and Warren Hastings? The spectacular impeachment trial of Hastings is a natural subject for any historian of India or empire. Indeed, it has been much written about. Historians of India have explored the meanings and larger contexts of the various events featured in the trial; imperial historians have investigated the political contexts for the trial in England as well as for the history of the East India Company; and literary critics along with cultural historians have used the trial to think about some of the larger implications of early colonial rule—its anxieties and ambivalences, as well as its significance for the unfolding of the gendered, racial, cultural, and national entailments of early empire. What more could I contribute to the discussion?

Significantly, I began thinking seriously about the trial during the years when President Clinton was impeached. The impeachment of Hastings had been the second last use of impeachment provisions in England, though there had been talk of impeaching Hastings's associate, Elijah Impey, who was the first supreme court justice in India and the man who had condemned Hastings's nemesis, Nanda Kumar, to death by hanging in 1775. The last impeachment also had India connections; in 1806 Henry Dundas, who had been for years the most powerful dispenser of patronage in his position as member and then president of the board of control for the Company, was brought up for impeachment on grounds of corruption. But in the United States, impeachment took on a more modern career, with (unsuccessful) prosecutions of Andrew Jackson and Bill Clinton, and preliminary charges against Richard Nixon around the Watergate break-in and cover-up. In the last decades of the twentieth century, impeachment has provided some of the great moral spectacles of our time, and allowed us to see in dramatic ways the peculiar relationships that have grown up around, and in recent years changed significantly, political ethics, public responsibility, and private virtue. The impeachment trial of Warren Hastings takes on special interest in this context.

But if I came to consider writing about the impeachment trial in the wake of the massive effort to bring down a relatively progressive President—an effort that failed to impeach but succeeded in distracting attention from many of Clinton's domestic policy agendas while probably bringing Bush to the presidency—the urgency of rethinking the origins of British empire increased dramatically after I had begun the project. I spent a year of sabbatical leave in 2000–2001 reading the transcripts of the trial, consulting archival collections in the British Library, and reading works of and about Edmund Burke, only to return to my teaching duties in New York a week before September 11, 2001. Soon thereafter, the U.S. administration began to use the terrible events of that day to provide an alibi to attack Iraq and establish what increasingly looked like, and even came to be popularly described as, an American imperial presence in the Gulf. The use of the charge of weapons of mass destruction as the false pretext for the invasion, the direct economic interests of many of the masters of war, the atrocities associated with the invasion and the occupation as well as with the internment facility in Abu Ghraib, all began to look very similar to an earlier period of imperial history, that of the British conquest and occupation of India in the eighteenth century. As I thought about the various historical parallels, I realized how important it was to revisit the most scandalous origins of imperial history in Britain. And I realized that the impeachment trial of Hastings, far from being the moment when scandal was genuinely expunged from the imperial record, played a much more complicated role in the history of empire. As I continued to research and write, I felt I was writing the history not just of the eighteenth century, but of the present as well. Never has the history of the eighteenth century seemed so self-evidently relevant.

If the corruption of power and money has been the main story of empire, then and now, I have always been more interested in the justifications of corruption than in corruption itself. In particular, I have focused on the way in which sovereignty was a key part of the imperial story: how the contradictions of early empire played themselves out through theories about sovereignty in India, assumptions about the meaning of military victories and political treaties, and proclamations about legitimacy—both for the East India Company in relation to the English state and for British imperial activity in relation to the sovereignty of the Mughal rulers (as well as myriad other Indian political powers). Few contemporary commentators were unaware of the need to address issues of sovereignty in the Indian context, and no contemporary was as exercised about the duplicity of Company rule as Edmund Burke. Nevertheless, the sad irony was that the impeachment trial seemed to consume this concern. By the end of the trial there was a consensus that the 1765 grant by the Mughal ruler to the Company of the "Diwani" (the right to collect revenue in Bengal) was a sufficient basis on which to predicate imperial occupation. At the same time, the Company was newly ennobled as the legitimate agent of British interests in political as well as commercial and economic matters. The trial had brought the corruption, venality, and duplicity of the British presence in India to the attention of the world, and yet in enacting the reformist agenda of Edmund Burke, it had ironically made empire seem a natural extension of British sovereign and commercial rights and interests. Burke's extraordinary empathy for colonized India and Indians, something that has seemed to many as inconsistent with his conservative political ideas, is still moving, even as it unintentionally helped to sanctify the colonization of India. After the trial, as scandal become identified increasingly with India itself—Indian customs and culture—it became the principal justification for empire rather than the unfortunate means of empire's creation.

My previous book, on the colonial history of caste, explored this shift in how empire was justified, and I was already well aware of the imperial role in the representation (not to mention the constitution) of India as a land of backward and barbaric custom. The aim of the present book has been to understand how the well-known scandals of the East India Company in the eighteenth century became either forgotten or subsumed within the larger and more compelling imperial narrative of an exhausted land that virtually invited the British to conquer it. Historians of India have frequently observed that the social, political, cultural, and economic buoyancy of India in the eighteenth century was not just forgotten but suppressed by a narrative in which the decay of India became the primary reason for the ease, and inevitability, of European conquest. These same historians have documented with increasingly detailed and robust arguments the extent to which the subcontinent was far from decadent in the decades before imperial conquest. But while most historians have also been well aware of the scandals of early empire, the implications of these scandals, either for the impoverishment of India's own history or for the history of Britain itself in the late eighteenth and early twentieth centuries, have been little noted of late. They have also been largely ignored in much of the recent resurgence of writing, either in imperial history or for that matter the new critical histories of colonial South Asia, much of it inspired by work in subaltern studies, and concerned with the late nineteenth and twentieth centuries in the larger historical context of nationalist mobilization.

As I delved into the scandals of empire, I soon realized that along with the rampant greed of Company traders (who were far more interested in using Company access and perquisites for the purposes of their own private trade than they were in stocking the coffers of their employer), the greatest scandal in fact concerned the matter of sovereignty—the principal subject of my own early work. Much of the ruinous private trade was in fact predicated on the unscrupulous use of a Mughal imperial decree of 1717, which granted a suspension of tariff for some Company trade under limited conditions. This situation set the tone for the systematic misuse and abuse of other grants, treaties, agreements, and understandings, each of which—most dramatically in the case of the Diwani grant of 1765—became the pretext for the assumption of sovereign rights over trade, revenue, law, and land on the part of a monopoly joint stock company that was at the same time systematically violating the terms of its own relationship to the Crown and Parliament of England. As I read further into the archive, I found myself rereading debates over the relative sovereignty of different Indian rulers, some of which had been principal sources for my own early dissertation work on the princes and principalities of southern India in the eighteenth century. And I realized anew the extent to which even my early "ethnohistorical" efforts to unpack the indigenous meanings of sovereignty in the eighteenth century had been affected by the imperial context of scandal. In particular, as I situated the arguments of Edmund Burke, the chief interlocutor of this book, alongside those of James MacPherson—the forger of Ossian fame and a major beneficiary of corruption around the nawab of Arcot (the Mughal "governor" of southern India)—I realized that arguments about sovereignty in India were almost always contingent on the particular political relations that were in play during the years of conquest and scandal about which I was now writing.

And so it is that writing this book has brought me back to my first efforts in historical scholarship, begun thirty years ago. While seeking to address topical issues having to do with the crimes and misdemeanors of high office and the reclamation of the idea of empire as a legitimate political form in the new world order of the twenty-first century, I found myself rereading arguments over whether the princes and kings of southern India were independent rulers or part of a complexly layered political system culminating in Mughal sovereignty. I read anew arguments made by Burke and others about the relationship between sovereignty and culture—Burke made the specious (but ironically prophetic) argument that sovereignty depended on a shared religious culture between ruler and ruled, an argument that must have caused embarrassment when he subsequently crafted the universalist basis for British sovereignty in imperial settings. And I came to see once again how historical questions have a way of resurfacing, even as they are regularly reframed and recontextualized over time. It has been refreshing to return to texts and questions I first considered more than a generation ago, and humbling to realize how flawed was my naive belief that I could simply reconstruct Indian understandings of sovereignty without considering contemporaneous European debates about sovereignty. But it has also been gratifying—and more than a little exhilarating—to come to appreciate the ways in which the arcane ethnohistorical ambitions of a young graduate student marinated in the enthusiasms of 1970s area studies continue to seem relevant not just to the larger global history of the eighteenth century, but also to the pressing global issues that confront us today.

I began working on this project during a year of sabbatical leave from Columbia in 2000–2001, and finished writing the book during subsequent summers spent in our quiet and sustaining retreat in the Berkshires. Although I used materials I had consulted in the library of the Tamil Nadu Record Office and the Connemara Library in Madras many years before, I found most of the sources for this project either in the British Library (which includes the records of the India Office as well) or in the library at Columbia University; I am grateful to the archivists and librarians of both institutions for their assistance throughout this project.

My principal interlocutor from the beginning to the end of the project has been my wife and colleague, Janaki Bakhle. Although during my work on the book she struggled with the daunting tasks of writing her dissertation and then her first book, she never hesitated to take time off from her own work to read, edit, and comment on drafts or discuss my persistent questions about Burke's contradictions, the debts of the nawab of Arcot (which she still thinks I haven't explained properly), or more generally how to frame this book for the multiple audiences I hoped to address. She has lived with this book as much as I have over the past five years, and yet not only has maintained her (and my) enthusiasm for the project throughout, but also has made sure that I worked to keep a balance between the historical subject and the contemporary issues that have made this history so relentlessly compelling.

I owe much to my friend and colleague Partha Chatterjee, who has read the entire book twice and given enthusiastic encouragement and advice along the way. Meanwhile, he has begun his own exciting project to rewrite parts of the imperial narrative of eighteenth-century India. We indulge our preoccupation with the Indian eighteenth century in a graduate seminar we have given together at Columbia each fall since 1998, a seminar where I have tried out many of the ideas behind this book. Gyan Prakash, too, read an early chapter and made terrific suggestions at critical stages in the development of this project.

I have benefited from the opportunity to give lectures based on this project in a number of venues, including Columbia, New School University, Harvard, Heidelberg, UCLA, and three conferences: one on history in Ann Arbor, Michigan, and the other two on empire in Santa Fe, New Mexico, and Volos, Greece. Akeel Bilgrami, Stathis Gourgouris, Mahmood Mamdani, Peter Perdue, Sudipta Sen, Ann Stoler, and Sanjay Subrahmanyam have all given their critical encouragement and made important contributions to the conceptualization of the project. I am also grateful to Sunil Agnani, Andrew Arato, Amiya Bagchi, David Bromwich, Jane Burbank, Jean Cohen, Fred Cooper, Fernando Coronil, Val Daniel, Peter Dimock, Prasenjit Duara, Dedi Felman, Chris Fuller,

Catherine Hall, Adeeb Khalid, Arjun Mahey, Ussama Makdisi, Karuna Mantena, Rama Mantena, Carole McGranahan, Uday Mehta, Aamir Mufti, Gyan Pandey, Neni Panourgia, Anupama Rao, David Scott, Patricia Seed, Tom Trautmann, and Deborah Valenze. My graduate students at Columbia have provided suggestions, encouragement, and critique through the years I worked on this book: I would especially like to thank Yogesh Chandrani, Rahul Govind, Anush Kapadia, Elizabeth Kolsky, Nauman Naqvi, and Karin Zitzewitz. Philip Stern, whose dissertation on the East India Company in the seventeenth century will soon be the basis for a landmark book, read an early draft and made extremely detailed comments.

Joyce Seltzer has been a wonderful editor. She evinced excitement for the project from our first conversation about the trial of Warren Hastings and has made me think seriously about the obligations historians have to write for a broader public. She kept me focused on the details of preparing the book for publication even when I was distracted by various crises in my new position in university administration at Columbia. And she arranged for two extremely useful readings of an earlier draft of the manuscript by readers whose astute comments made me view the book afresh from the perspective of British history and historiography. Julie Carlson has immeasurably improved my prose and citations. I am extremely grateful to Yogesh Chandrani and Natalja Czarneki, who labored tirelessly to help me locate, and then footnote, many of the sources for the project, as well as the illustrations in the book. I must also acknowledge the immense debt I have to my mother, Annabelle Dirks, for supporting this project in innumerable ways.

In writing about the history of empire, I have been inspired in particular by the work and teaching of two mentors, Bernard Cohn and Edward Said. Bernard (Barney) Cohn was my graduate advisor at the University of Chicago and continued as my unofficial advisor for the rest of his life. He was an erudite scholar and incisive critic of colonial history in South Asia; his pathbreaking writing and teaching on South Asia helped to reinvent imperial history and bring it into serious engagement with the study of early modern and modern South Asia. Edward Said, whose monumental work *Orientalism* was published just as I was leaving graduate school, launched the larger field of critical colonial studies and cast into sharp relief the continuing power of colonial knowledge. I was fortunate to become his colleague and friend when I moved to Columbia in 1997, and I discussed this project extensively with him. Neither will be able to read the book, since they both died within months of each other in the autumn of 2003. *The Scandal of Empire* is dependent on their work, and dedicated to their memory.

James Rennell, "A General View of the Principal Roads and Divisions of
Hindoostan, 1792." From *Memoir of a Map of Hindoostan: or, The Mogul
Empire* . . . (Calcutta: Editions Indian, 1976 [1793]).

⊰ *Prologue* ⊱

Every schoolchild in Britain, at least during the years of Britain's imperial glory, knew of the atrocity of the "Black Hole" of Calcutta. According to the canonical account, the Mughal governor, or nawab, of Bengal, upon capturing the English fort of Calcutta in June 1756, forced all remaining English prisoners, along with a motley collection of Portuguese, Armenian, and other soldiers, into a detention cell used by the British to house their most troublesome prisoners. On the stifling night of June 20, this cell, known as the "Black Hole," became a death trap for the 146 unfortunate souls who were crammed into the tiny eighteen- by fourteen-foot space, which had only two small windows "strongly barred with iron, from which we could receive scarce any the least circulation of fresh air." In the morning, when the guards finally reopened the room, 123 of the prisoners were dead, "smothered in the Black-Hole prison." As Jonathan Holwell,—the self-appointed scribe among the survivors—put it, "The annals of the world cannot produce an incident like it in any degree or proportion to all the dismal circumstances attending it."[1]

An unparalleled event to be sure, the Black Hole became a legend of and for the atrocities committed by the natives of India against the heroic traders of the East India Company, at least until the atrocities of the 1857 "Sepoy Mutiny"—when English men, women, and children were slaughtered in Kanpur and Lucknow—eclipsed the earlier ones and filled the schoolbooks with new parables of the horrors of empire. Although the Black Hole event was little reported at the time—only coming to the attention of the English authorities in London a year later when Holwell himself arrived by ship—it was seen in retrospect as the necessary occasion for the defeat of the nawab (provincial governor) in late June 1757. Holwell himself, then the governor of Bengal, made sure to erect a monument of the Black Hole in a central square in Calcutta in 1760. He profited personally as well as politically from the sympathy extended to him for his woeful part in the atrocity that prefaced the recapture of Calcutta and the assumption of dramatically new powers over Bengal.

Holwell wrote his account of the atrocity during the winter of 1757, when he spent five months aboard the *Syren* sloop in transit from Calcutta to London. His narrative gives pitiful details of the deadly night. Desperate for air, the men disrobed, drank their own sweat, and clambered for position in their pit of despair. "Figure to yourself, my friend, if possible, the situation of a hundred and forty six wretches, exhausted by continual fatigue and action, thus crammed together in a cube of about eighteen feet, in a close sultry night, in Bengal," he wrote, before describing in melodramatic detail the situation itself.[2] Friends dropped dead with growing regularity: "I traveled over the dead, and repaired to the further end of it, just opposite the other window, and seated myself on the platform between Mr. Dumbleton and captain Stevenson; the former just then expiring . . . Here my poor friend Mr. Edward Eyre came staggering over the dead to me, and with his usual coolness and good nature, asked me how I did? But fell and expired before I had time to make him a reply."[3]

As for Holwell, he felt his own death was unavoidable, only lamenting "its slow approach, tho' . . . my breathing grew short and painful." While Holwell took care not to blame the nawab for any deliberate cruelty, the prison guards were contemptible. "Can it gain belief, that this scene of misery proved entertainment to the brutal wretches without? But so it was; and they took care to keep us supplied with water, that they might have the satisfaction of seeing us fight for it, as they phrased it, and held up lights to the bars, that they might lose no part of the inhuman diversion." But the story was full of internal contradictions: the ease of Holwell's movement was belied by the claims about numbers of people in such a small space, the windows were apparently barred shut but nevertheless the guards enjoyed peering in, and there was even great uncertainty about who was actually inside the cell, dead or alive.[4]

According to Holwell, he himself was found alive the next morning, and immediately hauled before the nawab, who was incensed by the fact that he had found no treasure in the fort. When Holwell tried to describe to the nawab the horrible suffering of the prisoners, the nawab merely "stopt me short, with telling me, he was well informed of great treasure being buried, or secreted, in the fort, and that I was privy to it; and if I expected favour, must discover it." But it was not to be found, possibly because it had already been removed, perhaps by Governor Drake, who had retreated from, or in Holwell's prose "deserted," the fort with fifty-nine merchants and military men a few days before.[5] Part of the mystery surrounding why Holwell himself did not quit the fort revolves around another possibility, namely that he was arranging for the transfer of some of the treasury's contents for his own use. Historians have begun to cast considerable doubt on Holwell's general account of the events during the siege and leading up to the infamous night of June 20, suggesting that even the entry to the fort of the nawab's soldiers might have been prearranged.[6] Moreover, serious historians doubt that the story of the Black Hole itself is true.[7] At the very least, it seems likely that most of the deaths of Englishmen in the fort were the result of combat rather than imprisonment, however unpleasant imprisonment might have been. Whatever else happened, the account of the Black Hole turns out to rely entirely on Holwell's "eyewitness" narrative; all but one of the fourteen standard accounts of the Black Hole have been traced back to Holwell's general narrative, and the fourteenth was narrated sixteen years later.

If the great atrocity story of eighteenth-century imperial history was fabricated, it was of course based on the facts surrounding the nawab's efforts to drive the British out of Bengal. When Siraj-ud-Daula became nawab in April of 1756, taking over affairs of state from his grandfather, Alivardi Khan, who had just died at age eighty, he was well aware that the British were engaged in more than simple trade of the sort they claimed. Even one British sea captain, Captain Rennie, wrote about the injustice accorded the nawabs by various agents of the Company just after the fall of Calcutta (without a mention of the so-called Black Hole): "The injustice to the Moors consists in that, being by their courtesy permitted to live here as merchants—to protect and judge what natives were our servants, and to trade custom free—we under that pretence protected all the Nabob's servants that claimed our protection, though they were neither our servants nor our merchants, and gave our *dustucks* or passes to numbers of natives to trade custom free, to the great prejudice of the Nabob's revenue; nay, more, we levied large duties upon goods brought into our districts from the very people that permitted us to trade custom free, and by numbers of impositions . . . caused eternal clamour and complaints against us at Court."[8] It was small wonder that the nawab had become concerned, and no surprise either that he began to feel that the Company's treasure represented ill-gotten gains at his own expense. But however one might represent the siege of Calcutta, the most conspicuous violence had been done to the Indian part of the town, which was set ablaze by Company soldiers on the first word of the nawab's advance.

For the British, the fall of Calcutta was short-lived, reversed dramatically by the victory at Plassey in 1757. Plassey itself was not a major military victory—despite the reputation it subsequently received around the putative military genius of Robert Clive—so much as it was the negotiated outcome of the decision by Mir Jafar to conspire with the English. But by 1757, the British had begun on a trajectory of military conquest and occupation that gave them control, at least for a time, not just of growing swaths of India, but of Indian history too.[9] It is the story of this last, and perhaps most important, conquest that constitutes the real subject of this book. Built on fabrication, colonial history mirrors the general distortions and displacements of imperial self-representation—the use of imputed barbarism to justify, and even ennoble, imperial ambition. As this book shows, empire was only able to realize itself once its ignominious origins were recast, once its scandal could lead to, and make necessary, the triumph of empire itself. But first we must turn to the scandals themselves, for they will provide the themes that make the fabrications of empire relevant not just for those who were colonized, but for those who did the colonizing as well. For in the scandals of empire we see not just the basis for the creation of British imperialism, but also the origins of modern understandings of corruption, sovereignty, public virtue, the market economy, the bureaucratic state, history, and even tradition, the final repository of scandal for empire.

A 1788 caricature showing Edmund Burke about to hang Warren Hastings, with Lord North and Richard Sheridan as accomplices.

❈ 1 ❈

Scandal

Europe is literally the creation of the Third World.
—FRANTZ FANON, *THE WRETCHED*
OF THE EARTH, 1965

Empire was always a scandal for those who were colonized. It is less well known that empire began as a scandal even for those who were colonizers. Imperial expansion for England began either with the explorations of adventurers and often less-than-honorable men (such as pirates) or with the outright expulsion of less-than-desirable subjects. One of the many lessons of America for England was the need to control the circulation of its own people. Otherwise they would first claim to be more English than the English—startled into identity politics and national claims by their violent if often also intimate encounters with other "races," then they would siphon off the potential profits of empire, and finally they would declare independence. And if the loss of America led to the heightened realization of the importance of India, it also heightened concern about scandals of the East. And there was scandal aplenty.

The East India Company was launched in 1600, but it conducted its first century in relatively desultory fashion, establishing coastal forts; engaging in trade; forming alliances; contesting the Portuguese, the Dutch, and the French; and on occasion attempting to take on the Mughals themselves. Late in the century, the Company tried to develop an imperial foothold, without success. The Mughal empire was at its peak in the seventeenth century, when Maratha power rose across western and southern India in the wake of the withdrawal of Vijayanagara rule. Fortunes were made, battles were fought, trade was expanded, and territories were claimed, but the seeds of empire were slow in germinating; the British imperial presence did not take on major significance, even for Britain, until the "long eighteenth century" commenced in 1688. The Glorious Revolution might have been designed principally to alleviate the political turmoil of the previous century, but it also had important economic effects, not least the establishment of the English stock market. And the most prominent stock shares traded on Exchange Alley were of East India Company. Empire and capitalism were born hand in hand, and they both worked to spawn the modern British state.

Scandal was the crucible in which both imperial and capitalist expansion was forged. When the East India Company's charter was technically forfeited in 1693, Company shares were used to influence parliamentary support for charter renewal. In 1695 the report of the parliamentary investigation into the developing scandal over quick fortunes made through bribery and insider trading led to the dismissal of the speaker of the House of Commons, the impeachment of the lord president of the council, and the imprisonment of the governor of the East India Company. If the Company did in the end secure its renewal, the experience left a bad taste, suggesting to many that the only choice was between a licensed monopoly and a free-for-all in which pirate vessels could vie with East Indiamen for control over a new global marketplace, as well as new territories. Nevertheless, the Company not only survived into the new century, it soon also became a steady source of wealth for parliamentarian and investor alike. In addition, the Company took much of the credit for—and profits from—the new trade in tea. In the last years of the seventeenth century and the first of the eighteenth, tea from China, laced with sugar from the West Indies, became the staple that it has remained in the English diet. Spices, silk, cotton, and an increasing array of other Asian commodities established Britain's dependence on the global economy even as they secured growing legitimacy for the role of the East India Company.

But scandal, and its deep association with mercantile trade and imperial venture, hardly disappeared. In fact, the eighteenth century could be said to be the long century of imperial scandal, a time when trade and empire led to successive crises around the fundaments of English politics, culture, and society. By 1788, when Edmund Burke passionately denounced imperial excess at the spectacular impeachment trial of India's governor-general Warren Hastings, it had become generally recognized throughout England that India had been pillaged by a growing succession of increasingly unscrupulous nabobs. (Nabob was the term used for Englishmen who returned from the East with huge fortunes that allowed them to live like princes, with "nabob" itself an English corruption of "nawab," the term used for governors of provinces in the Mughal empire.) In a speech about the need to regulate the East India Company in 1783, Burke had painted a terrifying picture of nabobs marrying into the families of the old gentry, buying their way into Parliament, and destroying stable patterns of investment and economy.[1]

Imperial corruption had been at its highest point well before the time of Hastings, cresting during Robert Clive's years of greatest influence—from the 1750s through the 1770s. And there had been two major and several minor parliamentary inquiries into Eastern scandal and a successful—if somewhat limited—attempt at regulatory legislation, in 1773, amid many other efforts to stem the rising tide of corruption. But major concern about this corruption came later, only preoccupying the metropolitan conscience in the 1780s, a new era of reform both at home and abroad. During this decade, the Pitt Act of 1784, which was designed to rein in Company excesses, was one of the most important measures passed by Parliament.

The most significant inquiries concerned the personal activities and acquisitions of Robert Clive. Clive, later knighted and christened the "founder" of empire, was unabashed in his extraction of loot and his collection of "presents." He was almost brought to disgrace because of his insistence on keeping a *jaghire* (land grant) given him by Mir Jafar, the nawab of Bengal. This thank-you gift came at the expense of Company profits and was much criticized by Clive's enemies. But Clive was not only able to convince everyone that it was a present from the Mughal emperor (and not part of some sort of underhanded negotiation); he also secured from the Company the right to draw £27,000 a year from the Bengal revenues for the rest of his life.

The Battle of Plassey in 1757 had indeed been the occasion both for the establishment of the first stages of imperial rule in eastern India and for the massive private enrichment of Company servants. The select committee of the House of Commons that sat in 1772–1773 estimated that "presents" worth over two million pounds had been distributed in Bengal between 1757 and 1765.[2] A growing number of Company servants were amassing extraordinary fortunes simply by taking bribes from successful contenders in the internecine quarrels of state.

Presents, as they were called, were perhaps the most direct, and speedy, means of enrichment (and the one preferred by the higher echelons of Company employees), but they were only one way to amass a fortune. While the Company maintained a monopoly on trade between England and India, it allowed great freedom for its servants in India to engage in "country" trade, both up-country trade in India's hinterland and trade between India and other ports in Asia. Despite some impediments for Europeans trading in Bengal in the eighteenth century, profit margins were two to three times what a merchant could expect in Britain, and on some commodities— such as salt, betel nut, and tobacco—that were in effect reserved for European trade, profits in the 1760s were routinely 75 percent or better. The Battle of Plassey led to increased British control over trade to China—both because of new access to commodities such as opium, and because of the amount of new capital circulating in European hands—as well as additional opportunities, and capital, for inland trade.

In southern India during the same period, vast sums were being extracted by Company servants from the nawab of Arcot (the putative governor of the Mughal empire in the south but in fact a largely independent ruler), as fortunes were made not only from trade but also from a complex web of relations centering on his growing indebtedness. Successive Company officials returned from Madras with huge fortunes after only a few years, some returning to London with the promise of a regular salary for representing the nawab in political circles there. Presents were given by the nawab both to these lobbyists, as a way to secure influence with the king, and more immediately to Company representatives, many of whom were senior Company servants, as a way to defer (and supposedly guarantee) repayment of debt. These unscrupulous representatives not only made vast fortunes from extortionate rates of interest, they also came to dictate the nawab's political and military policy in the interest of securing greater revenues. The nawab's vulnerabilities in the faltering Mughal empire were thus translated into ever greater profits for the English.

Perhaps the greatest beneficiary of the nawab's "generosity"—and associated Company policies and politics—was Paul Benfield, who though vilified by Burke in Parliament was never subjected to parliamentary review of the sort experienced either by Clive or Hastings (in 1786, however, he was banished from India by Cornwallis).[3] But associates, representatives, and beneficiaries of the nawab of Arcot continued to exert pressure on Company politics for years: some contemporary observers have suggested that as many as twelve members of Parliament—most of them with parliamentary seats purchased with money from Arcot—continued through much of the century to advance the interests of the nawab.[4]

It is thus small wonder that the growing number of Company servants who returned to England with fortunes to invest in huge estates, titles, and seats in Parliament were called nabobs and roundly condemned, and scorned, by older gentry and rising mercantile elites alike.[5] For some observers, such as Lord Chatham, these nabobs brought with them the corruption of the East: "The riches of Asia have been poured in upon us, and have brought with them not only Asiatic Luxury, but, I fear, Asiatic principles of government. Without connections, without any natural interest in the soil, the importers of foreign gold have forced their way into Parliament by such a torrent of private corruption as no hereditary fortune could resist."[6] That this new "Asiatic corruption" was very like the "old corruption"—the system described by historians as a network not just of any particular class or interest, "but as a secondary political formation, a purchasing-point from which other kinds of economic and social power were gained or enhanced"[7]—only highlights the claim by Chatham that the nabobs had been contaminated by "Asiatic principles of government." Indeed, the more that both political and economic corruption could be pinned on the activities and servants of the East India Company, the better "old corruption"—with its own circuits of patronage, power, and wealth—could protect itself. This fact was nowhere more dramatically illustrated than in the widespread support for Edmund Burke's assault on Hastings—even among many with little specific interest in Company affairs. But if the servants of the Company were seen to carry with them the fruits of this Asiatic corruption, and the accompanying threat to the stability of gentry privilege when they returned to England and played their part in the eighteenth-century transformations of English political economy, the Company itself represented scandal of an even higher order. What was supposed to have been a trading company with an eastern monopoly vested by Parliament had become a rogue state: waging war, administering justice, minting coin, and collecting revenue over Indian territory.

Those Company servants who survived the rigors of the steamy Indian climate not only accumulated massive private fortunes; they also engaged the British state in actions and commitments that occasioned considerable skepticism and sometimes widespread disapproval. The Company waged almost constant warfare, both against the French—making Asia not for the last time a principal theater for European conflict—and against a growing array of Indian armies. Even the much heralded assumption in 1765 of Bengali Diwani rights—the transfer of the right to collect revenue directly from Bengal's landholders—which led to a negotiated commitment to pay Parliament a subvention of £400,000 a year, hardly compensated for Company deficits, which were also the result of the spectacular profiteering of Company "servants." The subvention was in part a massive bribe to Parliament to maintain the Company monopoly, but it was also part of a compromise to stem the force of the assault on the Company from the Chatham Ministry, concerned as it was with the statelike character of the Company.

Indeed, acceptance of the subvention effectively gave the Company sovereign rights over conquered territories.[8] But it also increased financial pressure on the Company, especially when it turned out that Clive's exuberant estimates were vastly exaggerated. Military victories had come at great cost to the Company and the British state, and speculation in Company shares after the assumption of the Diwani put unsustainable pressure on profits. Such financial crises put pressure on Company support at home and often led to greater exploitation in India, where the Diwani led to the outbreak of grievous famine conditions throughout Bengal in 1770. The Diwani also led to an exploding bull market in Company shares, a bubble that burst by the end of the decade after news of Company military setbacks.[9] By 1772, the Company had not only brought about a world credit crash; it had also come close to bankruptcy, in both financial and political terms.

The parliamentary inquiry into the acquisitions of Lord Clive in 1772, combined with the near bankruptcy of the Company, occasioned the passing of Lord North's India Bill of 1773, also known as the Regulating Act. Hailed as an effort to control the independence of the Company leadership in India, in reality the act was little more than a justification for bailing the Company proprietors out of a huge financial hole, since Lord North had arranged for the state to lend the Company £1.4 million to avert bankruptcy.[10] The bailout in part demonstrated the extent to which Parliament itself had come under the sway of nabob money and influence, because it had become clear from the previous decade how many sitting members had significant shares, and often proprietary interests, in Company fortunes. Clive himself had been completely vindicated by Parliament in 1772, despite widespread concern about the means he had used to assemble his fortune, not to mention policies to which he had committed the Company. Horace Walpole wrote,

> The oppressions of India and even of the English settled there under the rapine and cruelties of the servants of the Company had now reached England and created general clamour here. Some books had been published, particularly by one Bolts and Mr. Dow, the first a man of bad character, the latter of a very fair one, which carried the accusations home to Lord Clive; and the former represented him as a monster in assassination, usurpation and extortion, with heavy accusations of his monopolizing in open defiance of the orders of the Company . . . To such monopolies were imputed the late famine in Bengal and the loss of three millions of the inhabitants. A tithe of these crimes was sufficient to inspire horror.[11]

Such criticisms and scruples notwithstanding, Clive was still seen by many in Britain as the only man—whatever his moral character—with the courage and the vision to secure Company interests in India.

Robert Clive, by all accounts an impetuous man who was judged a bully by his contemporaries, had become a "writer" for the East India Company at the tender age of seventeen, and had begun his Indian career in Madras. After establishing a reputation for heroism in southern India (especially in the famous siege of Arcot), he was given primary responsibility for relieving Calcutta after its seizure by the nawab Siraj-ud-Daula in 1756. His troops defeated the nawab at Plassey, a haphazard encounter that only emerged as an English victory because of Mir Jafar's negotiated support for Clive. And yet the Battle of Plassey sealed Clive's reputation as the conqueror of India and founder of empire. Shortly thereafter he was named governor of Bengal, and then, after a brief return to England between 1760 and 1764, he was sent back as governor with the mandate to restore Company authority and to accept the Diwani (right of revenue collection) over Bengal from the Mughal emperor. Although he only arrived after the more important battle of Baksar was concluded in the Company's favor, he attained his public apotheosis in the acceptance of the Diwani and his inauguration of a new form of territorial rule for the Company. In his speeches in the House of Commons, exhorting parliamentary approbation for and recognition of the extraordinary accomplishments of the Company under his leadership (often in the context of defending himself against charges of personal corruption), he proudly boasted that the Company had been transformed from its earlier status as a band of merchants engaging only in commercial enterprise. He told the House in 1769 that he had been solely responsible for the transformation of Company rule from its origins as a minor and inconsequential trading operation to a great sovereign power. For now, he claimed, "The East India Company are . . . sovereigns of a rich, populous, fruitful country in extent beyond France and Spain united; they are in possession of the labour, industry, and manufactures of twenty millions of subjects; they are in actual receipt of between five and six millions a year. They have an army of fifty thousand men. The revenues of Bengal are little short of four million sterling a year."[12] Three years later he spoke even more confidently, asserting, "By progressive steps, the Company have become Sovereigns of that Empire."[13] But in the intervening three years, the famine, the stock crash, and then the collapse of Company fortunes put a rather different spin on his remarks.

Clive's personal actions, then—in particular his acceptance of certain presents as well as his *jaghire* (land grant)—were in the larger scheme of things small beer. On the one hand he explained that it was customary in India to give and receive presents. On the other hand, having compared himself to the nawab at the same time he charged all of his Company colleagues with corruption, he claimed his own relative virtue. As he went on to say when concluding his defense in 1772: "A great prince was dependent on my pleasure, an opulent city lay at my mercy; its richest bankers bid against each other for my smiles; I walked through vaults which were thrown open to me alone, piled on either hand with gold and jewels! Mr. Chairman, at this moment I stand astonished at my own moderation."[14] Although Clive was vindicated, his self-defense led to many more questions, both about his own actions and about the character of Company rule in India, leaving a taint on the origin story of empire for many years to come.

Clive himself had chastised Parliament both for insufficiently appreciating his contributions and for not acting boldly enough to consolidate Company gains. "It was natural to suppose," he argued, that such a glorious imperial conquest "would have merited the most serious attention of administration, that in concert with the Court of Directors, they would have considered the nature of the Company's charter and adopted a plan adequate to such possessions. No they did not. They treated it rather as a South Sea Bubble, than as anything solid and substantial."[15] But given the misfortunes of the Company between 1769 and 1772, these comments were largely dismissed, and although Clive was allowed to retire with his fortune intact, the select committee recommended a different kind of intervention than that argued for by Clive. Indeed, Clive correctly understood the consequent Regulating Act of 1773 as a personal rebuke. He committed suicide—though perhaps in part for reasons of ill-health—the next year.[16]

Warren Hastings was elected governor of Bengal in 1772, and elevated to the position of governor-general in 1773, precisely to oversee the reform of Company activities in India. Hastings's first act was to take direct control of the financial administration of Bengal. He also took direct responsibility for the administration of justice in Bengal, establishing a supreme court in Calcutta and implementing his own plan to draft new codes of civil law for Hindus and Muslims. With a hefty annual salary of £25,000, he was supposed to not only be above corruption but also root it out across the range of Company activities. He was given the difficult task of ensuring a reasonable financial return for the proprietors and political accountability for Parliament while keeping the peace, assuming new forms of administrative control, and extending Company operations more generally. Successful in much of his agenda, he spent most of his time in an epic struggle with Philip Francis, one of four appointees to

Hastings's executive council. Francis opposed all of Hastings's expansionist activities in an enmity that became personal because of competing political ambitions and mutual disdain, which included moral censure over sexual scandal on both sides. Injured in a duel with Hastings in 1780, ostensibly over the war against the Marathas, Francis returned to England intent on continuing his war by other means. He became the close confidante of Edmund Burke, and soon after his arrival in England began to supply the detailed information that led directly to Burke's decision to pursue Hastings's impeachment.[17]

The famous Articles of Charge that were drawn up by Burke and presented to the House of Commons in 1786 provide a clear picture of the new forms of scandal that had accumulated around Hastings in the decade after Clive's departure from the scene. Hastings was an educated man, unlike Clive. Schooled at Westminster, a committed administrator rather than a soldier, he worked his way patiently up the Company ladder and got into trouble for reasons that even Burke construed as having more to do with political ambition than with personal gain. In holding Hastings accountable to Parliament, Burke believed that he was interrogating the duplicity of empire itself. The two principal charges concerned Hastings's relations with Indian rulers. In the first charge, Burke argued that Hastings had deliberately violated the Company's agreement with the raja of Benares, making a variety of unauthorized demands on him and ultimately provoking him to rebel, an act that led to the raja's defeat and the annexation of Benares in 1781. In the second charge, Burke held that Hastings had also violated the Company's guarantee in regard to the lands held as *jaghires* by the mother and grandmother of the nawab of Awadh (who were also known as the "begums of

Awadh" because of their high rank). Other major charges brought by Burke against Hastings were of a more traditional sort. Burke alleged that Hastings had received "presents" in a way (and on a scale) much like Clive before him, though he acknowledged that many of the documented presents in fact were handed over to the Company. He also charged Hastings with using a wide variety of contracts, from selling opium to provisioning the army, for reasons of patronage.

And yet Hastings came to be known as the savior of empire in large part because his relations with the rulers of Awadh and Benares were driven by his assessed need to both protect the territorial gains of Clive and check the expansionist ambitions of the Marathas. In fighting the Marathas, Hastings—like Clive before him—ran up huge debts, and clearly used a variety of irregular means to balance the budget. But he also followed the successful Company strategy of deliberate deception, professing disinterest in expansion while working relentlessly to secure greater and greater power, and territorial authority, over those fertile regions that constituted a buffer between the Mughals to the north and the Marathas to the west. Even though his political methods spanned a period when standards of public virtue and private corruption—especially for the British in India—changed dramatically, his own relative moderation (compared, that is, to Clive) came to seem scandalous from the hindsight of the impeachment trial. In fact, most of the presents that could be documented were taken before the 1773 Regulating Act went into effect (though even then it had been nominally illegal for Company servants to take presents), and those received afterward were declared to the Company, and in most cases returned. As for the first two charges, Hastings defended himself by noting that both the raja of Benares and the begums of Awadh had forced his hand by engaging in acts of hostility first. He also argued that he had made reasonable demands—given the relations of protection between the Company and both Benares and Awadh—for financial contributions to war efforts that had been precipitated by the threatening activities of the Marathas. But his most successful defense was in fact that his methods had worked, that by the time he stepped down from the governor-generalship he had secured India for the Company. Burke's tirades against Hastings might have been the national expression of a bad conscience, but Burke no more offered to give India back to the Mughals than did Hastings offer to return his early winnings to the Company. Indeed, the trial of Warren Hastings was at one level simply the continuation of earlier parliamentary efforts to take control over a rogue English state, to harness imperial power—and wealth—securely to Britain. And once that was accomplished, whatever the particular political, or financial, fortunes of Warren Hastings, empire would no longer be a scandal.

The trial was in part the extension of the India Act of 1784, known as the Pitt Act. The act was meant to bring the Company under control by stemming its territorial expansion and reforming the politics and finances of the Company and its servants.[18] But while the Company was put under the authority of a board of control that itself was now answerable to the Crown and Parliament, the governor-general was given far greater powers in India than Hastings had possessed. The first new governor to benefit was Lord Cornwallis, fresh from his defeat at Yorktown, but with a reputation for probity and reform that he sustained until his retirement in 1793. Cornwallis implemented new regulations concerning private trade and presents, increased salary scales, and standardized procedures for recruitment and promotion. He also dealt Mysore's Tipu Sultan, adopted son and successor of Haidar Ali, his first major defeat in 1792. His crowning achievement was the Bengal Permanent Settlement of 1793—a fixed-revenue agreement with local landlords *(zamindars)* fashioned in large part from the physiocratic proposals of Philip Francis—that was designed to provide the regular funds necessary to pay new salaries and maintain Company solvency.[19] He was succeeded by John Shore, a Company servant who had been a major player in debates over revenue systems. Shore continued the nonexpansionist policy of Cornwallis. But when the marquess Arthur Wellesley (later known as the "Iron Duke") took the governorship in 1798, the military profile of the Company escalated back to the level of Clive and Hastings. Despite much concern in London and the return of major financial woes, Wellesley used the power that had been conferred on his position to mobilize Company forces once again. His forces defeated, and killed, Tipu Sultan—whose alliance with the French made this victory all the sweeter—and engaged Hyderabad and Awadh. In so doing, Wellesley not only filled in more of the map of British India; he also worked to make the map itself seem the natural outcome of British interest. And unlike Clive and Hastings, he did not get into trouble. Instead, he was catapulted by a new aggressive, and militaristic, nationalism to a position of national hero for his exploits. Empire was no longer a scandal; trade was no longer the primary mission of English enterprise; patriotism in the imperial theater was no longer a vice. Burke had done his work well.

Although Wellesley's profligacy landed the Company in a new set of financial troubles—the India debt rose from £18 million in 1802 to £32 million in 1810—subsequent debates over charter renewal no longer focused on the spectacles of corruption that had characterized the long eighteenth century.[20] But the debt made arguments for free trade increasingly persuasive. When the Company charter was renewed in 1813, all trading privileges and monopolies were removed, save for the tea trade with China. Indeed, the greatest controversy of the renewal debate concerned the role of missionary activity in India; before 1813 missionaries had been prevented from proselytizing in Company territory because of the potential disruption it would cause. The rising influence in Company politics of Charles Grant and William Wilberforce, prominent evangelicals, forced a change, and the directors reluctantly accepted the entry of missionary activity.

The public debate around charter renewal, much of it generated by missionary publicists, worked to focus public attention on spectacular examples of "barbarism" in India. Now when scandal was associated with India, it was attached to Indian customs rather than British activities.[21] Indeed, India became a land of scandal in an entirely new way, with scandal now a feature of generic Indian custom rather than personal English excess. Under new missionary pressure, it became a scandal that the Company allowed the continuation in British territory of the barbaric practices of *sati* (widow burning) or *thuggee* (highway robbery and murder with cultic overtones) or rituals such as "hookswinging" (a form of devotion involving hooks embedded in the back). After the first decade of the nineteenth century, it is hard to imagine a British parliamentarian—Whig or Tory—berating the British in India for their barbarism as Burke had done just a few years before. Even as nabobs were replaced by bureaucrats who were earnest, mostly middle class, and increasingly professional, Indian rulers were progressively converted from their positions as either allies or enemies into puppets of a new imperium. And even as scandal itself became institutionalized, it was displaced onto a civilizational map shared by British progressives and conservatives alike. "Anglicists" such as James Mill and Thomas Macaulay might have criticized Orientalists such as William Jones for their rosy view of India's past and their disinterest in India's potential progress, but they were all committed to the imperial project at least in part because of a shared condemnation of the Indian present.

The new imperial mandate was as congenial to the next generation of Company leaders—including Thomas Munro, Mountstuart Elphinstone, John Malcolm, and Charles Metcalfe—as it would have been much earlier to Clive and Hastings. And although after Wellesley's departure from India in 1805 imperial expansion proceeded in fits and starts, even as it continued to be condemned in Britain for its expense and sometimes for its appearance, it continued unabated for the next half century. The Gurkhas were defeated in 1814–1816, the Marathas were brought down in 1817–1818, Sind was taken in 1843, and Punjab was annexed after the Sikh wars of 1848–1849. By the time Lord Dalhousie annexed Awadh in 1856 there could be little doubt that the Battle of Plassey had inaugurated a century of relentless imperial expansion, whatever dissension there had been either within the Company or between it and the British state. Charles Metcalfe, one of the early nineteenth century's most respected Company grandees, wrote in 1820 what appears now as the creed of all imperial powers to the present day: "I abhor making wars, and meddling with other states for the sake of our aggrandizement—but war thrust upon us, or unavoidably entered into, should, if practicable, be turned to profit by the acquisition of new resources, to pay additional forces to defend what we have, and extend our possessions in future unavoidable wars."[22] As he made clear, while the British preferred not to take responsibility for their imperial aggression—shifting their own agency onto India—they were more than happy to take advantage of Indian "agency" whenever they could. Only the Great Rebellion of 1857 put a stop to formal expansion, but by that time expansion was no longer necessary. What the British state—which finally declared itself as the imperial authority and dismantled what had become the empty shell of Company rule—did not control directly, it could now control just as well by other means.[23]

Despite the taint of scandal that permeates British imperial history, what is perhaps most disturbing in retrospect is the extent to which the scandals that were at the heart of imperial beginnings—not to mention the scandal of empire itself—have been either laundered or converted into narratives of imperial, nationalist, and capitalist triumph. Burke's rhetoric and British reforms have been taken at face value, accepted as the end of an era rather than the basis for its reinvigoration and legitimation. The history of empire—or of the Company—in the eighteenth century has been written about as a problem of management and control, in which scandal was an impediment to the success of the Company rather than endemic to it.[24] At the same time, the overall importance of India for England in the eighteenth century has been largely ignored despite some efforts to break down the barrier between metropolitan and imperial histories.[25] And even historians who have accepted John Seeley's charge that most English history in the eighteenth century took place overseas also accept his conviction that empire was won more by accident than by design, in a "fit of absence of mind."[26]

Yet the scandals that came from both private profiteering and imperial aggrandizement were the necessary features of a system of conquest, expansion, and exploitation that has not only been seriously underplayed in imperial history but virtually erased from the history of early modern Britain. On the one hand, the traditional field of imperial history has been unable to accept either the fundamentally scandalous character of its principal subject or the extent to which that scandal—however much it is conceded to have been disadvantageous for the colonized—has been constitutive of the history both of colonizing nations and the modern world more generally. On the other hand, the history of Britain in the long eighteenth century is still written as if India (or for that matter the East India Company) was almost entirely irrelevant to the main events of the time.[27] New works in imperial history have made increasingly clear that empire has been constitutive for Britain, arguing that even the older work in imperial history that took on global themes has been deeply complicit in the celebration—and naturalization—of the national boundaries of knowledge itself.[28] As Kathleen Wilson has recently suggested, "Empire was, in a very real sense, the frontier of the nation, the place where, under the pressure of contact and exchange, boundaries deemed crucial to national identity—white and black, civilized and savage, law and vengeance—were blurred, dissolved or rendered impossible to uphold."[29]

During the last half century of decolonization, when new nations have been forged with all the contradictory legacies of their histories of imperial subjection and nationalist mobilization, new national histories have also emerged. First born as histories of freedom struggles, these histories have generated counterhistories, which in turn have spawned new kinds of historical controversies and debates. But with all the vital contention in these new fields of history that have challenged the neat divide between history and anthropology (in which history was accorded to Europe and North America, and anthropology was the domain for any real knowledge about the rest of the world), the one point of agreement has consistently been that imperial history had been written in the service of empire itself. Despite widespread recognition of the force of this critique, imperial history has persisted in upholding many of the perspectives of its own imperial past, despite revision, reformulation, and the occasional onslaught from other histories. Astonishingly, much imperial history is today still written as if the task of the historian is to achieve balance, and perspective, in the historical account of the costs and benefits of empire. Indeed, a postimperial sigh of relief has been almost audible in some recent writing, in which the historical stance of objectivity is said to be possible now that historians no longer need to take sides.[30] Imperial history—as is eminently clear from a brief perusal of the new five-volume *Oxford History of the British Empire*—has largely ignored the explosion of revisionist writing that has subjected most histories of empire to withering critique.[31]

New historical writing, much of it from the margins of the historical profession, has begun to excavate the range and intensity of the sometimes invisible, frequently unwritten, and often long-delayed effects of colonial rule on the colonized.[32] Indeed, it is now widely accepted that colonialism had a far greater influence on the colonized world than has been recognized even in accounts that take for granted that empire was driven by the relentless forces of economic and political exploitation. The institution of caste, for example, a social formation that has been seen as not only basic to India but part of its ancient constitution, was fundamentally transformed by British colonial rule. Colonial rule has often been depicted as weak, and yet it produced ethnic violence, religious exclusion, political weakness, civilizational embarrassment, and nationalist extremism, often in the name of precolonial tradition. Colonialism played a major role not only in the creation and delineation of institutions and formations that have been characterized as "traditional," but also in the fracturing and compromising of those that have been accorded at best only provisional status as "modern." "Colonial modernity" has become shorthand for describing forms of modernity—including, for example, democracy and the public sphere, secularism and cultural pluralism, as well as science, music, and the arts—that both bear the traces of colonial domination and expose the fundamental fissures of something that not long ago was widely presumed to be progressive, universal, and value free.[33] In many parts of the world, colonialism was the fundamental fact of modern history.

Colonizers were in some sense even more successful in erasing the enormity of the influence of imperialism on life at home than they were in suppressing the effects of their actions abroad.[34] After all, the self-representations of imperialism were hardly taken at face value by the colonized, even under the most apparently hegemonic conditions.[35] But things were different "at home," where self-representation was not only carefully fashioned to underplay the colonial encounter, but also deeply complicit in nationalist triumphalism and imperial bad conscience, if not from the start, certainly from the late eighteenth century. And that is where we return to scandal, for to focus on the scandals of empire and its representations—especially once Burke had done his work—is to reopen the history of Britain in the long eighteenth century and reexamine the foundational role of empire in the history of modernity itself.

Many of the elements we have come to see as fundamental to the rise of the modern West were produced in large part through the imperial encounter.[36] The scandal of empire is not merely the simple fact that empire has always been a scandal (even in the days before the full elaboration of racial theory and national suppression). Nor is it simply the larger history demonstrating the extent to which the history of empire is a history of one scandal after the next. The greatest scandal, in other words, has been the erasure of empire from the history of Europe (itself seen, even in some of the most critical accounts, as the fount of modernity). And so we will return time after time to the moment of erasure, when scandal became normalized in the assumptions and categories of modernity itself, for which the divide between the worlds of colonizers and colonized was fundamental. For this history, then, the trial of Warren Hastings will serve as the emblematic moment, when scandal was decried with public fervor and eloquence, and yet when scandal was not so much obliterated as it was appropriated by Britain's own launch into the modern world, with implications for its state structure, its national economy, its confident claims of modernity and civilization, its embrace of bourgeois reform at home and abroad, as well as its global political ambition. Thus we return to histories in which private corruption was converted into public virtue, a rogue trading state fashioned as the means to acquire an imperial jewel, a scandalous monopoly made the political basis for global capitalist domination, an invidious history rewritten as the national epic.

Scandal itself is a peculiar historical form that only reveals its real meaning long after the public outcry and formal investigations have ceased. Scandals point to the underlying tensions and anxieties of an age, even as they work ironically to resolve crises by finding new ways to repress these tensions and anxieties. Scandals require careful management, and they elicit widespread vicarious attention, because they invariably produce a spectacle in which we see how the mighty have fallen. Whether caused by sexual indiscretion, extreme political ambition, undue greed, or other appetites driven by the desire for self-fulfillment and self-aggrandizement, the public unfolding of scandal provides public titillation at the same time it becomes a morality play.[37] Despite the threat either that authority will be subverted or the rules and conventions of public (or private) life radically changed, scandals in fact usually lead to far more benign outcomes. For the most part, public scandals become ritual moments in which the sacrifice of the reputation of one or more individuals allows many more to continue their scandalous ways, if perhaps with minimal safeguards and protocols that are meant to ensure that the terrible excesses of the past will not occur again. Scandals often do lead to reforms, but the reforms usually work to protect the potential agents of scandal rather than its actual victims. Indeed, it is the scandal itself that must be erased, not the underlying systemic reasons for scandal. The scandal is only the tip of the iceberg, the moment of excess that in the end works to conceal the far more endemic excesses that, at least for modern times, have become normalized through our modern convictions about free trade, public virtue, corporate responsibility, political self-determination, and national sovereignty.

The scandals of Clive, Hastings, and Benfield were both parables of the larger structure of imperial greed and exploitation, and only the most extreme examples of imperial business as usual. If the early scandals of empire had been taken seriously, empire itself would have been the victim rather than Hastings. Not only was empire hardly abandoned; it was reformed precisely so that the private and idiosyncratic excesses of venality and corruption attached to particular individuals could be transformed into the national interest, both metaphorically and literally. As it turned out, the most egregious scandals of empire played a critical role in making empire safe for Britain—and for that matter much of Europe as well—in the nineteenth and twentieth centuries, for it was precisely the grandeur and scope of eighteenth-century scandal that allowed Burke to perform such powerful political magic. In the rhetorical excess—and as the historian Seeley would later say, "unreasonable violence"—of Burke's assault on Hastings, a century of "unreasonable violence" against the imperial subjects of India could be not only justified, but also institutionalized for an imperial future that would last another hundred and fifty years. Without scandal, in other words, it is possible that empire would not have emerged as so dominant a force in the history of the nineteenth and twentieth centuries. By the same token, it would have taken much more than these scandals of empire to bring down the British empire. Scandal both allowed empire to be "reformed" and made empire itself far less the issue than the scandals themselves.

Thus it is that the larger narrative of this book hinges on the indelible relationship between empire and scandal. The history of empire is narrated through the successive parliamentary inquiries that brought imperial scandal to national attention, culminating in the trial of Warren Hastings and his eventual acquittal in 1795. Edmund Burke is the key protagonist, and Robert Clive and Warren Hastings the major actors, of this drama. But the drama is not primarily about the excess of scandal, as fascinating as it is, so much as it is about the constitutive character of scandal for empire, and the constitutive character of empire for England. What follows, then, is a different kind of imperial history—an imperial history of modern Britain that uses scandal as the cover to investigate what became the normal, and legitimate, enterprise of empire. In the chapters that follow, the imperial "encounter" is the foundational moment of British modernity, not to mention a story with monumental relevance for the present. This encounter is used to set the stage not just for the history of the British empire in the nineteenth and early twentieth centuries, but also for the history of other empires, with implications for the twenty-first century as well.

Despite this large canvas, what follows only concerns the imperial encounter between Britain and India. As a consequence, perhaps the major scandal of imperial history is left unexamined. I refer to slavery, of course, the subject of extraordinary attention in Britain during the very years that Burke prosecuted his case against Hastings in Parliament. On May 12, 1789, William Wilberforce, a reformer who later denounced Britain for its failure to abolish *sati* (widow burning) in India, gave the first major abolition speech before the House of Commons, introducing multiple petitions calling for the abolition of the slave trade. In the years before this speech, the newly formed Society for Effecting the Abolition of the Slave Trade had begun its agitations to recognize the scandal of slavery and regulate the trade in slaves, for reasons that ranged from shame at the complicity of the British empire in such heinous activities to concerns about emancipating slaves as part of a Christian conversion effort. During the same years that Parliament considered the charges of impeachment, it also investigated and examined evidence on the slave trade. Parliament defeated a bill to abolish such trade that was introduced by Wilberforce in 1791, though it had, a few years before, sought to regulate the slave trade in some small measure. Edmund Burke was an early supporter of abolition, though by 1791, in part because of his desire to distance himself from Jacobin positions, he declared that "the cause of humanity would be far more benefited by the continuance of the trade and servitude, regulated and reformed, than by the total destruction of both or either."[38] But Wilberforce and the abolitionists continued to press their case, succeeding only in 1807 in finally pressing Parliament to call for an end to the slave trade.

The history of slavery thus tells a very similar story about efforts to cleanse the stain of scandal from imperial Britain. Since Eric Williams, historians have argued that the abolition of slavery was designed to allow an emerging market in labor to take over the task of slavery, controlling labor through the scarcity of employment and the use of cheap wages rather than through the egregious exercise of proprietary rights over people.[39] Other historians have viewed the abolitionist movement as a fundamental part of the general reformist concerns of the late eighteenth and early nineteenth centuries.[40] But recent work further suggests that the abolitionist movement was only able to secure any hope of success after the loss of the American colonies began to make it clear that empire itself was imperiled by slavery. While the assumption that empire could only be profitable with the use of slaves was widespread and little contested until the American Revolution, the concern of one clergyman in 1781 that slavery called into question the "moral state of the British Empire" was perhaps the real sign that slavery could become the scandal of record.[41] By the end of the eighteenth century, it was clear that scandals were no longer good for empire, and that scandals that could be seen as a blot on the moral justifications of imperial activity had to be exorcised once and for all.

In writing the history of the making of British empire, scandal thus occupies a key role. For empire to be both moral and secure, the principal scandals of Britain's global engagements had to be expunged from the imperial record, and then shifted inexorably onto the colonized subjects of empire. Slavery was an especially insistent problem, requiring further legislation and much greater vigilance after the 1807 Act of Parliament proved largely ineffective. But it was no accident that William Wilberforce shifted his attention from slavery to *sati* during the second decade of the nineteenth century, symbolizing the more general displacement of scandal from colonizer to colonized. As empire became the morally sanctioned expression of the national interest in the global context, the histories of imperial formation shifted in turn from the scandals of Europeans to the scandals that both explained and justified European rule. While these scandals were written into the cultures and customs of the colonized through an emergent ethnographic imperial imagination, they were also evoked with special sharpness in the use of atrocity stories to predicate imperial involvement. And so in the writing of a canonic history of empire in the nineteenth century we note the almost sacred status accorded to the gruesome tale of the "Black Hole" of Calcutta, a natural forerunner in many ways to the atrocities of the Great Rebellion (or "Sepoy Mutiny") of 1857–1858, which rehearsed the earlier horrors and gave rise to a generalized sense of the natural right of empire in late-nineteenth-century Britain. If Indian atrocity became the pretext for imperial conquest, Indian scandal became the clarion call for the imperial mission, based as it was on the idea of the burden of empire.

In thinking about the role of scandal and atrocity in the history of imperial formation and legitimation, it is impossible not to be deeply disturbed by the continuities with a present in which scandals, most recently of the U.S. relationship with Iraq—including the original arming of Saddam Hussein by the United States, the delayed reaction to Hussein's use of torture and genocide, the shameless use of the fabricated pretext of weapons of mass destruction to justify an imperial war, the use of the occupation to secure lucrative contracts for companies such as Halliburton, the horrific images of civilian casualties, and the systematic torture and sexual humiliation of Iraqi prisoners in Abu Ghraib—have failed to stem the tide of a new imperial resurgence. The final scandal of empire is that empire has not yet been consigned to the past tense once and for all. Empire, as many observers of contemporary globalization have observed, is transforming itself into new forms of global power that use markets, corporate influence, international banking systems, and law rather than military conquest, colonial occupation, or direct economic domination—but in recent years the United States has retreated to imperial ways and means.[42] Without prejudging the vast potential for globalization to rehearse and even enhance the past abuses of empire, it is, nevertheless, high time for the sun to set on all the empires of old. If history can ever serve as a lesson for our present and future, the history of empire as recounted here should remind us that no imperial ambition can ever be unencumbered by scandal. Indeed, scandal is what empire is all about.

Lord Clive, under examination by a committee of the House of Commons in 1772 and 1773, with a pointed reference to Clive's personal Indian estate (his jaghire).

⤙ 2 ⤚

Corruption

*Their prey is lodged in England; and the cries of India
are given to sea and winds . . . In India, all the vices operate by which sudden fortune is acquired; in England are
often displayed, by the same persons, the virtues which
dispense hereditary wealth. Arrived in England, the de-
stroyers of the nobility and gentry of a whole kingdom
will find the best company in this nation, at a board of
elegance and hospitality. Here the manufacturer and the
husbandman will bless the just and punctual hand, that
in India has torn the cloth from the loom, or wrested the
scanty portion of rice and salt from the peasants of Bengal, or wrung from him the very opium in which he forgot
his oppressions and his oppressor . . . Our Indian government is in its best state a grievance.*

—EDMUND BURKE, "SPEECH ON MR. FOX'S
EAST INDIA BILL," 1783

Private trade, the alleged scourge of Company integrity and managerial probity, might have begun with the Company itself, but in for-

mal terms it began in 1675, when the right to trade on a private account was extended to "any commodity . . . to any port or places in
the East Indies to the northward of the equator, except to Tonkin
and Formosa."[1] This new rule led to the rise of "interlopers" who operated on the high seas as virtual pirates until they were suppressed
in the early eighteenth century, and then to the use of trading privileges granted by Mughal authorities to the Company for private purposes. Despite periodic efforts to stem the tide of corruption, the
council in Fort William gave voice to what was a common perception when it noted, "If the Company allowed no private trade, their
servants must starve."[2] As early as the turn of the century it was clear
that there were great fortunes to be gained in India, and not from
the meager salaries granted to Company servants. Much political
capital was earned for and spent by efforts to secure appointments in
India for young men eager for the riches of the East. And while
some of these men perished at young ages from tropical disease or
mishap, a growing number secured fortunes of a kind unimaginable
at home.

Meanwhile, the Company grew in domestic importance as it became the chief financier for the public debt of the state through its
bonds, and as Company directors gained increasing influence in
Parliament. In 1709, the Company was obliged to lend £3.2 million—in effect its entire equity capital—to the state. In return, not
only did the Company secure major political favor—which helped
make Company bonds the most secure form of investment through
the first half of the century—it also was given a guaranteed monopoly for the East India trade. Between 1709 and 1749 the total value of
exports from Britain to Asia accordingly doubled to over one million
pounds a year; during these same years the Company failed to pay

yearly dividends to its stockholders only on two occasions.[3] But few histories of early eighteenth-century Britain note the extent to which Company interests were critical for the regnant Whig governments of those years, let alone call attention to the immense importance of Company stock for the state as well as the emerging global economy of investment and speculation.[4] Within India, Company restrictions on private trade were minimal, and especially after 1717—when a Mughal *firman* waived all customs fees for inland trade in commodities such as salt, salt peter, betel nut, opium, and tobacco—private fortunes were increasingly visible perquisites of Company service.

These fortunes soon came to play an important role in domestic politics and economics as well. Edward Stephenson, for example, became the first Bengal nabob to enter the House of Commons, having also purchased the estate of Lord Dawley from Lord Bolingbroke after his retirement from India in 1730.[5] Formal remittances ranged from £50,000 to £120,000 a year between 1731 and 1756, but this doubtless reflected only a small percentage of the actual wealth taken from India by Company servants, given both the formal restrictions on certain kinds of trade and the difficulties of currency exchange between India and Britain. In many cases, remittances became in effect other forms of international trade, in commodities such as diamonds and gold, and in illegal transactions with China (for tea) and other trading companies.

Despite dramatic increases both in actual Company trade and in private fortunes during the first half of the eighteenth century, dependence on silver bullion imports (Britain had little else to finance trade) and on the favors of Mughal officials made both the Company and its servants—in India and in Britain—anxious to secure a greater economic and political foothold. The military reversals in southern India against the French and its allies in 1751–1752 gave the first real indication that the Company could field a successful military campaign in India, either against Indian troops that had until then consistently overwhelmed them or against the French, who only a few years before had been the first to demonstrate the possible superiority of European field artillery over cavalry. At home, the formal policy of nonintervention and nonexpansion continued to be dogma for the Company's board of directors, for whom any major military expenditure threatened both profit margins and political fortunes. But Company aspirations were never contained by domestic complacency, even as the logic of state building was never fully apparent even to its own architects. The death of Alivardi Khan, the nawab of Bengal, in 1756 and the resulting contest over his succession provided the opportunity for an important victory, and, less than a decade later, the establishment of a new imperial order. That the new order led to almost immediate crisis no more diminishes the scale of transformation than it lessened the new, often extraordinary, opportunities for aggrandizement on the part of Company servants and investors alike. As it happened, a rather unpromising Company adventurer has been given much of the credit for this sea change in imperial history. I refer of course to Robert Clive, who was according to Thomas Macaulay (among many others) "the founder of the British empire in India."[6]

Clive, in some ways an improbable candidate for fame and fortune, began his Indian career like many other wayward youths of eighteenth-century Britain.[7] The son of lower-level gentry who lived beyond their means, he was sent to India at the age of seventeen with the hopes that his restlessness might be put to work to augment his family's position. Through his father's connections, young Robert secured an apprenticeship to the East India Company as a "writer" (clerk) in Madras. Bored with the bureaucratic banality of his job, he soon transferred to military service, possibly because of the turmoil attending hostilities with the French as a consequence of the War of Austrian Succession. With the luck of connections forged in his first military service, he was appointed commissary of provisions for European troops after the peace of Aix-la-Chapelle. This post unexpectedly earned him the huge sum of £40,000 between 1749 and 1753, in part because of opportunities that came with the mobilization required by renewed hostilities against the French. It was also during these years that Clive established a reputation for reckless valor on the battlefield, though the history of his actual military exploits is clouded by later imperial hagiography, first fueled by the voluminous writings of his associate and business partner, the historian Robert Orme.[8] Macaulay wrote that Clive quickly proved he was equal to any command: "Had the entire direction of the war been entrusted to Clive, it would probably have been brought to a speedy close."[9] He apparently played an important role in two key engagements, the first when he held the fort of Arcot in a sustained siege, the second when he led a force in Trichinopoly in support of Muhammed Ali, one of the two claimants to become the next nawab. The English forces were victorious despite their relatively inferior forces, and Chanda Sahib—the other claimant who had been supported by the French—was killed in the denouement of the battle. In a dramatic reversal of fortune, the British recaptured the balance of power in the Carnatic from the French and secured an important ally in the nawab of Arcot. And Clive took much of the credit. He returned home to England in 1753 at the age of twenty-seven, with a young bride and a substantial endowment.

Upon Clive's return, he bailed his family out of debt and redeemed the family estate, living a life of conspicuous opulence. He also sought to convert his economic fortune and military reputation into a political career, but failed to buy his way into Parliament because of an ill-advised alliance with the Earl of Sandwich, who in 1754 was on the wrong side of the prime minister. His fortune and prospects diminished, Clive decided after only eighteen months to return to India, a decision readily accepted by the Company directors given the likelihood of renewed hostilities with France. The death en route of the commander of Bombay gave Clive the opportunity to take over command, whereupon he used his position to take full credit for a successful assault on a Maratha fort accused of harboring pirates just down the coast. When he subsequently journeyed to Madras he found himself, once again by default, nominated for the largest assignment of midcentury, the Bengal campaign, undertaken to regain Calcutta from the new nawab of Bengal, Siraj-ud-Daula, and, as imperial history tells it, to avenge the horrible brutality of the Black Hole. Clive arrived in Bengal in early January and recaptured Calcutta in a surprise night raid. After several fits of indecision and indications—even to some of his most enthusiastic biographers—of military incompetence, he was nevertheless able to secure his position.[10] He renegotiated the right to settlement and fortification with the nawab, whose precarious political position was threatened by the resurgent energy of the French as well as by the delicacy of a number of other alliances in the immediate wake of his succession to the nawabship.

If the status quo was restored, the balance of power shifted irrevocably some months later when, in early May, Clive decided to back Mir Jafar, one of the nawab's most senior generals and a relative by marriage, in an effort to unseat the nawab. Delicate—and precise—

negotiations over the terms of the coup ensued, with a critical role being played by the most important merchant of Calcutta, a man by the name of Amirchand (Omichand). Clive was able to secure an agreement with Mir Jafar, but he deceived Amirchand by drafting two treaties, the forged version of which promised Amirchand £300,000 for his efforts. The great Battle of Plassey—commencing a year to the day after the "Black Hole"—that sealed imperial fortune was thus based on a double deception of former allies, the Indian prince and the merchant: a portent of things to come. And the battle itself, seen by many as evidence of Clive's military genius, was in fact a near disaster, saved in the end only by the early death of one of Siraj-ud-Daula's most trusted generals and the late but crushing defection of Mir Jafar. When Mir Jafar finally took the nawab's throne—after arranging for his son, Miran, to capture and murder Siraj-ud-Daula—it was clear that the political and economic fortunes of the English forces had changed for good. The Bengal nawab's treasury was opened for the distribution of booty and rewards, and in the aftermath of the coup, Clive secured plunder and presents that made him a fabulously wealthy man. Clive's presents alone amounted to well over £200,000, counting neither his share of the military spoils nor his subsequently granted annuity in the form of a *jaghire* (land grant) worth roughly £27,000, good for life.[11] The House of Commons select committee ultimately compiled a list of presents worth about £1.2 million that was distributed to the English in 1757 alone, and one imagines there must have been far more than so accounted.[12] The East India Company also secured effective political control over the wealthiest province of the Mughal empire.

Shortly after the Battle of Plassey, Mir Jafar made Clive a *mansabdar* (a high-ranking servant of the Mughal emperor) with the title Zubdat ul Mulk. At Clive's request, the nawab devised a scheme to attach the £27,000 *jaghire* to this award, but he did so using revenue on lands in the 24 Parganas, territory already ceded by the nawab to the Company. To many, Clive's *jaghire* seemed like a direct deduction from Company coffers, and it fueled a growing group of detractors who chafed at his new fortune and disputed his use of the state's military resources for spurious personal and political gain. In various letters, Clive began to articulate his own defense of his presents in language that anticipated the final reckoning of his career in the hearings of the select committee of the House of Commons some fifteen years later. He steadfastly maintained that presents were permissible if they were given voluntarily for genuine services and if they did no harm to the interests of the Company. Presents were not to be negotiated or agreed to beforehand, and they were to have no strings attached.[13] But even by contemporary standards in England, where "old corruption" flourished, his rewards seemed excessive and his defense suspect. Clive could hardly claim ignorance about the share he would reap of the conquest of Bengal, and the amount of his share eclipsed that of most other beneficiaries of imperial swindle. Concern about his presents was initially overshadowed by the enormity of Clive's military and political accomplishment, but it increased as pressures for reform grew, especially after the Company's financial crisis of 1770, the immediate pretext for the select committee's hearings. Indeed, most debates over corruption in India swirled around Clive's conspicuous lack of moderation, which his *jaghire*, more than anything else, came to symbolize.

Mir Jafar only arranged for Clive's *jaghire* after the passage of two stormy years in post-Plassey Bengal, during which *zamindars* (landlords) and other local leaders, merchants, and agents used the coup to test the power of the new nawab and the English. The English rivalry with the French had moved south to Hyderabad and the Carnatic, diverting troops (though conspicuously not Clive) away from Bengal, which itself suffered only minor threats from the Dutch. Much more serious were potential threats from continued Maratha ascendancy across the subcontinent, though luckily for the English this posed no direct challenge during these years. By 1759 not only did Mir Jafar seem to have consolidated his power; he did so in firm alliance with Clive and the Company, despite tensions over the discovery that the nawab's treasury did not come close to yielding the anticipated loot, and even though Clive was inflexible about his negotiated share. Indeed, Clive no more displayed moderation in his recognition of Mir Jafar's genuine financial difficulties than he did appreciation of the need for flexibility in his adherence to so-called Indian customs of exchanges, gifts, and honors. Moreover, Clive's acceptance of his *mansabdari* status and then of the *jaghire* exposed contradictions both in his own relationship to the Company (not to mention the Crown) and in his understandings of Mughal institutional and political forms. What, after all, was Clive doing proclaiming effective Company sovereignty over India while becoming a high-ranking officer of the Mughal empire?

Far more destructive for Bengal was Clive's deliberate expansion of the system of private trade, encouraging—doubtless for his material as well as political benefit—the use of the 1717 Mughal *firman* by Company traders. *Dastaks*, or free passes, had been used before, but their use escalated after 1752 when many local contracting merchants, who had handled most private trade, were replaced by Company servants who used their own agents, or *gumashtas*. In 1757, just after the Battle of Plassey, Mir Jafar proclaimed, "Whatever goods

the Company's gumastahs may bring or carry to or from the factories
. . . You shall neither ask for nor receive any sum however trifling for
the same . . . Whoever acts contrary to these orders, the English have
power to punish them."[14] This was a strong endorsement, and it was
used to combat the many ambiguities that had attended earlier uses
of *dastaks*. The *firman* itself was a document that by Mughal standards constituted neither a major concession nor the basis for the
kinds of uniform claims made by the Company or its servants. In particular, it decidedly did not sanction "private" trade in all the commodities assumed, and it granted "privileges" rather than "rights."
Trade in commodities such as salt and betel nut was based on specific privileges that had to be regularly approved by various political
agents of the Mughals—privileges that allowed, though only for a
fixed period, political as well as economic concessions.[15] Clive's
expansion of the "empire of free trade" exacerbated the aggressive
misreading of both Mughal privileges and the meanings of—and
terms of access to—local marketplaces.[16] As with Clive's culturalist
account of customs concerning presents, these misreadings were
clearly not unintentional. But they were used locally to excuse and
further imperial aggrandizement and they functioned importantly
to justify local actions in later parliamentary inquiries. The court of
directors was itself under no illusion about the nature of the problem. As they stated in a letter of 1765, "Treaties of commerce are understood to be for the mutual benefit of the contracting parties. Is it
then possible to suppose that the Court of Delhi by conferring the
privilege of trading free of customs could mean an inland trade in
the commodities in their own country at that period unpractised and
unthought of by the English, to the detriment of their revenues, and
ruin of their own merchants? . . . we do not find such a construction

was ever heard of until our own servants first invented it, and afterwards supported it by violence." Not that the Court was deeply concerned about the abuse of the representation of cultural difference; as they wrote some three years later: "Our chief object in confining our servants to the strict letter of the phirmaund *[firman]* has been to do justice to the natives in restoring them their rights, yet we never meant to give up such revenues as Government is justly entitled to for the protection it gives."[17] Indeed, the Company simply wanted the profits for itself, displaying no desire to atone either for its economic encroachment or its cultural misrecognition over the years.

Shortly before his return home in 1760, Clive wrote to William Pitt detailing the possible assumption of Diwani—or the right of direct rule—over Bengal, with the full permission of the Mughal emperor and the ripe promise of both full sovereignty and unparalleled riches:

I flatter myself that I have made it pretty clear to you that there will be little or no difficulty in obtaining the absolute possession of these rich kingdoms; and this with the Moghul's own consent, on condition of paying him less than a fifth of the revenues thereof. Now I leave you to judge whether an income yearly of upwards of two millions sterling, with the possession of three provinces abounding in the most valuable productions of nature and of art, be an object deserving the public attention; and whether it be worth the nation's while to take the proper measures to secure such an acquisition; an acquisition which, under the management of so able and disinterested a Minister, would prove a source of immense wealth to the kingdom, and might in time be appropriated in part as a fund towards diminishing the heavy load of debt under which we at present labour. Add to these advantages the influence we shall thereby acquire over the several European nations engaged in the commerce here, which these could no longer carry on but through our indulgence, and under such limitations as we should think fit to prescribe.[18]

However much of what he wrote Clive believed to be true, he was both prescient—if not entirely accurate—in predicting imperial expansion and self-serving in his representation of his own role in making it possible. But he was also characteristically disingenuous, for he was informing Pitt that whatever share of Bengal's wealth he had taken for himself (or directed to his colleagues) was only a small price to pay for the riches that now lay at the doorstep of England. Many in Britain were as ambivalent about imperial ambition as they were skeptical about Clive's altruism. Imperial historians have made clear the extent to which both leading members of government and the Company believed that territorial acquisitions would certainly involve greater expense than any possible gain, in managerial and administrative costs as well as military obligations. But if managerial concerns had indeed been triumphant—and in the end one cannot blame empire solely on the men in the field—there would have been no imperial expansion. And it is easy to believe that as much as Clive was resented, he was also envied. Envy and ambition made for a powerful combination.

Clive returned triumphant, and extremely wealthy, to England in 1760, coincidentally just after the French were defeated in a major battle in southern India. The *Annual Register*, edited by Edmund Burke, reported that Clive "may with all propriety be said to be the richest subject in the three kingdoms."[19] He did not, however, have a title to match, and he set about to use the patronage of the duke of Newcastle to procure one, though in the end he was only awarded an Irish peerage, of inferior stamp. This time he was successful in his bid to enter Parliament, but his political interests moved him into Company affairs and in short order into a protracted battle with Laurence Sulivan. Sulivan had been chair of the Company's court of directors from 1758 and he was horrified by the scale of Clive's enrichment, as well as the extent to which Clive raised the bar for corruption on the part of other Company servants. Sulivan was also in favor of commerce without war, since war was always expensive and the politics of empire potentially disastrous. During the 1760s his chief weapon against Clive was the *jaghire,* about which Sulivan raised early questions and sought to annul at every possible opportunity. Clive had unsuccessfully contested Sulivan's leadership, in the wake of the 1763 Treaty of Paris that ended the Seven Years War but gave the French what Clive believed to be inappropriate and dangerous privileges in India. Sulivan's first action was to suspend the payment of *jaghire* income to Clive.

In part because of the humiliation that attended this double defeat, Clive decided to return to India, a decision that, despite Clive's great reputation there, seemed perilous given the chaos of Company affairs after his departure. Indeed, Clive's successor Henry Vansittart had been overruled by his council in conjunction with a breach with Mir Jafar's successor, Mir Kasim; a disastrous massacre of British soldiers at Patna had occurred; and there was the prospect of new warfare against the nawab. But as Clive prepared to set sail for Bengal, his political prospects were enhanced at home. Sulivan was replaced by Clive's friend Thomas Rous, and Clive's *jaghire* was reinstated by the General Court. He left for India with two main goals: first, to reinstate the dependence of the Bengal nawab on the Company, and second, to reform Company corruption. In part because of his new persona as a political representative of the Company, but also because of the mess he had left behind in Bengal, he was now ironically to be the agent of Sulivan's reformist charter. He was to insist that Company servants abstain from trade in salt, betel nut, and tobacco, and he would enforce a new policy whereby "covenanted servants" could no longer accept presents above a set level. One can hardly blame many of his contemporaries who felt that once Clive had secured his own fortune, he wished to deny one to anyone else.

Despite Clive's claim that he had settled affairs in Bengal before his prior departure in 1760, he still had a lot to answer for. He had dramatically raised the stakes for imperial plunder and Bengal had been hit hard by the steady extortions of Company personnel. Clive had also raised expectations for local revenues, which caused the termination of Company remittances from England. Meanwhile, Mir Jafar had exhausted his treasury, in part by giving extravagant presents. Further, he was seen as insufficiently resistant to the efforts of the new Mughal emperor, Shah Alam, who had marched as far as Patna in an effort to take back some measure of control over eastern India. Shah Alam had also raised the question of customs and private trade, much to the distress of Company servants. Accordingly, Mir Jafar was made to step down as nawab on October 20, 1760, to be replaced by his son-in-law Mir Kasim. This succession was costly for the new nawab, who not only ceded Burdwan, Midnapur, and Chittagong for the maintenance of British troops, but also handed out various presents to "the English gentlemen," including £20,000 for the interim governor, Jonathan Holwell, £50,000 for the new governor, Henry Vansittart, and another £150,000 for the Company's council, along with a guarantee for another £18,000 a year for the governor. But these gifts just deferred the nawab's financial crisis, which came to a head two years later, again over private trade. When, after a series of altercations that turned river trade violent, Vansittart reached an agreement with Mir Kasim to waive some of his obligations to pay duty on all goods in transit (for a bribe of £70,000), the Company's council revolted and overruled the governor.

Faced with an unsustainable financial burden, Mir Kasim marched on a British garrison in Patna. The council responded in July 1763 by deposing him and restoring Mir Jafar. Mir Kasim executed fifty-six British prisoners in Patna, retreating to Awadh and allying himself with Shuja-ud-Daula, the nawab of Awadh, and solidifying his alliance with Shah Alam. The three engaged British forces several times over the next year, but were in the end decisively defeated—despite British casualties of close to nine hundred soldiers—in the Battle of Baksar in October 1764. Shah Alam settled with the British, Shuja-ud-Daula withdrew, and Mir Kasim fled in disarray. Mir Jafar meanwhile was squeezing Bengal revenues once again to secure his own succession, donating £375,000 to the army, £300,000 to the Company for their costs in the confrontation with Mir Kasim, and reportedly up to £530,000 for individual losses sustained because of the virtual cessation of private trade. He also signed a new treaty waiving all payments of duty except for a minor 2.5 percent on salt. But less than a year later, in February 1765, he died, and his son, Najm-ud-daula, succeeded him. Once again, presents were demanded, this time against the express orders of the Parliament's General Court. For some, it doubtless seemed their last chance to get rich quick. And in any case the bounteous riches of Bengal were fast disappearing.

When Clive returned to Bengal in 1765, he came to a land that was more securely under Company control than ever before thanks to the victory at Baksar. And yet he also returned to a land that had been squeezed dry by the very means that had earlier led to his own enrichment. His first act was to enforce the General Court's directive against taking presents, forcing Company servants to sign the new covenants. This would have been deeply resented in any event, but was resented especially because Clive's *jaghire* was widely seen to have been the cause of the government's directive, and because Clive enforced the new ban with despotic authority. His second act was to meet with the Mughal emperor, Shah Alam, in Allahabad, where on August 12, 1765, he accepted the grant of Diwani, or revenue-collecting power in Bengal, on behalf of the Company. The grant of Diwani meant that the Company had only to give £325,000 to the Mughal emperor in exchange for keeping the balance of Bengal revenues, now collected directly by the Company rather than by the nawab. Meanwhile, the nawab's position was much diminished, for although he maintained power over the police and judiciary, he no longer had a financial base. Despite Clive's belief that the assumption of the Diwani could have been accomplished six years before, this was a monumental moment in the history of empire, marking the final appropriation of direct authority over a vast tract of eastern India. Sovereignty was still ceded to the Mughal emperor, but given the Company's policy in such matters, the formal concession of sovereignty was meant to keep the peace both across the subcontinent and in Britain, while consolidating real economic as well as political supremacy in Bengal. In fact, Clive still relied on earlier systems of revenue collection, to be presided over by the newly appointed agent Muhammed Reza Khan, inaugurating what came to be known as Clive's dual system. Under this system, the role of the nawab became almost that of a pensioner to the British.

Clive's elevated position did not, however, translate into his being able to enforce any serious ban on private trade, despite efforts to centralize and control trade through a central committee known as the Society of Trade. Indeed, the society allowed Clive to control the use of tax exemptions, allowing him to reward his friends and associates and punish his detractors. It now became customary for a duty of 2.5 percent to be paid on most items, but if anything the Company's reliance on private trade for its compensation increased over the next few years, until the Regulating Act of 1773 brought salt and opium under formal Company monopoly and made private trade more difficult overall. Harry Verelst, Clive's successor as governor, wrote in 1769 that the agents of European traders had spread "the baneful effects of monopoly and extortion on every side of them."[20] Despite Clive's dramatic renunciation of private trade himself (although he never made much of his fortune from trade), nothing changed before Clive was asked to stand and defend himself before Parliament in the hearings of 1772. Nothing, that is, except the massive disappointment of the Diwani. Far from conferring the wealth that Clive promised—which was to justify a regular payment from the Company to Parliament of £400,000 a year in exchange for the ambivalent assumption of territorial sovereignty in India—the Diwani led to a major financial crisis. The monsoon in Bengal in 1769 and 1770 finished the depletion of Bengal's wealth that Company presents and trade had begun; according to some estimates, one-third of Bengal's population perished from starvation and disease during those years.[21] Bengal was a wasteland and the Company almost went bankrupt. Clive seemed accountable once again.

In the last act of his career, Clive was in fact brought to account, if feebly. He had returned for the last time from India in 1767, busying himself with buying estates and consolidating a political bloc in Parliament of old supporters and fellow India hands. His promotion of the importance of the Diwani grant led to Chatham's demand for national compensation as well as to a run on East India Company stock, which almost doubled in value the year of his return. But the problems in Bengal caught up with the price of stock in 1769, when it lost a quarter of its value almost overnight. A number of prominent figures lost thousands of pounds, including Sulivan, who had by then returned to the directorship, and Edmund Burke, who had invested his family fortunes with his cousin William, an agent of the raja of Tanjore. It soon became clear that the Bengal famine was in part caused by corruption in the trading of rice by Company servants, who had used the shortages to manipulate the market and make new fortunes. Alexander Dow's *History of Hindustan* was widely seen as a direct attack on Clive, especially the third volume published in 1772, as was William Bolts's *Considerations on Indian Affairs*, published in the same year, which charged Clive with selling his interest in salt for £32,000.[22] And then the Company's credit failed, leading directly to Lord North's Regulating Act of 1773, which set the terms for a rescue loan.[23] Before the act was passed, however, Clive was brought to Parliament to defend himself against charges that were raised first by a select committee and then a secret committee that looked into his Indian affairs.

Clive used his most recent sojourn in Bengal as a reformer to buttress his claim for approbation rather than condemnation, and he gave several speeches before Parliament that were judged brilliant, if sometimes excessive, rhetorical performances. He also attempted to put his own actions in India in the context of his version of imperial history, which took into account Indian customs, the transformations he had wrought to the East India Company, and the monumental benefits he had brought to England. He noted: "From time immemorial it has been the custom of that Country, for an inferior never to come into the presence of a superior without a present. It begins at the Nabob and ends at the lowest man who has an inferior. The Nabob has told me, that the small presents he received amounted to 300,000 pounds a year, and I can believe him, because I know that I might have received as much during my last Government." Clive here inserted not just his view of "native customs" but also his perspective of his own status, commensurate at least to that of any Mughal nawab, if not grander. He went on to say, "The Company's servants have ever been accustomed to receive presents. Even before we took part in the Country troubles, when our possessions were very confined and limited, the Governor and others used to receive presents, and I shall venture to say, there is not an Officer commanding His Majesty's Army . . . who has not received presents." And this was a small price to pay for the establishment of empire: "Let the house figure to itself a country consisting of 15 millions of Inhabitants, a revenue of four millions sterling, and a trade in proportion. By progressive steps, the Company have become Sovereigns of that Empire. Can it be supposed that their servants will refrain from advantages resulting from their situation?" What indeed would be the price of imperial sovereignty? Besides, and here he attempted to defend even those he had alienated through his own belated reformist zeal, "The Company's servants . . . have not been the authors of those acts of violence and oppression of which it is the fashion to accuse them. Such crimes are committed by the Natives of the Country, acting as their agents, and for the most part without their knowledge."[24] And he sought to defend all the Company nabobs from their reputation in England: "Their conduct is strictly honorable . . . there has not yet been one character found amongst them sufficiently flagitious for Mr. Foote to exhibit in the theater in the Haymarket."[25] Referring to Samuel Foote's scandalous play that directly satirized him in the leading role, he gave voice to a refrain that would over the years increasingly drown out concerns about British scandal: that the real abuses were performed by Indians themselves.

On the one hand, Clive defended himself by defending his colleagues, though he also made a great deal of his own probity in his last government as the Company reformer. He argued, for example, that there was no way a "monopoly of salt, betel nut, and tobacco in the years 1765 and 1766 could occasion a want of rain and a scarcity of rice in the year 1770," and that indeed his efforts had precisely been to end the excesses of private trade and the taking of presents during those years. But on the other hand, he refused to see anything wrong with the presents he had accepted on earlier occasions. In particular, he was steadfast in his defense of his *jaghire*, which in the eyes even of some of his most approving biographers constituted his Achilles' heel.[26] Speaking about himself, he said, "When presents are received as the price of services to the Nation, to the Company and to that Prince who bestowed those presents; when they are not exacted from him by compulsion; when he is in a state of independence and can do with his money what he pleases; and when they are not received to the disadvantage of the Company, he holds presents so received not dishonourable."[27] He went on: "Was I, after having resigned my life so often in the Company's service, to deny myself the only honorable opportunity I ever had or could have of acquiring a fortune, without prejudice to the Company, who it is evident would not have had more for my having less? Was I, when the Company had acquired a million and a half sterling specie, a revenue of near 100,000 per annum, when many individuals had through the influence of the success of our arms acquired fortunes of forty, fifty, sixty and seventy-thousand pounds, was I to have come home a beggar and depended upon the mercy of the Court of Directors?" In what then begged the credulity even of his closest associates, he proclaimed that he could "produce many witnesses now in England and in Bengal [all of whom know] that I made the honour of the nation and the interest of the Company my sole and principal study, even to my own private disadvantage. Had I been desirous to make use of those advantages which by being commander in chief and at the head of a victorious army I might done, even the jageer, great as it is, would have been an object scarce worth my consideration." As quoted earlier, after invoking both the wealth of captured Bengal, and the power he held in his own hands as the captor, he stood "astonished at his own moderation."[28]

Such moderation, of course, was not only fanciful, but rhetorically relative, both to the continued rapacity of other Company servants—keeping in mind that Clive had single-handedly raised the stakes for the corruption of the nabob—and to the supposed wealth, power, and grandeur he had garnered for England. Paradoxically, even as he failed to comment on the way in which his *jaghire* was seen by most to be a direct drain on Company wealth, coming as it did—even before the Diwani—out of territories that had previously been granted to the Company, he also failed to distinguish between private and public wealth when speaking of "England." As he noted, "It will appear by these calculations that the Company have obtained eight millions five hundred thousand pounds sterling and individuals three million five hundred thousand pounds, a clear gain to this nation of twelve millions sterling."[29] Not only was corruption business as usual, but also private gain and the public good did not have to be separated, least of all when the national interest operated in the alien theater of India. In these terms, empire was able to justify corruption and cleanse greed.

After months of hearings and two separate committees, one select and the second secret, Clive's affairs were finally considered in the debates that led to the passing of Lord North's Regulating Act of 1773. A week after North's bill was introduced, John Burgoyne, in presenting the secret committee's reports, proposed three resolutions: the first, "that all territorial acquisitions made by subjects belonged to the Crown"; second, "that it was illegal for private persons to appropriate the revenues of such possessions"; and third, "that there had been appropriation of such revenues."[30] The first was a direct challenge to the Company; the second and third, to Clive and his colleagues. After a long and sometimes raucous debate that lasted virtually through the night of May 21, the House not only rejected the resolutions but also passed another: "That Robert, Lord Clive did, at the same time, render great and meritorious services to his country."[31] He was accordingly allowed to keep his *jaghire* intact. As Burke wrote, Clive had "thus come out of the fiery trial much brighter than when he went into it."[32]

Despite Clive's momentary victory, the scandal around his vast fortune did not die. Soon after his parliamentary reprieve, the Regulating Act was passed. While some argued that Clive had played a significant role in drafting the provisions of the act, it was far more universally agreed that he had been the principal object of it. The act established a supreme court in Bengal, giving new powers to the governor-general—appointed now by Parliament—while balancing these powers by the establishment of a new and powerful council of four, appointed by the Company's directors. The bill sought to put in place a wide range of checks on the corruption of the Company servants, raising the salaries of key Company servants, while both prohibiting presents and placing some new restrictions on private trade. Significantly, an important provision for dealing with the excesses of Company merchants in southern India was dropped because of a deal with a group of powerful parliamentarians who represented the "Arcot interest."[33] And finally, the bill made possible the granting of a major loan of £1.4 million pounds to keep the Company afloat, with various provisions to ensure repayment but not, significantly, to claim direct rights to the Company's revenue in Bengal. Thus although in many ways the bill was an important marker in the history of Indian corruption, it was not only watered down due to the power of the Company both outside and inside Parliament; it was also in the end about management rather than about either morality or conduct.[34] But it was still seen as a rebuke by Clive, who as mentioned earlier committed suicide shortly after passage of the bill—ostensibly for reasons of ill-health (though this attribution might be due to the scandalous nature of suicide itself in eighteenth-century Britain).[35] Warren Hastings, who had become governor of Bengal in 1772, was appointed governor-general, with the mandate to become the Indian agent of reform. In many ways, he was in fact much better suited than Clive to be the inheritor of this new mandate, which had been designed precisely to undo what Clive had done.

Most imperial historians agree that the Regulating Act was too attenuated—and too internally contradictory—either to solve issues of Company management or to stop corruption, although it did put in place the structural conditions for the rivalry that was to bring Francis his disappointment and Hastings his disgrace. Significantly, Edmund Burke had been one of those who resisted the Regulating Act, a sign both of the general concern about increasing state control over commercial affairs and of the particular political loyalties of the Rockingham faction with which he was associated. Indeed, in 1773 Burke had claimed that "every capital disorder has b[een] either redressed, or is going to be so: the g[rea]t questions of presents are few; the business of monopoly, and oppressive trade is almost knocked in the head; the trade of the Company servants is almost knocked in the head; the anarchy of the Company—the greatest grievance—is reformed by the beginning of a system, one of the most beautiful ever seen established in any place."[36] And Burke had held that the proceedings against Clive were "illegal, unjust, and impolitick," arguing vociferously against the select and the secret committees that had been constituted to inquire into his affairs. Ironically, Burke's first realization of the complexity, and scandalous character, of Company affairs in India came through his kinsman William, who served as an agent for the raja of Tanjore from 1778 to 1782. William had been an enthusiastic investor in East India Company stock after the assumption of Diwani—a calamitous enthusiasm for Edmund since they pooled financial resources and were both seriously affected by the crash of 1769–1770. But while this setback did not turn Edmund against Clive, William's involvement with Tanjore did have a strong effect on him. Shortly after arriving in India in 1777, William had managed to persuade the raja of Tanjore to hire him as his agent, following the model of the nawab of Arcot. Rumor had it that he was put on a retainer of £8,000 a year, returning to England to press the claims of Tanjore against those of the nawab's many agents, not least the other pair of cousins involved in the affair, John and James Macpherson. In 1779 he joined forces with Edmund to write a tract countering the earlier historical treatise written by James Macpherson, blaming many of India's problems on the "Muhammedan conquest," but even then he was aware that the British were playing a less than benign role. Whether or not Edmund's sudden change on matters concerning Company affairs was driven by the prospect of profit for himself should the raja's position improve, his growing familiarity with the activities of the Company through his association with William clearly had a very strong effect on his views. Once one to shower accolades on Clive, he was soon to become Hastings's greatest critic. While the story of the debts of the nawab of Arcot rarely figures importantly in imperial histories of the conquest of India, it was in fact of critical significance for several reasons, not least its role in transforming Burke's views about empire.

Indeed, it was in southern India that the limits of the Regulating Act, and the excesses of the Company, were most egregious in the years after 1773. Beginning with the accession of the nawab, Muhammed Ali, in 1755, corruption associated with the European presence in Madras grew at a dizzying pace. By 1763, when George Pigot left the post of governor with a fortune of at least £300,000, the level of generalized corruption was staggering. Pigot had not only accumulated a major fortune; he had also secured the promise of a regular salary for representing the nawab in England upon his return, in what became a common extension of the politics of bribery and influence in Madras and London. It was also reported that he had led the nawab into further expenditure by persuading him to send his third son to London to present a diamond valued at £50,000 to the king. Every transaction in Madras, whether political or economic, was accompanied by escalating demands by individual Company servants for gifts, presents, and other considerations. In addition, Company relations with the nawab of Arcot, and their management of his relations with the other political forces in the south—most importantly Tanjore, Mysore, and Hyderabad—were driven by personal profit.

Ironically, the debts of the nawab turned out to be the basis of his political power and the reason for his economic survival. In the absurd colonial theater of mid-eighteenth-century Madras, it soon became clear that the best investment in town was in the debts of the nawab. Company servants vied with each other for the privilege of lending money to the nawab at usurious rates of interest. Becoming one of the nawab's creditors afforded the possibility of receiving lavish presents to substitute for regular repayments—which were themselves often made, at least in principle, as the offer of rights to collect revenue directly from villages or regions nominally under nawabi control. Under the system of "tax farming," this meant that any revenue collected over the contracted amount, by whatever means, would be profit. When combined with presents of diamonds and gold, this profit constituted a far better return on investment than the most lucrative private trade in Bengal or the most favorable East India Company stock on the home exchange, even when (especially when) the debts were not fully repaid. Meanwhile, the nawab would borrow more money to pay for additional presents, and save himself the bother, the uncertainty, and the expense of maintaining and administering an elaborate revenue collection system of his own. Indeed, the dependence of Company servants on the wealth and perquisites of local politics gave the nawab a new kind of political power, as he managed circuits of redistribution and entitlement that made him as indispensable as he was bankrupt. Given the list of creditors, the nawab was properly convinced that no matter how indebted he became, the Company would never force him into total bankruptcy, even as they would never take the trouble to regularize either his finances or his administration. Besides, the Company was embodied in the unparalleled avarice and venality of a growing group of Englishmen whose accession to the position of nabob was entirely dependent on the survival of the nawab. As a consequence, the debts of the nawab of Arcot were enmeshed in a form of Company politics that both parodied precolonial performances of sovereign authority and made the "old corruption" of midcentury English politics seem tame by comparison. By the late 1760s, there was not an Englishman in Madras who was not seriously on the take, and each new taker seemed to raise the stakes even higher.

By the time Muhammed Ali acceded to the nawabship in 1755, he was already deeply entangled in complicated and largely dependent political relations with the Company. He had granted the Company the tract around the town of Poonamalee in 1749, when he was still contending to be the nawab, and in 1763 he granted the Company a *jaghire*.[37] The *jaghire* was for an area consisting of 2,284 square miles in the region around Madras. He collected tribute from the rajas of Tanjore, Venkatagiri, Pudukkottai, Ramanathapuram, and Sivagangai, as well as a number of smaller "kingdoms" in the Tamil and Telugu regions of the south. As in Bengal and other parts of India, the Company nominally conceded its dependence on the sovereign authority of the nawab, and through him on the Mughal emperor. But given Muhammed Ali's political dependence on British power, no battles such as Plassey or Baksar had to be fought, and the distant relationship between the nawab and the Mughal emperor made the fiction of sovereign dependence far more chimerical than had been the case in Bengal before the Diwani. Muhammed Ali's first act as nawab was to set out with Company forces to collect tribute by force from any southern rulers who appeared vulnerable, agreeing to split all revenue proceeds with the Company. The nawab sent similar expeditions, again using Company forces, to engage the southern palaiyakarars in 1760, 1765, 1767, and 1783.

The nawab gave fabulous presents to senior Company servants, in large part to insure his own political survival in a context in which, especially after 1765, he was increasingly worried that he would be pensioned off. The nawab not only gave presents to a succession of Company servants who either had or pretended they had great influence on policy; he also employed a number of these servants to represent him in England. Between 1763 and 1792, at least a dozen Englishmen actually sat in Parliament with seats bought with nawabi money. The nawab also gave presents to defer the repayment of mounting debts contracted for a whole host of reasons, the most important of which was that the Company insisted it be given the full stipulated revenue for the *jaghire*. The Company's need for regular cash grew with its indebtedness, a result of its expensive wars first with the French, and later with Mysore. At the same time, Company servants lent money (against official Company policy) at usurious rates of interest to the nawab as well as to his revenue officers, or *amildars*. Although these same Company servants engaged in private trade, it was far more remunerative to invest whatever capital they could raise in the indebtedness of the nawab. The nawab offered interest of 20 percent or more and his bonds began to circulate widely across Madras. The creditors were usually repaid through combinations of cash payments and subcontracted revenue assignments, producing a complicated and interdependent fabric of rights and privileges both in the Company *jaghire* and in the extended territories of nawabi control. By 1766, almost every European in Madras was involved in some way with his debts, either as creditors or as executors for others. Since so many men connected to the Company had a vested interest in the indebtedness of the nawab—the creditors were especially notorious among the rich nabobs returning to England to buy estates and seats in Parliament—it was also assumed that if the nawab did in fact ever go bankrupt, his debts would be honored by the Company.

Despite the perverse logic of the system of corruption, there was never enough cash or revenue potential to stem the rising tide of indebtedness, given both the uncertain revenue base and the usurious rates of interest. Besides, the English creditors often wanted to take their money and run as quickly as possible back to England and their dreams of princely life. The nawab was thus encouraged to engage in periodic warfare to seek additional resources for the private as well as public needs of the Company. While a war with Mysore in 1767 began for defensive reasons, it was pursued in large part to protect financial interests. Many Company servants felt that if the revenues of Mysore could be assumed either by the Company or the nawab, it would provide a steady source of repayment for loans. As

Francis Browne wrote to Orme in 1769, "Such who were most considerably involved in the Nabob's misfortune greedily embraced every occasion that flattered them with a prospect of recovering their property, and there are not wanting those who conjecture that the war was commenced with a full hope of obtaining this end by extirpating Hyder Ally on that throne, who in turn was to resign the territory of Arcot to the Company for his private and public debts and all the expenses of the war."[38] The board of directors reprimanded the Madras government for its self-interest, writing, "We are alarmed that the debt to individuals should have been the real motive for the aggrandizement of Mahommet Ally and that we are plunged into a war to put him in possession of the Mysore revenues for the discharge of the debt." Indeed, the board went on to observe that their greatest apprehension was that any revenues procured from warfare—pursued with Company troops and money—would be "applied to the discharge of this debt instead of being applied to the support of the war."[39] The governor, Charles Bouchier (one of the nawab's largest creditors), was dismissed, and the directors sent a committee of three men out to Madras to investigate the scandal on the ship *Aurora*, which sank in a terrible storm off the Cape of Good Hope some time in 1770. Bouchier, allowed therefore to keep his fortune, was replaced by an even more corrupt governor, Joshua Dupre.[40]

Concern about the situation in Madras had mounted when news about the initial threat of the Mysore ruler, Haidar Ali, arrived. Meanwhile, John Macpherson, who had gone to Madras as a purser but managed because of his political connections to persuade the nawab to employ him as his agent, had returned to London in 1768 with dire reports of corruption and scandal.[41]

Madras might not have been the cause of the credit and stock crisis of the Company in 1769, but it contributed powerfully to a general sense of panic. When Bouchier was ordered to resign, a new council was appointed, and the directors at home decreed that the nawab's debts to the Company should be given precedence over the repayment of private creditors. They also commissioned Sir John Lindsay to serve as the Crown's plenipotentiary to investigate corruption and any causes for political concern in the Company's relationship to the nawab. Lindsay's chief assistant, George Paterson, soon became one of the leading figures in the nawab's court. In addition to boasting that he took great pains to help the nawab establish control over his debts and financial affairs, albeit in the end without success, during the four years he spent in Madras he managed to secure a fortune for himself. George Dempster, MP for Forfarshire, wrote in 1775, "There is lately come to Dundee a certain nabob from Madras. His name is Paterson. He has acquired a fortune of forty thousand pounds. This Eastern Prince has given a most splendid ball . . . They continued to drink very freely till five, and then beginning to turn a little riotous they display'd a truly British spirit by demolishing all the decanters, bottles, and glasses, and indeed everything that was breakable in the room."[42] This same Paterson earned an annual salary of only five hundred pounds and engaged in no private trade, nor did he lend money to the nawab or trade in his bonds. He made his fortune entirely from presents.

Paterson, who recorded his journey to India in a stylish diary of nine fat volumes, wrote of his steady efforts during his first months in Madras to be taken seriously at the court, or *darbar*. He worked assiduously to establish a personal relationship with the nawab, using an inflated representation of Lindsay's plenipotentiary powers to suggest that he carried with him some of the authority of the king of England. He praised the nawab's poetic sensibility, believing that he had developed a special relationship with a man who would on occasion shed tears when he thought Paterson displeased. Over the years he spent in Madras, however, he became increasingly suspicious of the nawab's motives, especially when the nawab appeared to be on more intimate terms with other Englishmen such as John Macpherson. He (like many earlier courtiers) called the nawab's court an Oriental den of intrigue once he no longer felt he controlled it.

Indeed, Paterson ultimately dismissed the nawab as someone who could not be trusted to honor either his word or his financial commitments. The leading impresario at the nawab's court in the first half of the 1770s, Paterson tried to mediate all of the nawab's relations with both the Company and its servants, telling him whom to trust and whom to avoid. He advised the nawab and his creditors about contract terms, interest rates, and political goals. He encouraged Lindsay to defend the nawab more vigorously than he first seemed inclined to do, and disapproved of Lindsay's efforts to demand presents from the nawab: "How everyone conspires to plunder the Nabob."[43]

Lindsay did amass a good fortune from the nawab, offering to become his agent in London upon his return (for which he pestered the nawab for additional salary until the nawab finally disowned him). When Lindsay left, to be replaced by Robert Harland, Paterson became both secretary to the mission and official representative to the *darbar*. By this time, Paterson had learned the rules of the game, and in making the nawab's interests his own, began to secure his own considerable fortune. He used the growing antipathy between the nawab and the governor, Joshua Dupre—who according to Paterson had "acquired a fortune of near three hundred thousand pounds by bribery, rapine, extortion and every species of corruption"—to foster closer ties to the *darbar*.[44] And he became increasingly tied to Paul Benfield, a man whose name came to stand for the corruption of the Company in southern India after he was vilified in Burke's famous speech on the matter.

Benfield had entered the Madras establishment in 1764 as a civil architect, engineer, and contractor, and he earned his initial fortune from the building boom in Madras during the early heyday of Company relations with the nawab. Benfield was an early enemy of Dupre, representing in part a new group of creditors who had initially been close to the raja of Tanjore but then gradually shifted their loyalties to the nawab, at about the time Dupre was making his own major break with the *darbar*. Benfield soon came to believe that the debts of the nawab were the most profitable investment in the colony, offering him some very large loans in 1772. Paterson was initially skeptical about Benfield, calling him a schemer wanting in integrity, but he soon began to support him, at various points advising the nawab that Benfield would be his most reliable ally. When Paterson was about to leave Madras, he even suggested that Benfield replace him as the nawab's chief confidant. In the end, however, Paterson became disillusioned with Benfield, whose self-interest was always several steps ahead of him.[45] By then Paterson had also become seriously disenchanted with the nawab. The last entries in his diary describe the nawab in the standard Orientalist terms that he had begun to use only during his last year in Madras. He wrote that the nawab was given to the importance of trifles and honors rather than reform and management, and that he ultimately doubted the nawab's steadfast loyalty to the English.[46]

Indeed, Paterson's final Indian musings trot out familiar terms of

colonial disparagement, expressing horror at Indian religious customs and unease at the systems of government that seemed endemic
in the East. As summarized by Pamila Nightingale, he also began to
see the Company with rather different eyes: "Whatever the failings
of individuals the company represented permanence, government
by rules and method, and respect for individual rights, as opposed to
the impermanence and insecurity of despotic and arbitrary power."[47]
In short, he judged his fellow countrymen less harshly from the perspective of the nawab's apparent failure. His "judgment" was perhaps not unaffected by his realization that he had used the same
methods to accumulate his wealth that had once seemed so unprincipled to him when done by others. The nawab's ultimate failure
was that he had not allowed Paterson the satisfaction of believing
that his own fortune was earned for the greater good of the nawab.
Paterson was also upset that the nawab never fully trusted him, or for
that matter any of the Company servants who had used his position
and entered his court. Of course, the question of political loyalty was
vexed for figures such as Paterson, who had to persuade themselves
that their own fortunes contributed to the greater wealth and prosperity of Britain, and not just because of the money they funneled
into the British economy. Nabobs were disparaged upon their return
to Britain not only because of class anxiety on the part of the aristocracy and landed gentry, but also because the admixture of public
and private good was hardly accepted as an unconditional benefit
even for those who accepted the levels of corruption that were common in domestic politics. In the logic of displacement that characterized most of the writing by English nabobs about Indian princes,
it was clearly far more convenient for Paterson to blame the inconstancy of Eastern "despots" than the greed of Western merchants
and adventurers.

For private as well as public reasons, the Company took great interest in the political and economic relationships between the nawab and his "feudal" dependencies, encouraging him to squeeze them for revenue and wage war for additional booty. Most important in this regard was Tanjore, the kingdom that controlled the rice bowl of southern India. Although Company servants tried to classify the raja of Tanjore as a simple *zamindar*, or landlord, of the nawab, he was in fact an independent king, and a collateral descendant of the great Maratha king Shivaji. Deeply in debt, the Company conspired with the nawab to initiate a predatory raid on Tanjore, using the rather flimsy pretext that the Maravar ruler of Ramanathapuram (just to the south of Tanjore), ostensibly a dependent of the nawab, had called for help. When the first raid in 1771 was largely unsuccessful, planning commenced for a second one. The only problem was that the Tanjore ruler had begun to establish relations of dependency through growing indebtedness as well, in particular with Paul Benfield. Soon, however, with the advice and concurrence of British officials, the nawab bought Benfield out, through a combination of presents and negotiated loans that made Benfield one of the nawab's principal creditors. After Dupre was replaced in 1773 by Alexander Wynch, a man who hoped to secure his fortune through the good graces of the nawab, the nawab was given the green light for another attack on Tanjore, using the argument that Tanjore had been fomenting rebellion among the southern *palaiyakarars* (chiefs). This time, the raid was successful. In taking Tanjore, the nawab doubled his revenues (from £1.2 million), though the cost of the two Tanjore expeditions was said to be closer to £950,000. Meanwhile Benfield, whose influence with the nawab had grown as quickly as his loans, demanded a share of the Tanjore revenues. Although the nawab gave the management of Tanjore to one of his two sons (already locked in battle over who would succeed the nawab), the acquisition of Tanjore did not in the end have the effect he had imagined. Instead, it both increased the nawab's indebtedness to, and dependence on, men such as Benfield, and intensified the pattern of mutual dependency and intrigue that dominated Madras politics during those years.

The directors in London had become increasingly concerned about the levels of corruption in Madras, with the delegations headed by Lindsay and Harland having availed little but new advocates for, and creditors of, the nawab. In 1775 they decided to replace Wynch as governor with George Pigot, who had been governor more than a decade before. Pigot had exhausted his fortune and become concerned that the nawab had neither sent him his promised pension nor honored the grant of a village to his Madras agent.[48] He represented the group of older creditors, most of whom had returned to England before the ascendency of Benfield and had become disappointed when the nawab ceased sending them money and gifts. Pigot was the most prominent of those who worked to persuade the directors not only that the nawab had to be restrained, but also that Tanjore had been badly treated by the nawab and his Company creditors. The Company's assumption of the Diwani in Bengal had made the power of the nawab (which given the intractability of the debts seemed to be on the increase) additionally suspect. There were those who even argued that the nawab was purposefully splitting the ranks of Company servants and using Tanjore as a resource base for recruiting alliances with other European powers to throw the Company out.[49] Pigot was sent to Madras with express orders to arrange for the restoration of Tanjore. Shortly after Pigot arrived in Madras, in December 1775, he announced the Company's intention, with the additional proviso that it house, and pay for, a Company garrison, which would offer military assistance to the nawab and the Company when needed (but also keep a check on the nawab). The news about the restoration did not go down well in Madras, where a vast majority of Company servants felt that this decision would seriously compromise their own fortunes by making it impossible for the nawab to repay their loans. Pigot's first concern was to control access to the nawab. Soon after he arrived, however, he also managed to persuade the Madras council to depose John Macpherson, who by that time had become the nawab's greatest supporter on the council, for attending the nawab's *darbar* without his permission.[50] He also had Benfield's *dubash* (agent) flogged for the same reason. When it seemed that the nawab would actively oppose him, Pigot threatened to imprison him, much to the consternation of most Company servants. Pigot refused the offer of a large Tanjore *jaghire* from the nawab, and traveled to Tanjore where, with great pomp and circumstance in March of 1776, he restored the kingdom to the raja. Benfield accompanied him to protect his claim to at least £200,000 granted as partial repayment of nawabi debt that had been secured on the Tanjore revenues.[51] Benfield subsequently petitioned the council to have Pigot acknowledge that these were private rather than public claims, and consequently could not be considered Company business.

It was only upon his return to Madras that Pigot began to realize the extent of disaffection with the restoration. He had only recently learned that the nawab's indebtedness had increased exponentially during the last few years, and was astonished to discover that the Company promissory notes (*qists*) were not paid directly from the Carnatic revenues but by European agents (*sahukars*). In June, the

Council formally opposed Pigot's efforts to ignore Benfield's claims and forced a reconsideration of the restoration itself. Eventually, in his deep frustration over the continued opposition of members of the Madras council, Pigot had his two principal opponents from the council, Stratton and Brooke, removed. He could now control the council, which was evenly split. But his opponents had too much at stake to quit easily, and, meeting in private, decided to stage a coup. On the night of August 24, 1776, Pigot was set up and waylaid on the streets of Madras, and surreptitiously put under house arrest in St. Thomas' Mount, some distance from the city. The council reconvened under the leadership of George Stratton and declared that the restoration was illegal. The nawab, according to many reports, opened his treasuries and distributed largesse to his principal supporters, thus increasing his debts to what at this point was close to two million pounds.

As soon as the Company's directors heard of the revolution in Madras, they ordered that Pigot be reinstated. But by the time their letter arrived on the shores of Madras in the late summer of 1777, Pigot had died in custody, ostensibly of ill-health. The bearer of the letter, John Whitehill, was made provisional governor, and the rebellious council was sent home in disgrace, though eventually they got off with miniscule fines and the incidental charge of a misdemeanor. The news of the Madras revolution caused initial consternation in England, and was the occasion for the publication of a raft of pamphlets and historical treatises, divided for the most part between those defending the nawab and those defending Tanjore. In large part because of the continued political influence of the Arcot group, however, the outrage disappeared into the vortex of factional politics. In the end, the two factions of creditors were so evenly arranged, and so much more interested in their own fate than in that of either Pigot or the raja, that the furor subsided with no major initiative for reform. Thomas Rumbold, a major creditor of the nawab, was sent out to be governor in 1778.

The failure to reform the corruption in Madras was made especially conspicuous when Rumbold returned to London in 1780, after a mere two years as governor, with a fortune of about £750,000, of which at least £180,000 had been procured as bribes from the nawab. Like other governors before him, he returned with a commission to act as the nawab's agent. He was soon elected to Parliament and apparently received a polite reception from Lord North. The impending loss of America, the growing political weakness of Lord North, and the news that no sooner had Rumbold left Madras than Haidar Ali asserted de facto control over the Carnatic hinterland, however, gave room to the Rockingham faction to agitate for inquiries into Rumbold's affairs. Edmund Burke, whose cousin William had been an agent for the raja of Tanjore, took up the charge, along with Admiral Hugh Pigot, a member of the faction (and George Pigot's brother). In particular, Burke made much of what he christened the "Arcot interest," claiming a corrupt relationship between the nawab, his creditors, and North's government. One member of the Rockingham faction proclaimed,

> The history of the India Company's servants was . . . for some years past, invariably the same: They went out to India; acquired great fortunes; returned home; aspired to seats in Parliament . . . They contrived to get themselves decorated with titles and distinctive appellations. Whatever was the object they had in view, they never failed to shew their attachment to Ministers, by enlist-

ing under their banners. But what was most singular, and most alarming too, was, if report could be credited, that the Nabob of Arcot had actually six or seven Members in that House. It was therefore to be feared, that in all enquiries of the nature of the present, it was more the intention of the Ministers to screen his good friends, than to bring them to justice.[52]

The committee that was finally authorized to look into Madras affairs produced voluminous reports and motions, "which together comprised a comprehensive critique of company policy in southern India."[53] But in part because of the feared Arcot interest, these recommendations produced little effect, aside from being sent to Madras along with a condemnation from the directors regarding the nawab's connections with his English creditors. James Macpherson, brother of John and by now an agent for the nawab (and author of one of his most cogent defenses), feared for wider political reprisals, only one of which was realized. This was the prosecution of Rumbold, who was charged with "Breaches of Publick Trust, and High Crimes and Misdemeanors."[54] In the end, the provisions of parliamentary inquiry, and resistance to the prosecution, saved Rumbold from a guilty finding. Nevertheless, it was widely acknowledged that the level of his corruption and political malfeasance was in large part responsible for the sorry state of Madras. And the fallout from the prosecution led to considerable support for the subsequent development of Pitt's reform bill of 1784.

Despite the enormity of the scandals in Madras, relatively little attention was paid to them, certainly in comparison to the scrutiny that was subsequently given to Warren Hastings. And despite Burke's personal interest in Rumbold, he was too small, and for that matter too venal, a villain to pursue for the kind of political drama he envisioned. So when Burke went to work for the select committee inquiring into East India Company affairs in 1781, his attention shifted to Bengal, and to Warren Hastings. It was not until 1785, in the interlude between his advocacy of the Fox reforms and the commencement of the impeachment hearings, that he turned back to Madras affairs. On February 28, 1785, Burke made a fiery speech about the corruption represented by the collusion between the nawab of Arcot and his creditors. Burke argued that the first set of debts to the nawab, those that had been made before 1767 and in that year received the attention of Parliament, had been genuine. But he believed that the new set of claims (amounting, he noted, to "two million four hundred thousand pounds") were a "gigantic phantom of debt" fabricated by creditors who worked in league with the nawab to defraud the Company and even more seriously the people of the Carnatic. He proclaimed that "the nawab of Arcot and his creditors are not adversaries, but collusive parties, and . . . the whole transaction is under a false color and false names. The litigation is not, nor ever has been, between their rapacity and his hoarded riches. No: it is between him and them combining and confederating, on one side, and the public revenues, and the miserable inhabitants of a ruined country." Burke continued, "It is therefore not from treasuries and mines, but from the food of your unpaid armies, from the blood withheld from the veins, and whipt out of the backs of the most miserable of men, that we are to pamper extortion, usury, and peculation, under the false names of debtors and creditors of state." The most fraudulent debts were contracted in the "ever-memorable period of 1777, by the usurped power of those who rebelliously, in conjunction with the Nabob of Arcot, had overturned the lawful government of Madras." He quoted from Henry Dundas's own findings of the time; Dundas had written that the debts "will not bear inspection, as neither debtor nor creditors have ever had the confidence to submit the accounts to our examination."[55]

In Britain, beneficiaries of the nawab ("the Arcot interest") attempted to mobilize support to reimburse the nawab's debtors, even in the face of concern that unscrupulous nabobs were draining the public coffers of England itself for their own private interests. Of all the corrupt nabobs, the one who was seen as most egregious was Paul Benfield. Burke called him "the chief proprietor, as well as the chief agent, director, and controller of this system of debt." Benfield's claims had been said to range between £500,000 and £800,000, though it was interest and commission on a wide range of transactions that garnered him a regular income of around £150,000 a year. But he had used his fortune well, securing the support of both Dundas and Pitt in his parliamentary bid of 1780. "Every trust, every honour, every distinction, was to be heaped upon him, Benfield. He was at once made a director of the India Company; made an alderman of London; and to be made, if ministry could prevail (and I am sorry to say how near, how very near they were prevailing) representative of the capital of this kingdom." Benfield, who had been sent back to London after Pigot's death, managed to use the system of rotten boroughs to buy a parliamentary seat as MP of Cricklade in 1780, which he held mainly as an absentee until he was finally banished from India by Cornwallis in 1786. That Benfield had both secured a seat for himself and funded seats of up to eight others brought the corruption of the Company into the sanctum sanctorum of Burke's own faith in English government: "A single Benfield outweighs them all: a criminal, who long ago ought to have fattened the region kites with his offal, is by his Majesty's ministers enthroned in the government of a great kingdom, and enfeoffed with an estate which in the comparison effaces the splendor of all the nobility of Europe."[56]

Benfield's electoral effort, Burke proclaimed, "was managed upon Indian principles, and for an Indian interest. This was the golden cup of abominations; this the chalice of the fornications of rapine, usury, and oppression, which was held out by the gorgeous eastern harlot; which so many of the people, so many of the nobles of this land, had drained to the very dregs."[57] The gorgeous Eastern harlot of which Burke spoke, of course, was the nawab of Arcot in drag. As concerned as Burke professed to be about the poor exploited peasants of India, he was most exercised by the seductive power exerted by the opulence of the east. Rapine, usury, and oppression were all joined under the name of fornication, and this golden cup of abomination was offered to distract and then corrupt the good citizens of Britain by the promise of instant gratification and untold riches. Burke not only played out the Orientalist fantasy of the East as female enchantress and victim both; he ultimately could not keep himself from blaming the East for the scandal. The charge of rape will never stick when the victim is judged a whore. The phantasmatic character of the nawab's debts were the illicit issue of collusion and desire, a combination that Burke found especially dreadful in his later years, long after he had penned his famous tract on the sublime and the beautiful.[58] Despite much rhetoric that claimed the suffering masses of India as "fellow-citizens," it is hard not to read Burke's words as anything other than his desperate concern to keep the scandals of the East firmly outside the borders of Britain. If Burke was signally aware that events in India were vital to

British politics, economy, and society, he never embraced the imperial ideal without ambivalence. India might have an ancient constitution of its own—and empire might be a worthy extension of Britain's own ancient constitution—but there were clear dangers in
bringing the two together. The underside of Burke's sympathetic
rendering of India was his sense of its horror. The nawab of Arcot
might have been a puppet of rapacious Britons, but he also became
a symbol of how India was corrupting the callow youth of the Company service not only with its immense wealth but also with its irre-
vocable, and deeply sexualized, alterity.[59]

When Burke began speaking out on Indian affairs in the debates
over Fox's ill-fated India Bill of 1783, he had been especially concerned about those returning nabobs who used their corrupt fortunes to buy themselves landed positions and political power. He
had provided as frightening an account of the class mobility afforded
by the imperial connection as any broadsheet rant or Haymarket
skit about nabobs. In ominous tones, he had inveighed against the
surreptitious entry of this corruption and its widespread influence:
"They marry into your families; they enter into your senate; they
ease your estates by loans; they raise their value by demand; they
cherish and protect your relations which lie heavy on your patronage; and there is scarcely a house in the kingdom that does not feel
some concern and interest that makes all your reform of our Eastern
government appear officious and disgusting."[60] This is where the
Burke in favor of reform in India and the Burke against revolution in
France merge, for his greatest concern seems to be about the consequences of imperial excess and corruption for the values in England
that undergird its ancient constitution. But Burke's famous sympa-

thy for the Indian peasant here too betrays its real motive in his fear that India has corrupted Britain. He contrasts the fortunes accumulated from imperial exploitation with hereditary wealth both because of the horrible oppressions that made them possible and because it was impossible to draw a veil across the origins of this new class of unprincipled, untutored, and uncultured nabobs.[61] What the rabble was soon to threaten in France was already knocking at Britain's doors. That nabobs bought their way into the gentry and into Parliament posed a fundamental, and deadly, challenge to the ancient constitution.

The worry that the corruption of empire would lead to the corruption of the metropole was not Burke's alone, for it underwrote the pervasive disdain for the nabob that used tales of corruption to justify fears of social transformation. Burke was more concerned than many of his contemporaries that these tales were at the expense of Indian peasants as well as princes. He was not sanguine that legitimate trade was the engine of progress and the development of a new worldly enlightenment. David Hume and Adam Smith, among other figures in the Scottish Enlightenment, had both argued that trade was to agriculture what agriculture had been to hunting and gathering, a mode at once of economic expansion and social betterment. Trade would create sympathy as well as wealth, the circulation of ideas as well as goods. Burke accepted the general premise that trade was both necessary and good, but he was worried that it would lead to revolutionary change, not least because of the easy slide from trade to credit, from credit to speculation, and then from speculation to peculation. He defended the role of the East India Company, but he read the excesses of its servants as the dangerous underside of trading society.[62]

When trade was uncontrolled—unanchored by the social charters of eighteenth-century English society—it could quickly develop this dangerous underside, nowhere perhaps with as much ease and success as in an imperial theater such as India. Empire thus had simultaneously to control the potential excesses of trade and to realize its political ambitions in an explicit political apotheosis. In order to prevent corruption abroad from engendering new forms and levels of corruption at home, it had to be guided by England's own ancient constitution, with its Parliament and its elite leadership firmly in command. Thus it was that the excess of imperial corruption, embellished with such rhetorical fervor by Burke, became the necessary ground for cleansing England. The corruption of Benfield and Hastings—though significantly not that of Clive—became the clarion call that would warn Britain against moral and political corruption. In the end, Burke used India to protect Britain from a revolution by shopkeepers and upstarts.

For Burke, at least, corruption in India was of critical importance for the future of Britain. But one must wonder why he spoke so much more about corruption abroad than at home, when "old corruption," that "parasitic system that taxed the wealth of the nation and diverted it into the pockets of a narrow political critique," seemed to many a far more dangerous threat to the body politic.[63] In the 1770s and 1780s most radical observers in Britain, from Thomas Paine to William Cobbett, were chiefly concerned about the local system of corruption that was most of all encapsulated in the patronage network, and expressed little concern for the corruption of the nabobs abroad. The domestic network enabled the elite to profit enormously through legal means, most of all from the influence afforded by the immense powers of patronage that directly connected wealth and political power. But these powers of patronage were imperial in a variety of ways, in relation both to appointments abroad and the purchase of estates and parliamentary seats at home with money plundered abroad. Popular discontent, meanwhile, was directed toward safe targets. Nabobs were figures of fun, or scurrilous critique, on the part of the older aristocracy, ever alert to the threats of new money. Burke too—who like Pitt was concerned that a failure to enact some reforms might allow the growing revolutionary fervor in France to cross the Channel—must have been tempted to deflect local critiques by making Hastings into a paradigmatic figure of evil, the embodiment of corruption itself. Pitt, attentive as he was both to popular and elite discontent, sided with Burke for some time, and his reforms both at home and abroad were hardly less conservative in intent. In the end, however, Pitt could not agree to ground all of Britain's discontent in the figure of Hastings.

Burke was both prescient and right to insist on the degree and extent of corruption in India. But why did he choose as the object of his vendetta Hastings, a man who was not just far less corrupt than Clive or Benfield (let alone all the other nabobs from Madras), but also admired by many Indians for his knowledge of Persian and his respect for things Indian?[64] Hastings was in many ways like Burke himself, a man of great intellect and sensitivity, hardly a figure who could carry the full weight of British corruption in India, the accumulated censure for the corrupt nabob. In the end, Burke's choice of Hastings was a fatal miscalculation, driven more by his concerns at home than by his real political engagement with the situation in India. The difficulty at home of course was that the radicals failed to understand the imperial dimensions of the political and economic crisis, while conservatives such as Burke used an imperial analysis at least in part to shift attention away from domestic politics. To insist that empire was constitutive for the emergent discourse of corruption, and that it played an important role in the performance of reform in the late eighteenth century, is to attempt to combine Burke's imperial perspective with the more radical critique of "old corruption." Few contemporaries within the British political scene were able to imagine such a combination.

These stories of corruption by the likes of Clive and Benfield, which set the stage for Burke's assault on Hastings, say little about the extent and influence of corruption, beyond giving figures to suggest the enormous dimensions of wealth plundered from India by the most unscrupulous of the Company's servants. It is doubtless true that the distinction between public good and private benefit changed considerably during the period under review. The conceptual contours of corruption were given new meanings by efforts to not just reform the Company but also end the "old corruption" that had driven so much of business and politics in contemporary England. This kind of historical context is necessary, but it can also reduce the sense of shock at the level of corruption and provide additional background for the claim that "corruption" alone, however defined, hardly provided the means either of India's impoverishment or Britain's industrialization. Meanings of corruption might have changed over the last decades of the eighteenth century, but the scale of corruption is staggering however we look at it, and the effects of this corruption were overwhelming for India as well.

For now, however, we will defer the discussion of the relationship of imperial formations to the wealth of nations, in order to consider the next great scandal of Britain's relationship with India. I refer of course to the governor-generalship of Warren Hastings, who was put on trial in the great impeachment hearing in the English Parliament from 1786 to 1795. For if the scandals of Clive and Benfield were spectacular on their own, the scandal of Hastings became, literally, the greatest spectacle of late-eighteenth-century Britain, and the symbol for many of what the imperial relationship between Britain and India had become. And yet the greatest irony of this spectacular scandal was not that the trial fizzled out after nine long years, but that it led to the regeneration of the imperial idea. Empire emerged from the trial stronger than ever. The imperial enterprise had been cleansed of corruption, but what replaced it turned out to be far more deleterious and long-lasting.

*Opening day of the impeachment trial of Warren Hastings
in the House of Lords.*

⇥ 3 ⇤

Spectacle

To the Commons of England, in whose name I am arraigned for desolating the provinces of their dominion in India, I dare to reply, that they are . . . the most flourishing of all the states in India. It was I who made them so. The valor of others acquired—I enlarged and gave shape and consistency to—the dominion which you hold there. I preserved it . . . I gave you all; and you have rewarded me with confiscation, disgrace, and a life of impeachment.

—WARREN HASTINGS, JUNE 2, 1791

The trial of Warren Hastings was by many accounts not just the trial of the century, but the most extraordinary political spectacle in Britain during the second half of the eighteenth century. Thomas Macaulay wrote: "There have been spectacles more dazzling to the eye, more gorgeous with jewellery and cloth of gold, more attractive to grown-up children, than that which was then exhibited at Westminster; but, perhaps, there never was a spectacle so well calculated to strike a highly cultivated, a reflecting, an imaginative mind . . .

Every step in the proceedings carried the mind either backward, through many troubled centuries, to the days when the foundations of our constitution were laid; or far away, over boundless seas and deserts, to dusky nations living under strange stars, worshipping strange gods, and writing strange characters from right to left."[1] Gilbert Elliot, one of the trial's managers, commented, "[The audience] will have to mob it at the door till nine, when the doors open, and then there will be a rush as there is at the pit of the playhouse when Garrick plays King Lear . . . The ladies are dressed and mobbing it in the Palace Yard by six or half after six, and they sit from nine till twelve before the business begins . . . Some people and, I believe, even women—I mean ladies—have slept at the coffeehouses adjoining Westminster Hall, that they may be sure of getting to the door in time."[2] The formal trial commenced in the House of Lords on February 13, 1788. Elaborate arrangements were made to control and accommodate the crush of people who attended the opening days. In addition to nearly 170 lords, there were judges, lawyers for both sides, and two hundred members of the House of Commons, which had voted to impeach Hastings the year before. The queen—"dressed in a fawn coloured satin, her head dress plain, with a very slender sprinkling of diamonds"—took her place in the royal box, along with the young prince, the duchess of Gloucester, and other attendants, among them the dukes of Cumberland, Gloucester, and York.[3] The prince of Wales was there, with Charles Fox, who, after Edmund Burke, led the team of "managers," along with such prominent figures as Charles Grey and Richard Sheridan. And the throng who pressed to procure tickets for the public seats of Westminster (spending as much as fifty guineas for tickets to key speeches) made up the rank and fashion of London society. During the opening days of the trial, the galleries were graced by Joshua Reynolds, Edward Gibbon, and the diarist Fanny Burney, whose colorful account of the trial furnishes many details that were not part of the official transcript.

Surveying the vast assemblage, Burney described the entry of the accused man, Warren Hastings: "The moment he came in sight, which was not for full ten minutes after his awful summons, he made a low bow to the Chancellor and Court facing him . . . What an awful moment for such a man!—a man fallen from such height of power to a situation so humiliating—from the almost unlimited command of so large a part of the Eastern World to be cast at the feet of his enemies, of the Great Tribunal of his Country, and of the Nation at large, assembled in this body to try and to judge him! Could even his Prosecutors at that moment look on—and shudder at least, if they did not blush."[4] Macaulay, many years later and with a view far more ambivalent than Burney's, painted a similar picture: "The culprit was indeed not unworthy of that great presence. He had ruled an extensive and populous country, had made laws and treaties, had sent forth armies, had set up and pulled down princes." Macaulay questioned neither his greatness nor his glory, only his virtue. But his virtue was on trial precisely because of his greatness and glory. As Burke made clear in his opening speech: "We have brought before your Lordships the first man in rank, authority and station; we have brought before you the head, the chief, the captain-general in iniquity; one in whom all the frauds, all the peculations, all the violence, all the tyranny in India are embodied, disciplined and arrayed."[5] By the time he brought the charges of impeachment against Hastings, the "savior of India" had become a symbol for him of all that was rotten in the East, both of the capricious abuse of Brit-

ish power and position and of the alarming possibility that the corruption of India would enter Britain through the sanctioned success and fame of Hastings.[6] All the sins of Robert Clive and Paul
Benfield, who had bought their estates, their titles, and their political positions with the ill-gotten gains of empire, were laid at the feet
of Hastings.

The first two days of the trial were taken up by pageantry and the
reading of the impeachment charges. On the third day, as Macaulay
famously put it, "Burke rose."[7] It took four sittings for Burke to complete his speech. Macaulay wrote, "The energy and pathos of the
great orator extorted expressions of unwonted admiration from the
stern and hostile Chancellor, and, for a moment, seemed to pierce
even the resolute heart of the defendant. The ladies in the galleries,
unaccustomed to such displays of eloquence, excited by the solem-
nity of the occasion, and perhaps not unwilling to display their taste
and sensibility, were in a state of uncontrollable emotion. Handker-
chiefs were pulled out; smelling bottles were handed round; hysteri-
cal sobs and screams were heard; and Mrs. Sheridan was carried out
in a fit."[8] Fanny Burney, less undone than some others among the ladies because of her fondness for the culprit, was still impressed:

> When he narrated, he was easy, flowing, and natural; when he
> declaimed, energetic, warm, and brilliant. The sentiments he in-
> terspersed were as nobly conceived as they were highly coloured;
> his satire had a poignancy of wit that made it as entertaining as it
> was penetrating; his allusions and quotations, as far as they were
> English and within my reach, were apt and ingenious; and the
> wild and sudden flights of his fancy, bursting forth from his cre-
> ative imagination in language fluent, forcible, and varied, had a

charm for my ear and my attention wholly new and perfectly irre-
sistible.[9]

Burke was known as a great orator, but on many previous occasions
he had overdone his performance, and had not always chosen his issues well.[10] Now not only was he near perfect in seizing and shaping
the spirit of the moment; he had also found an occasion that seemed
worthy of his full eloquence.

Burke had worked unceasingly to create this occasion, spending
virtually all of his hard-earned political capital in an epic struggle
that, once he had unexpectedly secured Pitt's support in the House
of Commons in 1786, catapulted India to center stage for the next
two years. As Burke noted at the end of the 1786 session, "India is no
longer new to the ears or understandings of the nation, you know
that one great difficulty in our way was the opinion that nothing relative to the East was to be made intelligible or, to come nearer to
the truth there was something like a resolution taken; not to know or
to care anything about it. That difficulty is in a great measure got
over."[11] Burke had immersed himself in East India Company affairs and impressed the galleries with his deep and extemporaneous
knowledge of Indian events and Company doings. He made the Indian victims of Hastings—from the begums of Awadh to
Nandakumar—household names. In his opening speech to the
House of Lords, he "described the character and institutions of the
natives of India, recounted the circumstances in which the Asiatic
empire of Britain had originated, and set forth the constitution of
the Company and the English Presidencies."[12] By painting Hastings
as a villain who was to be held entirely responsible for Company
policy, Burke sought to put all the iniquities of the British in India

on trial. By suggesting that Hastings was the single cause of the Company's defiance of morality and public law in India—"if you strike at him you will not have need of a great many more examples: you strike at the whole corps if you strike at the head"—he attempted to make a debate on India the occasion for the cleansing and regeneration of the imperial mission.[13] Generations of historians, all of them struck by the passion and irrationality of Burke's obsession with Hastings, have judged him—and the trial—a failure, both because of Hastings's eventual acquittal and because of the ultimate ignominy that was attached to a trial that squandered nine long years of public attention. But that Burke was responsible for creating such a great public spectacle around British activities in India—however it turned out—is remarkable, even if India had hardly been unimportant in British society and politics for the previous thirty years at least. And, as it turned out, the trial was no failure at all.

In some ways, Burke was an unlikely champion for India. He had regarded the proceedings of Parliament against Clive in the early 1770s as "illegal, unjust, and impolitick," and did not believe that the reports of abuses in those earlier years justified greater state regulation of the Company.[14] A prominent member of the Rockingham political group, Burke was also no champion of Lord North's Regulating Act of 1773. His real interest in India began only after his cousin William went to Madras in 1777. Arriving after Pigot's death in prison, William became an agent of the raja of Tanjore, a post he held for the next five years in England and India. Biographers and historians have discounted the importance of this connection, though Peter Marshall has noted that Edmund was "perhaps insufficiently critical of William's version of the rights and grievances of

Tanjore."[15] The dispute between the creditors and supporters of the nawab of Arcot and the raja of Tanjore was the occasion for active politicking and pamphleteering during the late 1770s, and many prominent figures in British public and political life were drawn into Indian affairs as a result.[16] Whether or not Burke took a dislike to Warren Hastings—who had supported the nawab—because of his cousin, it was surely the case that Burke first became concerned about Company corruption in the context of the debts of the nawab of Arcot.

Burke played a key role in the activities of a select committee that was established in 1780 to report on the renewal of both the 1773 Regulating Act and the Company charter. Because the Regulating Act had been responsible for creating the supreme court of Calcutta, the committee's review also entailed a serious examination of the court's influence, especially in the wake of the Nandakumar case. Nandakumar, who had been the diwan of the nawab of Bengal in 1764, was a prominent player in the complex politics between the nawab's court and Company servants. In March 1775, he alleged that two critical appointments at the young nawab's court in 1772 had been made as the payoff for a major bribe of £35,000 to Hastings. Nandakumar had not always been Hasting's enemy, but by the mid-1770s he had made an alliance with the governor-general's councilors who, led by Philip Francis, opposed Hastings on almost every matter of Company policy. Soon, however, Nandakumar's accusations sparked a dangerous conflagration beyond his control. He was sued for forging a document in an earlier struggle in 1769 by other contestants for power in the nawab's court, even as the councilors used his evidence to sully Hastings's reputation in England. Hastings responded by accusing Nandakumar of forging the letter from the nawab's mother that had been the only evidence for his own acceptance of a bribe for an appointment that, in any event, he made with the full approval of the councilors. And so when Nandakumar was tried and sentenced to death in the supreme court for the earlier forgery, many assumed that Hastings was behind what some later called a "judicial murder."[17]

Burke's select committee examined a whole series of documents that portrayed the court as having trampled on Indian customs and traditions, all while considering European concerns about the racial composition of juries. Although the select committee did not in the end accuse either Hastings, or the chief justice, Elijah Impey, of malfeasance, Burke's unease about Company politics outside of Madras, and his concern to discover more, stems from his work on this committee. It was reconvened in the winter of 1781 with the much wider mission of examining the relationship between the East India Company and the "native inhabitants" of India.

It was during this time that Burke came into close association with Philip Francis. Francis had just returned to Britain after spending seven tumultuous years as one of four members of the supreme council that had been constituted and given wide powers (including veto power over the decisions of the governor-general) under the 1773 Regulating Act. Francis, widely thought to have been the anonymous author of the wicked Junius letters concerning British politics in the years leading up to (and ending abruptly with) his departure for India, was both brilliant and ambitious. An improbable candidate for the council, he soon became its most vigorous opponent of Hastings, in alliance with two of the three other councilors. Before going to India Francis was briefed extensively by Clive, who had turned against Hastings because of his alliance with Laurence Sulivan, and when he arrived in Calcutta in 1774 he was ready to do battle. Quickly determining that Hastings was not going to consult him in any serious way, Francis began by questioning the propriety of the "Rohilla War," a matter that was later to become the first charge for impeachment, though it was defeated in the House of Commons.[18] Excoriated by most observers well into the nineteenth century, but later seen as yet another necessary defensive move on the part of Hastings and the early Company, the bloody annexation of Rohilkhand was conducted by the nawab of Awadh with the use of Company troops.[19] Hastings had clearly pressed the nawab for quick cash to cover Company debts, and had shown no more concern about the campaign than he did about another one to annex Etawah that had been conducted without the use of Company troops.[20] But he had enforced Clive's earlier, broader stipulations that had placed Company troops, for a not inconsiderable sum, in Awadh to stem the nawab's efforts to become more independent from the Company. Francis, anticipating (and later fueling) Burke's charges, held Hastings accountable as well for his efforts to contain the Marathas, another factor in Hastings's support for the annexation of Rohilkhand. In devising military strategy for Company dominance over the subcontinent, Hastings was certainly no more ruthless than Clive before him, though in fact he pursued policies that were at once more sustained and more long-lasting in their effects. But Francis was adamant in his opposition, and went on to oppose Hastings on almost every matter that came before council until he left in 1780.

Francis believed that the majority opposition to Hastings in the supreme council—Francis was supported by John Clavering and

George Monson, with only Richard Barwell in Hastings's camp—
would lead to a speedy recall and his own replacement of Hastings.[21]
But in 1776 he lost his majority—first Monson died, followed shortly
by Clavering in 1777—and his personal relations with Hastings
steadily worsened. Still convinced that he was about to be named
governor-general, Francis was also embittered because of Hastings's
response to a scandal involving Francis and a young, married
Frenchwoman.[22] He was discovered climbing down a ladder from
the woman's bedroom, but nevertheless took special umbrage at
Hastings's censure. In a letter to Lord North, dated December 16,
1778, he wrote:

> Permit me now my Lord to solicit your Lordship's personal favor
> and protection on a point purely and exclusively personal to me,
> of which the meanest and most ungenerous advantage has been
> taken by Mr. Hastings. You will probably hear of a supposed im-
> proper connection (of which I assure your lordship no direct
> proof ever did or ever can exist) between me and a French woman
> whose Husband is a writer here, and who, I understand, intends
> to prosecute for damages. This business, Mr. Hastings, forgetting
> the uniform history of his own private life, has endeavored to turn
> into an affair of state, and to bring it formally as a matter of crimi-
> nal charge against me before the Court of Directors.[23]

Just the year before, Hastings had wed Marion von Imhoff, after providing a generous settlement to her ex-husband, who had been an
impecunious portrait painter in Calcutta. Hastings's first wife had
died two years after they were married. In the years after his wife's
death, it was widely assumed that he had a longtime affair with the

wife of a medical officer, Thomas Hancock, posted first in Madras and then in Bengal. This affair—with Philadelphia Hancock, who was also Jane Austen's paternal aunt—did not lead to a divorce, but it did produce a daughter, whom Hastings supported until she reached her majority.[24] Given Hastings's compromised life, Francis was doubtless especially incensed by his moral censure. Although Francis never formally admitted his own transgression—refusing a formal challenge from the cuckolded husband and fighting a suit that was brought to the supreme court of Calcutta—he later took the Frenchwoman as his mistress (Francis's wife had stayed behind in England during the years he was in India). He did so, however, only after having been forced to pay a considerable sum to the Frenchwoman's husband, per the judgment mandated by the chief justice, Elijah Impey, Hastings's good friend.

Relying on the belief that the court of directors would not look kindly on Hastings's continued military expenditures, Francis failed to realize the extent of Hastings's support in England, as well as the degree to which even those in Britain were clearly conflicted about their political ambitions in the subcontinent. During the 1770s there was growing recognition that the Marathas did constitute a major threat to the British presence in India. After a decisive defeat by forces from Bombay in 1779, in alliance with the one Maratha leader who had made a treaty with the Company, Hastings attempted to secure Francis's support for an all-out assault. Francis, however, reversed an alleged understanding with Hastings, opposing any military actions either against the Marathas or against Haidar Ali in the south. As convinced as Francis was that Hastings's actions would be rebuked by Company directors and stockholders in England, Hastings was nevertheless systematically supported for almost all the actions that later occasioned his impeachment. Francis, never one to understand that his very tenacity made him steadily more unpopular, was adamant in opposing Hastings in all his military ventures, but this last disagreement almost had fatal consequences. Soon after learning that Francis had reversed their understanding, Hastings sent him a letter that he planned to present to the council the following day. In it he stated:

> In truth, I do not trust to his promise of candor, convinced that he is incapable of it, and that his sole purpose and wish are to embarrass and defeat every measure which I may undertake, or which may tend even to promote the public interests, if my credit is connected with them. Such has been the tendency and such the manifest spirit of all his actions from the beginning. Every fabricated tale of armies devoted to famine or to massacre have found their first and ready way to his office, where it was known they would meet the most welcome reception. To the same design may be attributed the annual computations of declining finances and an exhausted treasury, computations which, though made in the time of abundance, must verge to truth at last, from the effect of discordant government, not a constitutional decay. I judge of his public conduct by my experience of his private, which I have found to be void of truth and honor. This is a severe charge, but temperately and deliberately made from the firm persuasion that I owe this justice to the public and to myself, as the only redress to both, for artifices of which I have been a victim, and which threaten to involve their interests, with disgrace and ruin.[25]

Francis responded by challenging Hastings to a duel. "I am preparing a formal answer to the paper you sent me last night," he wrote.

"As soon as it can be finished, I shall lay it before you. But you must be sensible, Sir, that no answer I can give to the matter of that paper can be adequate to the dishonor done me by the terms you made use of. You have left me no alternative but to demand personal satisfaction of you for the affronts you have offered me."[26] They met in the early hours of Thursday, August 17, 1780. Shots were exchanged and Francis was wounded—though not mortally—by a bullet that lodged in his left shoulder. He recovered soon and returned to the council in the third week of September to declare that he had never been party to an agreement with Hastings. Defeated and dejected, he sailed for England on December 3.[27] Despite his departure, the duel in fact had only begun.

Soon after Francis returned to England, he established contact with Burke, whose opinion of Hastings took a decided turn for the worse. Francis, who supplied Burke and the select committee with a mass of inflammatory documents, clearly played a major role in turning Burke against Hastings, and in supplying him with the material that led to the charges of impeachment. Burke spent much of his time between 1781 and 1783 working on the newly reconstituted select committee, looking into abuses of Company rule in India beginning with the causes of Haidar Ali's invasion of the Carnatic and then moving on to "rise, progress, conduct, and present state of the Maratta War."[28] With the news of Chait Singh's revolt in Benares, Burke moved for a recall for Hastings, only to find that East India Company stockholders were overwhelmingly opposed to such a move. During the summer of 1783, Burke began work on what became Fox's India bills. The bills were defeated in the House of Lords because of the express disapproval of King George III, as well as because Burke was unable to rouse any major support for his view that Hastings was the root of all evil in Britain as well as India. But by the time the Pitt bills were passed in 1784—looking very much like Fox's earlier legislation—there was widespread agreement that Hastings should be brought home and replaced by a less controversial figure.

Nevertheless, when Hastings did finally return to England in 1785, he was well received by many, including the royal court. Meanwhile, Burke worked at a relentless pace to publicize his concerns about Hastings, and by 1786 even Pitt was willing to accept that some of Hastings's actions were "censurable."[29] Francis was in regular contact with Burke, commenting on the drafts of all his speeches, supplying him with the local knowledge he needed. Boasting in various letters that he, along with Burke, had together changed the course of British politics, Francis worked closely with Burke on the "first scene of the first act—the Rohilla War."[30]

The formal assault on Hastings began on February 17, 1786, when Burke requested that certain papers concerning his conduct be laid before a committee of the House of Commons. During several sessions in April, Burke presented twenty-two charges of "High Crimes and Misdemeanors." Beginning with the Rohilla War of 1774, they included the "Benares charge," in which it was alleged that Hastings had driven the raja Chait Singh of Benares to revolt in 1781; the charge that Hastings had confiscated in 1781 and 1782 the landed income and treasure of the begums of Awadh; the awarding of corrupt and extravagant contracts; the illegal receipt of presents from Indians; Hastings's revenue policy; the conduct of the Maratha War; and Hastings's treatment of the Rohilla Faizullah Khan. The allegations were drafted in dramatic prose, to establish general criminality but more to make an impression than to convict according to the legal standards used in impeachment trials. As Burke wrote to Francis, his purpose was "not to consider what will convict Mr. Hastings (a thing we all know to be impracticable) but what will acquit and justify myself to those few persons and to those distant times, which may take a concern in these affairs and the actors in them."[31] Burke did not at first believe there was any real chance of conviction. He was also more concerned to play to the gallery, and, as his own words make clear, to vindicate his campaign, than he was to open himself to a charge of excessive legalism.[32] Even when Pitt anticipated that Burke's inattention to legal procedure might doom his cause, politically as well as legally, Burke resisted the language of law.[33]

In the short run, however, Burke's rhetorical attacks had unexpected success, even though his rhetoric worked to collapse the whole problem of India onto the person of Hastings. And when Hastings gave his own tedious and legalistic defense over two days in early May before the House, he discovered, much to his surprise, that he had lost more support than he had gained. Pitt, for example, believed that Hastings's failure to admit some faults in the larger context of the meritorious services he had performed on behalf of British imperial interest, justified—even necessitated—the trial. While the first charge on the Rohilla War was defeated by a vote of 119 to 67—leading many observers to believe that the impeachment was doomed—the second, on Benares, was judged grounds for impeachment by a reversed majority of 119 to 79. Pitt, who had voted against the first despite his reservations about the Rohilla War, began his own speech by justifying a monetary demand on Chait Singh but then pronounced that a fine of £500,000 was excessive. Pitt seemed most disturbed that the Benares episode could be read to imply that matters of political policy and financial interest had become too entangled. In voting against Hastings, Pitt astonished many observers who believed that government officials would seek to protect Hastings, both because of their enmity with Fox and because of the royal court's support for Hastings. Pitt's vote accordingly made clear that Burke's mission could now be seen to transcend party politics. All of a sudden, impeachment seemed possible.

As the drama unfolded, seven of the twenty-two articles were accepted, with the charge concerning various aspects of Hastings's policy in Awadh ("Misdemeanors in Oude"), broken into thirteen separate charges, making for a total of twenty actual "Articles of Impeachment" brought before the House of Lords. The managers of the impeachment presented complete evidence only on the four principal charges, namely Benares, the begams of Awadh, presents, and contracts, completing their case for the prosecution on May 30, 1791, without addressing the other charges. In the Benares charge, Hastings was accused of forcing Raja Chait Singh to make various additional military contributions in 1778, in direct violation of the Company's settled agreement with the raja, and of provoking Chait Singh into rebellion not only by making other extraordinary demands but also by attempting to arrest him in his own palace in 1781. When Hastings had assumed the governor-generalship, Benares had been formally subordinate to Awadh, but with the death of the nawab of Awadh in 1775, the Company assumed sovereignty over Benares. Hastings was concerned to maintain Benares as a buffer state between Awadh and Bengal, and felt this could only be done by allowing it a significant measure of autonomy. The Company thus issued a *sanad* [decree] that stipulated that Benares pay an annual revenue of slightly more than £250,000, and be asked to maintain a cavalry of two thousand horses for the service of the Company. From that time on, the raja was frequently referred to as a *zamindar,* or landlord, even though he was granted greater rights than most others denominated in that way. After several years, Hastings became increasingly suspicious that the raja was hiding great wealth that could be extremely useful for the Company, stretched as it was due to major expenditures associated with the Maratha campaign, and began to worry about the continued loyalty of the raja given the resurgent political position of the Marathas and of Mysore. He thus used the ambiguities of the treaty relationship to ask for greater subsidy and more emphatic proofs of loyalty.

The managers presented Hastings's actions as violations of the treaty rather than as logical extensions of Company sovereignty, as if there was in fact no contradiction in a larger field of political relations in which the ultimate sovereignty of the Mughal was completely elided and the nature of the *zamindari* relationship totally undefined. *Zamindars* were both revenue agents and local sovereigns, and were treated very differently depending on which part of the definition was taken most seriously at any given time. In attempting to use both sides of the classificatory coin—collecting a steady revenue, and expecting political, military, and financial support from a subordinate—Hastings was only doing what the Company had done before and would continue to do for the rest of its tenure in India. This is not to absolve Hastings of his personal excesses, so much as to say that in larger historical terms the question of excess was irrelevant, given overwhelming historical evidence that this was the way the Company was able to expand from being a trading corporation to a sovereign power. Besides, although Francis opposed Hastings on the matter of military policy with respect to Benares, Awadh, and the Marathas, he had no objection to the Company formally declaring sovereignty over most of India and acting accordingly. In other words, in the prosecution of the impeachment, Burke was right to say that Hastings stood as a symbol of British rule in India, but was wrong to believe that he was in any way an exception. The Benares charge could therefore be seen as emblematic of the entire political history of the Company from the seventeenth century to its demise as a result of the Great Rebellion of 1857–1858.

Hastings was certainly aware of the extent to which his relations with Benares were direct extensions of previous Company strategies and policies. He can therefore perhaps be excused, if not for his actual crimes, for being dumbfounded by the turn of events in the trial. He found it almost impossible to believe that what he saw as his narrowly defined quarrel with Francis would have surfaced on the national stage in so dramatic, and personally threatening, a way. Convinced that he had saved the Indian empire virtually on his own, he believed that he would return to a hero's welcome. He doubtless found it difficult to comprehend the force of Burke's personal disdain. He must also have failed to understand why he was impeached, in some fundamental sense, not only for doing what all of his predecessors had done, but for doing it better (and in some respects less egregiously). Given his quarrel with Francis and his sense that Burke was in Francis's thrall, he initially refused to take seriously the need to mobilize support, beyond licensing his private agent, David Scott, to publicize his cause (though eventually he spent a huge sum to try to obtain such support). His hurriedly prepared and tediously delivered defense in the House of Commons was symptomatic of his general attitude. Although after the negative vote on the Benares charge he seemed to wake up to the political realities of his return, he was unable to take control of his life once he had left India behind. And his image was hardly helped by the fact that a diamond that he had been given by the nizam of Hyderabad, and then sent on to present to King George III, arrived the day after the vote on Benares.

When the House reconvened after a summer recess to consider further charges against Hastings, his position was very precarious indeed. And any lost momentum was immediately recaptured by the rhetorical flourishes of Richard Sheridan, the brilliant playwright who presented the case concerning extortion from the begums of Awadh with an eloquence that exceeded his most successful thespian efforts. Once this vote went against Hastings, impeachment seemed inevitable. In May 1787, Hastings was formally impeached by the House of Commons, and the case was referred for trial to the House of Lords. Hastings's only consolation was that Francis had by that time so alienated parliamentarians, his venom so transparent that he had angered even those who supported the impeachment, that he was voted off the team of managers.

By the time Burke made his opening speech, in February 1788, he was at the height of his career, with political and rhetorical power to match. His words of indictment rang across Westminster Hall and across the nation: "I impeach, therefore, Warren Hastings, in the name of our Holy Religion, which he has disgraced,—I impeach him in the name of the English Constitution, which he has violated and broken,—I impeach him in the name of Indian Millions, whom he has sacrificed to injustice,—I impeach him in the name, and by the best rights of human nature, which he has stabbed to the heart. And I conjure this High and Sacred Court to let not these pleadings be heard in vain!"[34] Even if Burke miscalculated the legal possibilities for success in planning his political strategy, he can hardly be faulted for his belief that in impeaching Hastings he was putting empire on trial before the entire nation. He asserted, "It is according to the Judgment that you shall pronounce upon the past transactions of India, connected with those principles, that the whole rule, tenure, tendency and character of our future government in India is to be finally decided." And more than empire was at stake: "My Lords, it is not only the interest of a great Empire which is concerned, which is now a most considerable part of the British Empire; but . . . the credit and honour of the British nation will itself be decided by this decision . . . We are to decide by the case of this gentleman whether the crimes of individuals are to be turned into public guilt and national ignominy, or whether this nation will convert these offences . . . into a judgment that will reflect a permanent lustre on the honour, justice and humanity of this Kingdom."[35]

The moral and political stakes were thus very high indeed. As Burke went on to say, "They were crimes, not against forms, but against those eternal laws of justice which you have assembled here to assert." These laws were universal as well as eternal, at least in their fundamental principles. Burke neither wished to allow a different standard for the actions of the British when in India, nor to provide even the whiff of a suggestion that universal law would not be as applicable to events in (British) India as to events at home. In part this was because the corruption of empire threatened Britain itself: "It is no derogation to us to suppose the possibility of being corrupted by that by which great Empires have been corrupted."[36] But Burke was committed to the idea of the universality of law for larger reasons as well:

God forbid it should be bruited abroad that the laws of England are for the rich and the powerful; but that for the poor, the miser-

able, and defenceless they afford no resource at all . . . God forbid it should be said that no nation under heaven equals the British in substantial violence and informal justice . . . that, in order
to cover our connivance and participation in guilt, and our
common share in the plunder of the East, we have invented a set
of scholastic distinctions abhorrent to the general sentiments of
mankind, by which we are to deny ourselves the knowledge of all
that the rest of the world knows, and what so great a part of the
world both knows and feels.[37]

Indeed, the reputation of British justice, all that was good and sacred about the ancient constitution, was on trial as well. To convict
Warren Hastings was to uphold the foundations of British sovereignty.

In one of his most ringing phrases, Burke protested against
what he characterized as Hastings's "geographical morality." He proclaimed, "We think it necessary in justification of ourselves to declare that the laws of morality are the same everywhere, and that
there is no action which would pass for an action of extortion, of
peculation, of bribery and of oppression in Europe, Asia, Africa, and
the world over." Dissecting and ridiculing Hastings's own defense,
Burke argued first that India had its own laws and constitution, and
that in any case no British subject could be exempt from British law.
In May 1786 Hastings had asserted, "The whole history of Asia is
nothing more than precedents to prove the invariable exercise of arbitrary power." In the hurry and general disorganization of Hastings's
preparations for his defense, he had asked his friend, the Orientalist
Nathaniel Halhed, to write the section on Asiatic government.
Hastings himself, though he had a pragmatic, and hardly disinter-

ested, view of the powers assumed by various rulers in India, was in fact far more committed to Indian law and political precedent than Clive and other British officers had been before him. So embarrassed was he by this part of Burke's attack that he had his council later disavow the entire section of his defense, and in his later speeches he always took great care to emphasize his record of commitment to legal process and codification rather than mention anything touching on the notion of "Oriental Despotism."

Meanwhile Burke scored full points in this part of his oration, painting Hastings as scornful both of the lawful exercise of power in imperial theaters and of the principles of British law itself. In one of his most dramatic flourishes, he said:

> He have arbitrary power. My Lords, the East India Company have not arbitrary power to give him; the King has no arbitrary power to give him; your Lordships have not, nor the Commons, nor the whole Legislature. We have no arbitrary power to give, because Arbitrary power is a thing which neither any man can hold nor any man can give away. No man can govern himself by his own will, much less can he be governed by the will of others. We are all born in subjection, all born equally, high and low, governors and governed, in subjection to one great, immutable, preexistent law, prior to all our devices, and prior to all our contrivances, paramount to our very being itself, by which we are knit and connected in the eternal frame of the universe, out of which we cannot stir.[38]

Burke did not suggest here that there were no differences between India and Britain. Laws differed not in form but in substance, and

Burke gave the law of caste as an example of difference. But he argued that universal ideals encompassed these particular expressions of difference in custom and convention. Indeed, Burke went even further to assert that Hastings would be held accountable by both Eastern and Western law. In yet another flourish, he suggested that Hastings would have been far more horridly treated under the law of Tamerlane, for example, than even Burke could countenance for the punishment of "any human creature."[39]

In subordinating his own conviction about universal value to these scattered references to Eastern constitutionalism, Burke caricatured both Hastings and his intended audience, since Hastings knew far more about Indian law than Burke did, and the parliamentary audience cared little about the ancient constitution of India itself. Throughout his speeches he stressed that Indian difference was as important as universal morality; ridiculing the position of the defense that the people of India had "no laws, no rights, no distinctions of rank, no sense of honour, no property" of their own.[40] He expounded the virtues of "Mahometan law, which is binding upon all, from the crowned head to the meanest subject—a law interwoven with the wisest, the most learned, and most enlightened jurisprudence that perhaps ever existed in the world."[41] And yet he confessed that in India too there was a yawning gulf between the ideal and the real, between the theory of the law and its practice. And besides, his heaviest criticism, aside from Hastings, was for Indian agents, or "banyans."[42] Judging them to be a "low caste," he characterized this group of agents as *vaisyas*, or merchants, on the one hand, and as *diwans*, or agents, on the other.[43] Burke began by blaming Hastings for confirming, establishing, and increasing this system—"the instrument of the greatest tyranny that ever was exercised, of the basest peculations, and the most scandalous and iniquitous extortions upon the Country." He soon gave away his prejudice, however, by blaming the banyans themselves. "Through them Mr. Hastings had exercised oppressions which, I will venture to say, in his own name, in his own character, daring as he is (and he is the most daring criminal that ever existed) he dare never have entered into." Reserving his greatest scorn for Hastings's principal agent, Krishna Kanta Nandy, he went on to castigate the entire breed. "While we are here boasting of British power, we are in more than half the service nothing but the inferior tools and miserable instruments of the tyranny which now the lower part of the Natives exercise, to the disgrace of the British power and to the ruin of all that is respectable among their own countrymen."[44]

Indeed, these natives had been the instruments of the ruination of British character, the cause for the degradation of British law and justice in the East. Despite Hastings's official abolition of Clive's dual system of rule, he had—unwittingly—exacerbated its worst features. In these passages Burke thus betrayed uncharacteristic scorn for Indians, and for Indian institutions, revealing the extent to which these gestures toward the importance of cultural difference in the end only sustained his own conflation of the ancient constitution of Britain with his actual commitment to universal norms and values.

Burke's scorn for certain Indians came out most clearly in his use of John David Paterson's report on disturbances in the district of Rangpur in northern Bengal. Paterson alleged that the disturbances stemmed from the use of extortion and torture by the revenue agents of Devi Singh, the man who had contracted with Hastings to squeeze revenue from Rangpur. Although the report was not only unreliable but also hardly Hastings's responsibility, the supposed atrocities incensed Burke, who put them to extravagant use in his speech. Burke described the use of public floggings to obtain the revenue demand, sometimes the flogging of a man's children in front of him. But there was more. "Virgins," Burke went on, "whose fathers kept them from the sight of the sun, were dragged into the public Court, that Court which was the natural refuge against all wrong, all oppression, and all iniquity. There in the presence of day, in the public Court, vainly invoking its justice, while their shrieks were mingled with the cries and groans of an indignant people, those virgins were cruelly violated by the basest and wickedest of mankind." Now he had his audience virtually aghast, and he continued: "It did not end there. The wives of the people of the country only differed in this; that they lost their honour in the bottom of the most cruel dungeons . . . But they were dragged out, naked and exposed to the public view, and scourged before all the people . . . they put the nipples of the women into the sharp edges of split bamboos and tore them from their bodies."[45] Just as Burke went on to say at last, "My Lords, I am ashamed to go further," Mrs. Sheridan swooned and had to be carried from the hall. According to observers at the trial, "In this part of his speech Mr. Burke's descriptions were more vivid—more harrowing—and more horrific—than human utterance on either fact or fancy, perhaps, ever formed before. The agitation of most people was very apparent—and Mrs. Sheridan was so overpowered, that she fainted."[46] Shortly thereafter, Burke himself collapsed from stomach cramps, and had to be persuaded by the Lord Chancellor to continue his speech the next day.

Sexual scandal, of course, was the most riveting of all, and appealed to the general theatrical character of the trial, which many prominent women attended. The use of sexual violence as a means to blame Hastings not just for all he did himself but also for the actions of Devi Singh—the torturer who was said to have virgins delivered to his bed each night—was especially drawn to the increasing importance of women in the mobilization of political opinion in late-eighteenth-century England. Much of Burke's rhetoric seemed calculated to mobilize the paternalism of men and the sentiment and sensibility of women. As Sheridan explained in his parliamentary speech, "They could not behold the workings of the hearts, the quivering lips, the trickling tears, the loud and yet tremulous joys of the millions whom their vote that night would snatch or save from the tyranny of corrupt favour."[47] And while Burke horrified his audience with his carefully rendered images of the torture of women's breasts, he was setting up his subsequent assault on Hastings for the violation of women in the case of the begums of Awadh, where the sanctity—and by implication the sexual propriety, if such it could be called—of purdah (the seclusion of women) and the Oriental harem had been so cruelly violated by Hastings and his men. India itself was cast as feminine, in a way that dramatized its exoticism and difference, and rendered into the object of Britain's protective, and patriarchal, benevolence. Burke's rhetoric consistently highlighted the gendered, and sexualized, character of imperial scandal, but nowhere was this more clear than in his opening speech on the impeachment.

Less dramatic, but far more potentially damning, was Hastings's role in the "judicial murder" of Nandakumar. Burke did refer to this incident in his opening speech, condemning Hastings in particular for refusing to allow his council to hear Nandakumar's charges, presuming that if false the council (still with a majority opposed to Hastings) would surely have found them so. In a subsequent speech

to the House of Commons in the spring session of 1789, Burke proclaimed that Hastings had murdered Nandakumar, only to receive a
censure from the House for having spoken of a crime of which
Hastings had not been accused. But Burke had decided not to include this charge in the impeachment trial for several reasons, chief
among which was that Elijah Impey, the supreme court justice, was
brought to the House for possible impeachment in May 1788. Despite having a far less enviable reputation than that possessed by
Hastings, Impey defended himself ably, and was protected in part by
the concern of government (and Pitt in particular) not to appear to
overuse the impeachment process when so much was at stake with
Hastings. Although the letter produced by Nandakumar was widely
believed to have been forged, it was clear that execution was considered extreme for an act that had had little material impact (in India,
too, forgery had never been considered a major crime). It was also
clear that Hastings stood to benefit from Nandakumar's speedy demise. That Burke was unable to use this charge was certainly injuri-
ous to his ultimate success. As it happened, by the time Burke was
censured for invoking the charge in such a direct manner, both Pitt
and Fox wished to use the occasion as an excuse to drop the trial. By
this time, many of the managers felt that while the impeachment
had raised important issues, it had no chance of success. Sheridan
was one of those heartily sick of the whole affair. Despite his repeat
performance in the House of Lords of his celebrated speech concerning Hastings's extortion from the begums of Awadh (which concluded with his staged collapse into Burke's arms), by late 1788
Sheridan was reported to have said that he wished that both
Hastings and Burke would leave town for good.[48] Burke resisted their
entreaties—indeed he was reinvigorated by the renewed opposi-

tion—and the trial dragged on for another six years.[49] And it dragged on in part because Hastings's defense team had successfully persuaded the House of Lords to insist that all the charges be heard before any vote would be taken. As time wore on, England grew weary of the trial.

By 1789 more had changed than just the outlook of the trial. King George III had descended into madness in the autumn of 1788, shortly after Sheridan's last speech, bringing England close to a major political crisis. And then, in the summer of 1789 as Burke carried on his parliamentary show, the Bastille was stormed and Britain's international attention was once more firmly fixed on the land just across the Channel. Burke himself became one of the first to condemn the events in France, defending France's ancient (and monarchical) constitution with all the rhetorical excess he had used to characterize India before Hastings. As he did so, he not only broke with Francis—who supported the French Revolution from start to finish—he parted with Fox and his Whig allies as well.[50]

Shortly thereafter, the king dissolved Parliament and new elections were held. By the time the trial convened again, it was February 1791. By early June, given all the disruptions that kept deferring parliamentary attention to the impeachment, only four of the twenty charges had been examined. Hastings had already petitioned for a speedy conclusion to his trial (forgetting, or ignoring, the fact that it had been in large part his lawyers' strategy to prolong the considerations). Now he asked for a day to speak in his own defense, despite his previous desire to defend himself only after all the charges had been brought. He knew that the political climate in England had changed irrevocably, and he seized the opportunity to defend himself in far stronger terms than he had used when he first spoke in Parliament years before.

"You have been told," he began, "that I have ruined and depopulated the provinces entrusted to my care; that I have violated treaties, and brought disgrace and discredit upon the British name in India; that I have oppressed the native inhabitants by my extortion, or arbitrary demands of money; that I have wasted the public treasure by profusion; and that I have been guilty of disobedience to the orders of my superiors. This is the substance of the general charges urged against me."[51] In reply, he said that he had "increased the revenues of my government from three millions to five." He held up the testimonials of countless Indian rulers that he was still held in high esteem for his liberality and uprightness, to which he added myriad other testimonials from "native inhabitants" who made him proud of his actions in India to this day. He confessed that he had on occasion deviated from the precise instructions of the court of directors, but answered that in each case he had, and could still, justify his decision. And he noted that the court had repeatedly honored him in ways that could only imply their fundamental satisfaction with his service.

Hastings then went into greater detail. Regarding the charge that he had violated the treaty with Chait Singh of Benares, unjustly extorting huge sums from him to pay for his military debts, Hastings asserted that Chait Singh was "not an independent Prince." He was, like his father and grandfather before him, the vassal of the nawab of Awadh, who had transferred Benares (along with Ghazipur) to the Company before Hastings's administration. On the one hand, Hastings now took pains to stress that Chait Singh was a proper *zamindar* (landlord), and had the full rights attending to that status.

"My Lords, I scarcely need tell you, that whatever our various resolutions or opinions might be, individually or collectively, they could not affect the right or title of Chait Sing to the Zemindary, nor the tenure by which he held it. He was neither more nor less than a Zemindar." On the other hand, he argued that his demand for additional support from Chait Singh in a time of need was neither exceptional nor indicated anything that might be construed as an exercise of "absolute power." "It follows from what I have said," he maintained, "that if every Government has, in time of danger and necessity, a right to increase the taxes and revenues upon their subjects, we had also the same right to increase the tax, rent, or revenue or whatever name be given to Chait Sing's year payments, upon him, who was our subject, whenever necessity should require it, and of that necessity Government only could judge." Hastings added that he had only made the demand after he had commenced the war with the Marathas and had received intelligence that there was a danger of renewed war with the French. And then he took care to revise his earlier formulation: "I certainly did not use the words arbitrary power in the sense which has been imputed to me. The language, it is true, was not my own, for I was indebted for that part of my defence to the assistance of a friend; but this I can aver, that nothing more was meant by arbitrary power than discretional power. I considered myself and Council as invested with that discretionary power which Commanders in Chief have over their armies, which the Legislature has lately conferred in a greater extent on Lord Cornwallis singly." Yes, he had arrested Chait Singh when his request was ignored, but he did not do so with any "disgraceful restraint." Indeed, he had acted with prudence, and consistent "with the interest of my superiors, and of the people whom I governed."

On the subject of the second charge, concerning the extortion of money from the begums of Awadh, Hastings disavowed the charge that any acts of cruelty accompanied the resumption. He admitted, however, that he had not only consented to the nawab of Awadh's request that he resume the confiscation of the begums' treasure, but had also encouraged the nawab. After all, Hastings reasoned, the begums had given clear evidence of their support for Chait Singh. But beyond that, Hastings argued that the begums had in fact no real right to the treasure they claimed as their own. They had simply appropriated a large sum of money, left in their custody by the older begum's late husband upon his death, against the dictates of Islamic law. They gave their consent neither for any of this money to be used to discharge the considerable debts of the late husband, nor to help his son upon his succession. This was far from being a case of a son's heartless theft from his mother with the support of the Company, as alleged by the prosecution. Inasmuch as Hastings had an interest, he once again argued that the Company was in dire straits, committed beyond its means to the desperate military effort to fend off threats from the Marathas and other enemies of Company rule. "My Lords, I do most solemnly declare that I acted to the best of my judgment, paying due regard on the one hand to the laws of justice, and on the other to the interest of my employers."

The charge concerning the begums of Awadh had been presented by Richard Sheridan, and it was perhaps the most electrifying event of the early trial days. In his first speech before the House of Commons, Sheridan's oratory had played an important role in recruiting Pitt to support the charge, and when he expatiated on Hastings's iniquities before the Lords, he played to a House in which many in the audience had paid dearly for admission. Speaking for four days,

Sheridan claimed that Hastings had ordered his troops to invade the women's quarters of the begums of Awadh, despite his full knowledge as to "how sacred was the residence of women in India." As he went on to say, this "threat, therefore, to force that residence, and violate its purity by sending armed men into it, was a species of torture." Hastings was thus charged with violating the special purity of these Indian women, and desecrating the shrine of Indian womanhood with mercenary soldiers—who were themselves neatly affiliated with the retainers of Devi Singh, who had performed such gruesome torture on the naked bodies of Indian virgins. Sheridan also emphasized the terrible breach of "filial piety" in forcing Chait Singh to turn against his mother and grandmother, a charge also noted by Burke when he declaimed that Hastings had made "the pious hand of a son to tear from his mother and grandmother the provision of their age, the maintenance of his brethren, and of all the ancient household of his father." Burke went on to say that the begums had been "bereaved even of their jewels: their toilets, these alters of beauty, were sacrilegiously invaded, and the very ornaments of the sex foully purloined."[52] Once again, this explicit language of sexual violation and violence was intended to present a gripping portrait of the rape of India, a literal as well as metaphorical condemnation of Hastings as a vicious man with neither scruple nor even a shred of moral concern. Burke thus assumed the mantle of universal morality against these threateningly stark and sexualized images, which evoked the horror, and the eroticized fascination, of an audience that had already been accustomed to descriptions of the East as feminine and, behind the veil of purity, deeply licentious.

Hastings did not rise to the bait; instead, in his response he talked about the political context, and the financial needs, of the bureaucratic entity he had to manage in such difficult circumstances. Nevertheless, the charge concerning the begums did more political damage to Hastings than any other, and the resonance of this supposed crime against two Oriental matriarchs made the facts of the case largely irrelevant. As in the Benares charge, the complexity of the actual case revolved around the ambiguous relations between the Company and Awadh, in this case with direct reference to the obligations of Awadh to maintain a military force for the Company as well as to provide Company coffers with significant subsidies after 1775. The Company was frustrated by the extent to which the resources of Awadh had been alienated through grants of benefices and *jaghires* to extended members of the royal family as well as to local lords, *zamindars* and other landholders among them. But of all the wealthy retainers in the kingdom, none seemed to control more resources than the begums themselves, both through their *jaghires* and in the treasures they controlled. Hastings could hardly have been accused of prurience solely for desiring some access to this wealth, given the larger claims he could make about the level of nawabi debt, which was close to £625,000 when the celebrated events occurred. And in the end, the begums were neither impoverished, nor in fact violated, because strict precautions had been taken to prevent any real intrusion into the *zenana* (harem). Hastings was vulnerable for having intervened, both directly and through his resident, in local palace affairs, first guaranteeing the integrity of the begums' *jaghires* and then managing their resumption; and he was certainly not wise to associate himself with the attack on Fyzabad in the larger context of his own rhetorical claims about noninterference. But once again these were crimes of empire itself rather than of the dastardly excess of the governor-general. These charges, however, especially as painted by the fevered rhetoric of Sheridan, were precisely the kind that fascinated and compelled the British public, who found it more difficult to forgive Hastings for this than for his other alleged misdemeanors.

As for the charge that he had taken presents for his personal enrichment, Hastings had little difficulty disposing of its force, especially in the changed context of 1791. In his final defense, he succinctly noted that the only genuine evidence that was held against him was in fact his own word, which he would hardly have supplied had he thought he had something to hide. Second, he argued that the presents in question were really nothing more than the "common Zeasut," or entertainment allowance, granted routinely by the nawab on the occasion of any dignitary's visit. "I will not pretend to deny, I never did deny, that I accepted the usual entertainments which were then (for it was previous to the Act of Parliament prohibiting the receipt of presents) usually given to the visitor, by the visited . . . It was usual in the country, and it is impossible for any person to read any oriental history without knowing that the custom has prevailed all over the East, from the most ancient times to the present. My predecessors, as I was informed, had received the same, and it was never held criminal in them." Hastings also defended himself against the charge that he had taken other presents, and only credited them to the Company after he feared disclosure and scandal. Most commentators on the trial have observed that Hastings kept his own accounts very crudely, and that he seemed confused about basic budgetary matters. While Hastings was rightfully accused of carelessness—including failing to report and itemize presents and on occasion neglecting to return them—he was clearly far less avaricious than his predecessors.

Although Hastings seemed to fall between the cracks by having accepted hospitality in the years after the 1773 Regulating Act had tried to clamp down on all Company corruption, the truth was that most of the presents he was accused of taking were either subsequently handed over to Company coffers or used to defray Company expenses during his own tours outside Calcutta. Hastings was certainly no Clive, and when he returned to England he knew he had to depend on a handsome Company pension rather than his own ill-gotten gains to support his admittedly aristocratic tastes. Unlike Clive, he accepted that he had made errors, but steadfastly denied that he did so with any intent to defraud the government for his private gain. "I never did harbour such a thought for an instant," he remarked, adding quickly, to put things into perspective once again, that he had in any case been "too intent upon the means to be employed for preserving India to Great Britain, from the hour in which I was informed that France meant to strain every nerve to dispute that empire with us, to bestow a thought upon myself, or my own private fortune."

Sensing at last his final vindication, Hastings dealt with the other charges in even more peremptory a fashion, protesting his innocence, correcting misrepresentation and misinformation, and frequently resorting to the larger context of his great accomplishments. Hastings emphasized the strategic and military crises that he managed, noting that he simply had come up against the same limitation that Lord Cornwallis was presently also confronting, namely that "the resources of India cannot, in time of war, meet the expenses of India." He went on, "Your Lordships know that I could not, and Lord Cornwallis cannot do, what every Minister of England has done since the Revolution—I could not borrow the utmost extent of my wants during the late war, and tax posterity to pay the interest of my loans." By comparing his plight with that of Corn-wallis, who was that very year forced to assume a large loan to sup-port his own military preparations for an assault on Haidar Ali, Hastings clearly attempted to have some of Cornwallis's reputed glory, and unblemished moral reputation, reflect back on him. He also neatly characterized the extraordinary financial strictures placed on the imperial mission in India. But he went on to stress his accom-plishments rather than any failings. He had not only saved the em-pire; he had done so at a time when Britain had lost America and had put itself at risk of losing its imperial position altogether. He had also brought the Indian empire to the point where Cornwallis could proclaim his own successes:

> In this long period of thirteen years, and under so many succes-sive appointments, I beg leave to call to the recollection of Lord-ships, that whilst Great-Britain lost one half of its empire, and doubled its public debt, that Government over which I pre-sided, was not only preserved entire, but increased in population, wealth, agriculture, and commerce; and although your Lordships have been told by the House of Commons, that my measures have disgraced and degraded the British character in India, I ap-peal to the general sense of mankind, to confirm what I am now going to say, that the British name and character never stood higher, or were more respected in India, than when I left it.[53]

Hastings also took credit for transforming the administration of land revenue in Bengal, for instituting courts of civil and criminal justice, for establishing a new form of government in Benares, and for cementing the Company's subsidiary alliance with the great province of Awadh. He created the conditions for Company trade in opium and salt, and held off famine even when it crept to the borders of Company rule. Finally, he had raised the Company's annual revenue from three to five million pounds. "I gave you all, and you have rewarded me with confiscation, disgrace, and a life of impeachment."

With these remarks, Hastings came close to assuring his own acquittal, even if he had to wait another four years. He had finally been able to take momentum away from Burke. During the last stages of the trial, Lord Cornwallis came in to testify, having finished his stint as governor-general of India. He defended Hastings's reputation and legacy. Despite Hastings's repeated requests to schedule parliamentary sessions so as to conclude the trial, judgment day kept being postponed. Over nine years, the trial had in fact consumed only a little more than a hundred days, but delays, adjournments, and the scheduling of sessions amid other business and crises conspired to make for inordinate delays (responsibility for which was in fact shared equally by both sides). By the end Burke, now expecting defeat, sought to drag things out further, using up the last nine days of the trial in 1794 for his concluding speech. Closure was only reached on April 23, 1795, before a packed house. With all the changes in the House over the years, only twenty-nine peers declared themselves willing to take part in the final deliberation. Warren Hastings was acquitted by large majorities of all the charges against him. The last impeachment trial in Great Britain had ended.

Peter Marshall, the leading historian of the impeachment, has suggested not only that the trial was a monumental failure, but also that its real victims were Hastings and Burke.[54] He writes, "Whatever view is taken of his shortcomings, there can be no doubt of the severity of Hastings's punishment, even though he was acquitted." He continues: "To Hastings, incapable of seeing that he had any real case to answer or that he was not the victim of lunatics and villains, the humiliation of being subjected for seven years to a ferocious prosecution must have been torture." Marshall cites Thomas Macaulay and James Mill, who accepted most of the charges but felt nevertheless that Hastings had been ill-used, as further evidence that Hastings did not deserve his ordeal. Burke, though his judgment was "disastrously at fault," was motivated only by a tenacious devotion to truth. Wishing in retrospect that Burke, for his own sake, had been defeated in the House, Marshall concludes by asserting, "The damage done to him by these years of frustration is incalculable." Perhaps Marshall cannot be faulted for feeling that both Hastings and Burke had been harmed, nay consumed, by the trial. But what does it mean for a historian to cast these two figures as victims, especially when it is implied that a sacrifice is especially tragic when it is in vain—when, as in this case, the whole process seemingly had no real historical effects? Like most other historians and observers, Marshall has judged the impeachment to have been a sham, with little ultimate influence on either Britain or India.[55] Although he would have wished Burke success, both to increase regulation over Company affairs and to generate greater interest in (and responsibility for) the events of India, he nowhere suggests that empire itself was a problem. While the trial could hardly have been expected to bring an end to empire, it could have led, he suggests, to something more than disillusion and apathy. In his view, not only was Hastings let off; the imperial project continued unreformed.

The trial, however, was hardly a failure, even in Burke's terms.[56] Burke succeeded in directing Britain's full attention to the iniquities of the nabobs and the corruption of power and wealth that attended the idea of India. The trial made it clear that even great men were answerable to the judgment of the ancient constitution when they abused their office in imperial theaters far away from home. The regulatory concerns of Pitt's 1784 bill that recalled Hastings and sent Cornwallis to India became both publicized and generally accepted in large part because of the trial. Even more dramatically, the trial produced the conditions not just for empire's success but also for its transformation into a patriotic enterprise by allowing Burke a platform on which to make clear that empire was a sacred responsibility. Empire was to be no longer the province of unprincipled pirates, but rather an affair of state answerable to the nation. If the massive personal corruption of old was no longer acceptable, neither was a total separation between a monopoly trading company and the British government (even though they continued formally to be separate). When British leaders—from Arthur Wellesley to Lord Dalhousie—would wage war and annex territory in far-off lands, they were now to do so in the name of Britain, with all the presumed glory, justification, and (in the end) profit that attended this new imperial mission. The trial not only put paid to the scandals of empire; it also raised empire above the possibility of scandal. The only scandal that remained, of course, was one that neither Burke, nor for that matter subsequent historians of empire, would conceive as such: the scandal of empire itself.

The disillusion and apathy so bemoaned by Marshall provided proof of the trial's imperial success. India had been a sensation in Britain's public affairs for so long because of the sensational scandals associated with Clive, Benfield, and Hastings. For much of the eighteenth century, the economic, social, and political consequences of Company activities were palpable in myriad ways across the full spectrum of British society. Even before the trial was over, however, empire began to drift from view, along with the sins of Hastings, which were increasingly seen as excessive only in degree. Hastings could now be viewed in the context of his growing reputation as the savior of India, and at a time when empire was naturalized as a normal state project. Ironically, its very normalization also made empire seem less interesting, both less destabilizing and less important. Even more ironically, the legitimizing process enacted by the trial also worked to sever India's affairs from Britain's, exempting Britain from imperial danger at the same time that Britain could claim an autonomy that made empire seem largely epiphenomenal to the national story. Sir John Seeley was right to declare, when he delivered his famous lectures on imperial history at Cambridge in the 1880s, that "we seem, as it were, to have conquered and peopled half the world in a fit of absence of mind."[57] The trial of Warren Hastings was in large part responsible for creating the conditions of this national amnesia. But although Seeley was correct that Britain had taken an insular view of its history, he was in fact unable to fold India into the story of the foundation of "Greater Britain."

Burke at least had been clear that empire was not produced in a fit of absence of mind. But his ultimate concern was not to rehearse the story of empire's origins so much as to transform its future, not to arrest imperial expansion so much as to launder it (and thus sanction more of it). Despite his impassioned excoriation of imperial excess, he neither condemned empire nor did he seek to question its origins. Conor Cruise O'Brien has asserted that Burke became exer-

cised about India as a coded expression of critique concerning England's treatment of Ireland. But Burke's obsession always seemed to
be far less about India (or for that matter either Ireland or France)
than about England itself. Burke believed that the case of India
could be used not just to sanctify empire but also to bolster his idea
of the ancient constitution. The origins of this constitution might be
shrouded in violence and legend, but its reality was for him the necessary foundation for all that was worth saving in contemporary Europe. His great despair over the French Revolution betrayed both his
own monarchical leanings and his monumental terror at the prospect of change. And India had been both the engine of undesirable
change and a source of temptation and fantasy that undermined traditional forms of privilege and protocol. India represented a whole
host of threats to the structures of British society that had to be preserved at all costs. In a peculiar sense, the same French Revolution
that made India seem to most Britons so far away made India all the
more important to Burke—which is another reason he refused to
back down when invited to do so by both Fox and Pitt.

Burke's demise came soon after that of the trial itself. He retired
from Parliament in 1794, just after his final speech on Hastings. On
the day before his retirement, some members of the House moved a
vote of thanks to the managers of the impeachment, only to face opposition from a small but determined group who sought to separate
Burke's extreme and irresponsible actions from those of the rest of
the managers. The vote carried, though with a sizeable negative
vote. Not long after Hastings's acquittal, Burke became ill and was
sent to Bath to recuperate. He went into a slow but steady decline
and died on July 9, 1797. During the last year of his life, he wrote
several letters suggesting his desire to attain vindication for having

spent the last fifteen years of his life on the Indian question. In one letter to French Laurence, to whom he had entrusted the task of preparing a history of the impeachment, he wrote,

> Let not this cruel, daring, unexampled act of publick corruption, guilt, and meanness go down—to a posterity, perhaps as careless as the present race, without its due animadversion, which will be best found in its own acts and monuments. Let my endeavours to save the nation from that Shame and guilt, be my monument; the only one I ever will have. Let every thing I have done, said, or written be forgotten but this. I have struggled with my active Life; and I wish after death, to have my Defiance of the Judgments of those, who consider the dominion of the glorious empire given by an incomprehensible dispensation of the Divine providence into our hands as nothing more than an opportunity of gratifying for the lowest of their purposes, the lowest of their passions—and that for such poor rewards, and for the most part, indirect and silly Bribes, as indicate even more the folly than the corruption of these infamous and contemptible wretches . . . Above all make out the cruelty of this pretended acquittal, but in reality this barbarous and inhuman condemnation of whole Tribes and nations, and of all the abuses they contain. If ever Europe recovers its civilization that work will be useful. Remember! Remember! Remember![58]

These are stirring words, and as fine an epitaph as any enemy of empire might wish. But Burke's call to remember his Indian struggle betrays his real reason for outrage. The "dominion of the glorious empire"—that "incomprehensible dispensation of the Divine providence"—had been sullied by the cupidity of men such as Hastings. Britain's civilizational attainments and aspirations had been put at risk. In gratifying their lowest passions, the nabobs threatened not just to take empire down, but to destroy European civilization itself. While we cannot fail to be moved by Burke's passionate commitment to the cause of imperial reform, we cannot forget which civilization he sought to serve.

Burke was also distressed in his last years for less noble reasons. Hastings had been granted an annual pension of £4,000 (with a large advance to cover legal expenses) after his acquittal, a sum roughly three times more than Burke's own pension after his retirement. But this amount neither met Hastings's rising debts—incurred in large part because of his repurchase and rebuilding of his family estate in Daylesford—nor signified the end of the impeachment cloud. For Hastings was still shunned by Company directors even as he carried with him the taint of the trial. As long as Henry Dundas, who had turned against him in the early stages of the trial, ran the board of directors, there would be no place for him in Indian affairs.[59]

By the time the trial had ended, attitudes about India had changed as well. Britain was taking pride in its empire; a new nationalist fervor held imperialism as both an accomplishment of the nation and a continuing source of credit to it. It still took some time for Hastings himself to be rehabilitated, despite growing recognition that he had preserved the empire during the same critical years that he had set in motion many of the reforms carried on by Cornwallis. In 1813, when he was asked to appear before the House of Commons to testify on the subject of the charter renewal for the Company, the MPs "by one simultaneous impulse rose with their heads uncovered, and stood in silence."[60] He testified that he was horrified at orders forbidding Indian sepoys from wearing caste marks or symbols of their religion, and he was dead set against allowing Christian missions to proselytize freely. He argued strongly against allowing "the lower order of British subjects" to settle in India, for they "will insult, plunder, and oppress the natives."[61] He had also been much in favor of Wellesley's College, and the need to cultivate the learning of Persian, Urdu, and Sanskrit. Shortly after his triumphant return to the House of Commons, he received an honorary doctorate in civil law from Oxford. He died four years later at home in Daylesford, drawing a handkerchief over his face just minutes before he drew his final, private, breath.

It was not until well after his death, however, that Warren Hastings's historical vindication was complete. Histories of empire written in the late nineteenth century praised Hastings's role as the guardian of empire, noting little about any of his "misdeeds." By 1904, Lord Curzon had made canonic what was then widely accepted, that Hastings was "a great and ill used man."[62] Subsequent biographies in Britain (and America) have continued Curzon's tradition, finding Hastings to have been mightily wronged, heroic founder of empire that he was.

Hastings has had his apotheosis. His portrait stares down at visitors to the reading room of the India Office Record room in the British Library, and his legacy as one of the most important icons of the imperial pantheon, even in a moderately chastened postimperial Britain, continues to this day.[63] If he was temporarily a victim of empire, he is now acknowledged as one of its most important founders. Yet Hastings's sufferings, not to mention the question of his historical guilt, are in some fundamental sense beside the point. Like Burke, if in a somewhat different way, Hastings was instrumental in the history of imperial formation at a critical time for Britain. Losing America might not have been the cause of King George's madness, but it would have brought considerably more national despair had the imperial theater not simultaneously been expanding and transforming in ways that were foundational for Britain's economic expansion and political development. Britain needed both Hastings and Burke for its modern empire—and for that matter its modern nation—to succeed. And it needed its modern empire to enter the nineteenth century with a hope for the kind of greatness it soon came to take for granted, and now mourns.

The history of how Hastings and Burke made modern Britain is also the history of how they made Britain modern. In producing, and then erasing, the scandal of empire, they both played epic roles. And the greatest episode of this epic was the impeachment trial of Warren Hastings. The trial was certainly no failure, even as it presaged, and worked to make possible, the establishment of a secure and legitimate British imperium in the east. At the same time that Britain's political right to claim sovereignty over India was secured, the economic basis of Britain's interest in India became transformed by the conversion of private trade into imperial commerce. And so it is to the story of the economic dimensions of the imperial relationship that we now turn.

Warren Hastings, mounted and attired, displaying (among other sayings)
"Territories acquired" and "Eastern Gems of the British Crown."

⤏ 4 ⤎

Economy

Such exclusive companies, therefore, are nuisances in
every respect; always more or less inconvenient to the
countries in which they are established, and destructive
to those which have the misfortune to fall under their
government.

—ADAM SMITH, *THE WEALTH OF NATIONS,*

1776

In his impeachment assault, Burke had condemned Hastings for his
personal greed and corruption, but he had also raised larger questions concerning the dire economic effects of British rule in India.
In fact, he had made his most eloquent and forceful denunciations
of the economic consequences of Company rule just a few years before the commencement of the trial. In the *Ninth Report of the Se-*
lect Committee—a committee that in 1783 had been "Appointed to
take into Consideration the State of the Administration of Justice in
the Provinces of Bengal, Bahar and Orissa," and headed by Burke
(who wrote all but a few words of the report)—the idea of a "drain of
wealth" or an "Annual Plunder" that would inevitably ruin the Brit-

ish provinces was developed in terms that were much later made famous by the great nationalist and economic historian Romesh Dutt
in his celebrated *Economic History of India*.[1] Burke used the *Ninth
Report* to attack the system of commerce that had developed under
Company rule, in particular lamenting a system in which a significant amount of the land revenue was used to finance its own
trade. As he wrote,

> A certain Portion of the Revenues of Bengal has been for many
> Years set apart, to be employed in the Purchase of Goods for Ex-
> portation to England, and this is called The *Investment*. The
> Greatness of this Investment has been the Standard by which the
> Merit of the Company's principal Servants has been too generally
> estimated; and this main Cause of the Impoverishment of India
> has been generally taken as a Measure of its Wealth and Prosper-
> ity. Numerous Fleets of large Ships, loaded with the most valu-
> able Commodities of the East, annually arriving in England in a
> constant and encreasing Succession, imposed upon the public
> Eye, and naturally gave rise to an Opinion of the happy Condi-
> tion and growing Opulence of a Country, whose surplus Produc-
> tions occupied so vast a Space in the Commercial World. This
> Export from India seemed to imply also a reciprocal Supply, by
> which the trading Capital employed in those Productions was
> continually strengthened and enlarged. But the payment of a
> Tribute, and not a beneficial Commerce to that Country, wore
> this specious and delusive Appearance.[2]

Burke's conviction that the notional "investment" represented by
land revenue and realized in trade was for Britain's prosperity alone,

and that the annual tax paid by the Company to Parliament (£400,000)—what Burke calls the "tribute"—paid by the Company constituted an unsustainable drain on the economy of India. Burke's critique became the basis for a critical economic history of British India, and has been invoked with approval in most important nationalist writing about the effects of British rule on India. Much of Burke's analysis here, as elsewhere, was derived in fact from the writings of Philip Francis, who worked out a comprehensive critique of the political economy of the Company during his time in Calcutta in the 1770s. Francis denominated four "articles of tribute" as critical for the drain of wealth from Bengal. The first was the "investment," which was described as a "clear acknowledged Tribute from Bengal to England"; the second was the remittances made to other presidencies (Madras and Bombay), another "direct Tribute"; the third was the transfer of private income to England; and the fourth was the transfer of income from private trade.[3] But Burke gave clear specification as well as rhetorical force to Francis's insight that the political economy of commerce between Britain and India was predicated on unequal, and unfair, terms of trade—on the part of both its private traders and its stakeholders—set by the political domination of the Company over the Indian subcontinent. And he painted the picture of a devastated Bengal in the stark and dramatic terms that would more than a century later be cited to explain why India became impoverished during the very years when Britain attained world economic power through both an industrial revolution and increases in its commercial capacity.

Burke addressed the economic effects of empire in a context in which arguments around the advantages of free trade were in ascendance, and in which the general disrepute of the Company had made clear that monopolies were good only for a few unscrupulous individuals rather than for national economies. Adam Smith had published his influential *Wealth of Nations* in 1776, and while he was not a critic of empire per se, he was a severe critic of monopoly. Merchants and manufacturers, he wrote, were always "demanding a monopoly against their countrymen," and since they were the ones who derived the greatest advantage from these monopolies, they were rational to do so. But he argued strongly that this not only disturbed the invisible hand of market forces, but worked against the public interest as well. He recognized that the interests of merchants and sovereign rulers were different. Merchants secured profits by buying cheap and selling dear. Sovereigns, however, were concerned to keep prices for imported goods as low as possible, and prices for domestic goods as high. It is in the interest of sovereigns, he insisted, "to allow the most perfect freedom of commerce."[4]

In the case of the East India Company, the monopoly par excellence, the interests of merchants and sovereigns were diametrically opposed not only for reasons of profit and national interest, but also because merchants claimed inappropriate forms of sovereignty. Smith wrote that the "administration [of the Company in India] is necessarily composed of a council of merchants, a profession no doubt extremely respectable, but which in no country in the world carries along with it that sort of authority which naturally overawes the people, and without force commands their willing obedience." In the case of India especially, "such a council can command obedience only by the military force with which they are accompanied, and their government is therefore necessarily military and despotical." Further, Smith noted that the government would be subservient to the interest of monopoly, "and consequently . . . stunt the natural growth of some parts at least of the surplus produce of the country to what is barely sufficient for answering the demand of the company." Indeed, Smith believed that if the policy of the English Company were to continue, it would prove "as completely destructive as that of the Dutch."[5]

Smith was aware that private trade could hardly be prevented under monopoly conditions. He argued: "The servants naturally endeavour to establish the same monopoly in favour of their own private trade as of the public trade of the company." And because private trade would likely be far more extensive than public trade, it would have even more dire effects on the country. "The monopoly of . . . the servants tends to stunt the natural growth of every part of the produce in which they chuse to deal, of what is destined for home consumption, as well as of what is destined for exportation; and consequently to degrade the cultivation of the whole country, and to reduce the number of its inhabitants. It tends to reduce the quantity of every sort of produce, even that of the necessaries of life." Referring to the Regulating Act of 1773, he noted that the regulations sent out from Europe had been well-meaning but structurally flawed. As Smith observed, "It is a very singular government in which every member of the administration wishes to get out of the country, and consequently to have done with the government, as soon as he can, and to whose interest, the day after he has left it and carried his whole fortune with him, it is perfectly indifferent though the whole country was swallowed up by an earthquake."[6] It was of course no accident that Smith was writing his great treatise in the mid-1770s, in the wake of the great Bengal famine and the parliamentary inquiries into the corruption of Clive and his group. The signal importance of the Company for Britain's national economy and its seemingly devastating effect on India must have deeply influenced Smith as he developed his own account of the nature of commerce and the role of the market in a global context.

Smith, like his various interlocutors who shaped the Scottish Enlightenment, was anxious to rescue the idea of commerce from the reputation it had developed in relation to the Company. The worry that the corruption of empire would lead to the corruption of the metropole was not Burke's alone, and Smith's critique of monopoly was deeply influenced by the scandals surrounding the Company during the years he composed *The Wealth of Nations*.

Smith, of course, had rather different concerns from those of Burke. He doubtless looked forward to a day when trade with India could be free not just of monopoly but also of political interference, though given his focus he was less worried about the specific outcome of political relations between India and Britain, as long as commerce could be free. Smith, like Hume and Robertson among others, had argued that trade would have beneficial national as well as global effects, creating not just a vibrant economy but a more advanced society as well. Trade would create interdependency and sympathy as well as accumulation and wealth, the circulation of new ideas and values as well as commodities and money. But despite Smith's dislike of the Company, his general confidence about the role of commerce necessarily came largely from a history that was deeply connected to that monopoly enterprise. After all, it was precisely the recognition of the riches of the East—the vast reserves of raw materials and other commodities that could generate the basis for global dependence on commerce—that drove the thinkers of the Scottish Enlightenment to theorize a world in which economic circulation, interdependency, specialization, difference, exchange, and understanding would predicate a new kind of social and political future.

Despite Smith's and Burke's rhetoric—and indeed many of the arguments that had been mounted against monopoly forms—the gradual demise of the Company monopoly in the early nineteenth century was not linked to the creation of a global economy predicated on free and unencumbered trade. Instead, the uncertainties of the loss of monopoly control were channeled into the growing political power of Britain over India. While critical concerns about both private and public corruption were allayed by the regulation and diminishment of Company economic autonomy, trade itself was hardly free to operate according to Smithian principles. While free trade and open markets became the most important ideological pillars on which empire consolidated itself, empire itself made free trade impossible for the colonized. The regularization of the imperial relationship worked ironically to make possible a new understanding of empire, as the necessary political vehicle for the consolidation of a global economic system in which political disruption to trade could be controlled, if not completely curtailed. The desire for perfect market freedom on the part of followers of Smith, like the desire for perfect individual freedom on the part of the great nineteenth-century British liberals James Mill, Jeremy Bentham, and Thomas Macaulay, existed alongside the acceptance of empire.[7] British liberalism, buttressed by beliefs in progress and the liberating potential of education and civilization, came to accept empire as a necessity, if only in the short term. And it was hardly surprising that empire became natural in part as a consequence of Britain's growing prosperity and dominance, constituting strong arguments in favor of a firm, if benevolent, imperial hand. The global utopia of the new world of commerce and exchange did not turn out quite as predicted by the thinkers of the Scottish Enlightenment after all.

The history of the East India Company's monopoly is thus the exception that proved the rule of capitalist modernity in Britain, both in its early phases through the end of the eighteenth century and later in its gradual demise and absorption into formal empire during the first half of the nineteenth century. In the first instance, the East India Company had been able to begin to compete with the Dutch and establish a reputation for quick and regular profitability precisely because it had been granted monopoly status and official sanction from the Crown, as well as because it established a system of internal governance that was as efficient as it was careful to maintain close relations both with the state and its investors. East India trade began with pepper, much of it from various Southeast Asian islands, and later diversified to include other spices such as cloves, nutmeg, mace, and cinnamon. Soon, however, goods from the Indian mainland became even more important, beginning with indigo (a textile dye) and including saltpeter (used in preserving meats and for making gunpowder) as well as light textiles such as calicoes and silk. A warehouse system was established in various port cities, where Company representatives set up warehouses (factories) that organized local trade and stored at the ready the goods that were to be exported upon the arrival of Company ships. Early on, the Company realized that its trade required the use of force, and in 1613, and again in 1615, the British had serious engagements with the Portuguese on India's west coast that allowed them to establish a base in Surat. Soon thereafter the Company was able to secure official permission, in the form of a *firman*, from the Mughal court to establish warehouses and settle its business agents in Mughal territory. From the start, military and political considerations were critical to the Company's success.

The early success of the Company did not mean, however, that there were no critics of its monopoly status; indeed, it only served to make the possibility of engaging in Eastern trade more attractive. The Company was put into crisis by the execution of the king in 1649, and Cromwell's subsequent decision not to renew the charter. But the ensuing chaos and loss of profit changed Cromwell's mind after a few years; in 1657 he issued a new monopoly charter for the London East India Company, and just a few months later £740,000 was raised for a new and permanent joint stock venture that led directly to years of steady prosperity for the Company. Charter renewal became a vexed issue once again in the years after 1688–1689, when there were several major bribery scandals (the speaker of the House of Commons was removed from office after he was charged with accepting massive bribes to persuade him to support renewal), and the establishment of a breakaway rival company chartered as the Scottish East India Company. The Crown, desperate for funds given William's war with France, and aware that Company trade had to be better managed, put the monopoly up for auction, selling it to a new East India Company in return for a loan of two million pounds. After years of intense politicking, however, and a hostile buyout from the largest stakeholders in the new Company, many of whom had been directors of the old one, a united Company emerged in 1709 that once again effectively blended the different factional parties into a single monopoly venture.

The price for this success was a loan to the Crown of slightly more than three million pounds. There had been myriad arguments about the question of the monopoly, and a profusion of tracts that had appeared to argue for free trade. But these debates can be misleading in retrospect, for they were driven by the recognition that by 1709 the East India Company had clearly established itself as one of the leading financial institutions in Britain. The growing number of merchants and investors who wished to secure better relations with the Company were united in their acceptance that some form of monopoly was necessary, and indeed that the Company could not succeed either at home or in India without the direct support of the state. By then, the Company was one of the key creditors of the Crown—second only to the Bank of England—and it was also a major source of contracts to London merchants and an integral component of what historians have characterized as the financial revolution of the period between 1688 and 1756. During those same years the Company was the single most important source of shares and stocks for the growing exchange market. When modern finance capital was born, it was clear that finance of this kind, and at this level, was necessarily global. It was also clear that the state was not about to lessen its involvement in Company affairs. The Company was literally the "state of exception."[8]

By the early eighteenth century, the range of commodities involved in the East India trade had expanded as well. Perhaps the most critical entry to the trade was tea, itself responsible for a massive change in the dietary habits of England, after an initial period in which it was viewed as a pernicious drug. Tea was introduced in the second half of the seventeenth century, and by the early eighteenth century had become an article of mass consumption, along with the sugar from Jamaica that also sweetened the bitterness of coffee and chocolate, two other tropical commodities that began to be imported into Britain at roughly the same time. That tea became the national drink of England was not unrelated to the fact that, as Sidney Mintz has put it, "the production of tea was developed energetically in a single vast colony, and served there as a means not only of profit but also of the power to rule."[9] The linked commodities of tea and sugar were thus both closely tied to empire. As Horace Walpole noted in a letter of 1779 to Horace Mann, "I am heartily glad that we shall keep Jamaica and the East Indies another year, that one may have time to lay in a stock of tea and sugar for the rest of one's days."[10] Although the trade in tea was made possible by the colony in the East Indies, in the eighteenth century all tea was grown in China. Tea was an ideal import; it could sustain tremendous profits, it did not compete with local manufacturing, and demand for it seemed steadily to rise; in the early eighteenth century some 200,000 pounds of tea were imported into Britain each year, and by 1757 this figure reached a staggering sum of three million pounds, by which point it had become the dominant commodity of trade. The duty on tea reached 112 percent before it was finally controlled by the Commutation Act of 1784, but tea continued to produce enormous tax revenues for the state, as demand rose to the point where nearly thirty million pounds of tea were imported in 1813–1814.

There were two problems with tea, however. The first was that the Chinese initially accepted only silver bullion in exchange for tea. Gradually the Chinese did become interested in various Indian products, including cotton piece goods and, increasingly, opium. The "country trade," as it was known, was developed in effect to produce and then export local goods for the China trade, to substitute "currency" for the bullion that had increasingly drained the Company's finances. The second problem, and this intensified as opium became the principal item of exchange for tea, was fear that reliance on a producer not controllable through direct colonial means could be dangerous. As a result, the development of tea plantations in India, first in Assam and Darjeeling, and later in Ceylon and southern India, was strongly encouraged, despite abiding concerns to control European settlement in India after the precipitous end of Britain's control over the thirteen colonies in North America. By the time of the Charter renewal of 1833, European settlement in India was made possible precisely to allow for direct control over the cultivation of crops such as tea, coffee, and indigo.

The East India Company had been concerned to maintain its monopoly both over commerce with its port settlements in India and with China, but in order to do so it established other monopolies as well. Even the reforming efforts to stem the tide of private trade, especially in the hinterland regions of India outside formal Company management, became opportunities to establish monopolies over the country trade. For example, the opium trade was subjected to monopoly control in 1773, with deleterious effects on Indian peasants. All opium was henceforth to be procured at fixed rates and delivered to Calcutta, the only place where it was to be refined. Curiously, after 1775 the revenues from opium were treated as tax or excise funds rather than as profit from trade, with the unintended consequence of disguising the extent to which this profit was connected to the colonization of the Indian economy.[11] Indeed, the China trade worked more generally to disguise the weaknesses of the Company as a corporate body and its growing level of debt in the years between 1769 and 1793. It is impossible therefore to evaluate the economic implications of British trade in India—both for India and for Britain—without looking at the larger global picture that Britain's colonial presence in India made possible, including country trade as well as profits from China, along with the private fortunes attained through informal, improper, and otherwise largely invisible means. The economies of both India and Britain were transformed through their relationship in the second half of the eighteenth century, and Britain's global dominance in everything from naval and military power to industrial and commercial capacity was inseparable from its empire. And yet the facts that the Company was so financially challenged and that military expenditures in India kept adding to these challenges have made early empire seem—at least in the annals of much imperial history—simultaneously a losing proposition for Britain, and one that was neutral or even advantageous for India. It was very much the other way round.

Some of the key British actors in the imperial drama of the late eighteenth century were among the first to decry the economic consequences of the Company's relations with India. The conviction that empire constituted a serious economic drain on India began with critics of Clive such as William Bolts and Alexander Dow, though even Clive's ally, Harry Verelst, advanced a similarly disturbing analysis of imperial economics. As early as 1772, Alexander Dow asserted that Bengal's decline had commenced with the Battle of Plassey, and that it was a direct result of foreign dominion. He calculated that Bengal lost approximately £1.5 million each year through extraction of specie and the use of monopolies in inland trade, especially in basic commodities such as salt, betel nut, and tobacco. He also claimed that the levels of taxation had risen to unprecedented levels, and that "seven entire battalions were added to our military establishment to enforce the collections . . . [that] carried terror and

ruin through the country." As he expostulated, "Though they exported the specie, though they checked commerce by monopoly,
they heaped oppression upon additional taxes, as if rigour were necessary to power."[12] British justice protected natives less than despots,
and property lost any security it previously had. He recommended
an end to monopoly, a reduction in revenue demand, the enhancement of the security of property, along with other political and cultural remedies for the lack of sensitivity and fairness in the rule of
Bengal. Verelst compiled figures concerning imports and exports for
the years 1766, 1767, and 1768 suggesting that Bengal exported ten
times what it imported, noting, "Whatever sums had formerly been
remitted to Delhi were amply reimbursed by the returns made to the
immense commerce of Bengal . . . How widely different from these
are the present circumstances of the Nabob's dominions! . . . Each
of the European Companies, by means of money taken up in the
country, have greatly enlarged their annual Investments, without
adding a rupee to the riches of the Province."[13] Verelst further observed: "It will hardly be asserted that any country, however opulent,
could long maintain itself, much less flourish, when it received no
material supplies, and when a balance against it, of above one-third
of its whole yearly value, was yearly incurred."[14]

The "drain" of wealth from the combination of revenue extraction and trade—what since Francis and Burke was understood as the
use of the "tribute" or the "investment" to fund the procurement of
commodities and various raw materials—especially when combined
with the forms of control exercised over the operations of internal
markets, has been seen as fundamental to the rise of imperial power
ever since. When Romesh Dutt wrote what in effect was the first
"nationalist" economic history of India, it seemed natural that he

would begin by quoting Burke and others to make the point that he was doing nothing more than working out the details of an argument that had already been made by the British themselves.[15] Subsequent debates over the economic effects of British rule in India have often hinged on the stress given to the relative enormity of investment and tribute. Historians who have downplayed the negative role played by the British have relied on official figures about trade and assumed that land revenue was merely reinvested in local government; those who have argued against them have observed not only that land revenue and trade were both part of the drain, but also that any calculations taking the official prices as the base would invariably serve drastically to undervalue the actual imports and underestimate the profits.[16] Critics of empire further adduce the extent of "private" corruption, adding that any reasonable estimate would have to take into account the enormous amount of smuggling, much of it conducted through contraband such as diamonds and transported out of India by a variety of means to continental Europe before it made its way surreptitiously to Britain. For example, the historian Irfan Habib has recently estimated that while the drain from Bengal and Bihar to England through the official channels of the Company alone was around £737,651 in 1779, a more accurate estimate in fact would be £1,823,407. Using a variety of calculations based on extrapolations of extra-official activity, he suggests that the total gain of Britain at the expense of India was well over two million pounds a year in 1789–1790, rising to over 4.7 million in 1801.[17] But even using more conservative calculations on the basis of official accounts, Habib has calculated that "the tribute amounted to 9 per cent of the GNP—a crippling drain for any economy."[18]

While the debate is in large part about the numbers, it is even more crucially about the evaluation of historical context. Holden Furber, for example, an economic historian from the United States who argued against the claims of nationalist economic history, has noted: "Those who believe that contact with the West tended to impoverish India at this period do not contend that Indians could themselves have built fleets and exported goods to Europe for sale at a profit." Instead, they merely "feel that the sum of Indian wealth would have been greater if the European empire-builders had not been abroad in the land." Beginning with the conviction that trade itself was a good thing, and had stimulating effects on the economy, he assumed that India's economy was fundamentally stagnant and certainly unlikely to participate in any global commerce that would commence the great transformation of capital. With these assumptions framing his analysis, he then estimated the difference between imports and exports for the years 1783 to 1793 in order to assess the magnitude of the drain, believing that "the only true 'drain' resulting from contact with the West was the excess of exports from India for which there was no equivalent import." His most liberal assessment, including private remittances as well as all official exports, is roughly £1.8 million annually. This, Furber noted, was a "drain" in goods. But he discounted completely the idea of a tribute. "A notion that India was paying a tribute of gold and silver to her European conquerors at this time can find no foundation in fact." He wrote that "Dutt and those who followed him were so preoccupied with the idea that India was being systematically looted by the invaders from the West that they failed to study the process of European expansion within India in all its aspects." That said, he remarked that he himself had only begun such a study, and had concentrated on the effects of this expansion on Europe. And yet he felt sure that the so-called drain had limited effects and could not be linked to a notion of tribute that took into account the collection of land revenue for the simple reason that most of the "profit" of empire was reinvested in India. "In so far as the monies received by European East India companies or European governments in return for bills of exchange or bonds sold to individuals in India were spent within India to maintain armies, wage wars, or pay for administrative services, there was certainly no drain of wealth from India to the world outside."[19] Aside from the fact that he still did not account for £1.8 million a year by his own calculation, this is an extraordinary assessment of the costs of an imperial occupation.

Whether argued with the passionate rhetoric of Burke or the political savvy of Dutt, the idea of the drain has been so powerful in part because it neatly captures the sense of India's wealth and potential being slowly but surely absorbed by Britain as imperial power. As an image to explain why the once opulent and productive land of Bengal had been so ruined, transformed into a place of famine and misery, it is easy to understand why "the drain" has taken such hold in the debates over the economic consequences of empire from the late eighteenth century to the present. But the drain is in fact only one way to measure the costs of empire. The drain only calls attention to economic loss through the balance of trade, defined as the net amount of commodities or specie lost to India in official and unofficial trade. This net amount has been calculated using official trade accounts with some estimates of other remittances, including illegal ones, and on the basis of rough notions of the surplus of country trade and the parliamentary inquiries that looked into the major corruption scandals of the time. It does not require a preoccupation "with the idea that India was being systematically looted by the invaders from the West" to suppose that official accounts are insufficient, and British parliamentary inquiries inadequate, as accurate measures for the costs of empire in macroeconomic terms. Monopoly control over country trade, the rampant use of the *dastak* (privileges giving preferential treatment to Company traders), monopolies governing the cultivation of crops such as opium and indigo, and more general control over pricing and markets would obviously skew official statistics in significant ways. Additionally, there were a multitude of ways in which wealth was removed from India—much of it, as noted earlier, as the result of private and often illicit trade—without commensurate forms of compensation that go well beyond even the analyses of Dutt and Habib.

But if many of the resources that stayed in India in fact simply reproduced and expanded the imperial apparatus itself (inevitably leading to more illicit remittances as well), what is the meaning of reinvestment anyway? This is why most critics of empire have insisted on the idea of the tribute, for it links the drain of wealth through unequal trade with the extractive powers of a colonial state. Furber's sense that the drain was of limited importance was inextricably connected to his notion that the colonial state itself was like any other state form. Thus his last assumption—the basic contention of every colonial occupation—was that when resources were invested in the costs of military preparedness or action as well as administration itself, this was classifiable as neutral "reinvestment" in India's economy. Reinvestment, in other words, was nothing other than the use of the "tribute" to support the colonial state itself. But the colonial state not only did almost nothing to invest in infrastructure or provide meaningful administrative services, for agrarian or

any other purposes; it was in fact designed entirely to extract resources from India for the enrichment of the Company in particular
and Britain more generally. In the end, the argument over how to
interpret the economic data concerning the impact of the British
presence on India hinges on whether one views the colonial state as
legitimate and benevolent, or as fundamentally extractive in a way
no indigenous state could be.

In the late eighteenth and early nineteenth centuries, the British
gradually appropriated revenue rights with the simultaneous aims of
taking direct political control and funding their own political and
military costs straight from the agricultural "surplus." They also per-
fected the art of asking their political allies to offer military aid in
the form of housing and supporting Company troops—the equivalent of requesting rights for military bases but also requiring funding
to maintain them, with the promise of additional resources in the
event of sustained military action (funds that would in fact support
those troops).

The progressive establishment of rights to revenue collection
combined political and military ends in a variety of ways that led to
the encroachment of de facto and de jure forms of sovereignty across
growing swaths of the subcontinent. But leaving aside the political
and strategic effects of early imperial policy, what were the immediate economic effects, in India and for that matter in the metropole,
of the Company presence? If, in fact, the annual "Indian Tribute to
Britain" during the 1780s and 1790s was approximately four million
pounds, it is hard to sustain the notion that the British presence in
its early phases was inconsequential, whether it was benign or not.
These were also the decades when land revenue rates went up as

dramatically as the efficiency in collecting this revenue across large portions of Bengal and Bihar. When in 1793 Lord Cornwallis enacted the "permanent settlement" of Bengal, an assessment of land value that was to enhance agrarian entrepreneurial investment because it was fixed in perpetuity, the consequences for nonpayment of the full taxes for that land—at a rate that was fixed at a rate optimal for the colonial state—were so draconian that close to 50 percent of the estates changed hands in the ensuing decades. During the same years, the pressure on peasants increased even in areas well outside formal Company control, as for example in Mysore, where the ruler Tipu Sultan was squeezed for money after the negotiated settlement of 1792 (ending the third Mysore War). Awadh, still the exemplary political ally, "was made to pay Rs. 87 lakhs annually for the nine years preceding 1785, and then Rs 50 lakhs annually until 1801, when the Company coolly annexed half of its territory."[20] And there were multiple other ancillary economic effects, from deflation resulting from the decline of bullion imports, to the demise of internal trade in textiles due to the diversion of Bengal's exports of silk and textiles entirely to Europe.[21]

And yet many imperial historians continue to discount the notion that empire had serious economic effects on India, protesting that the relatively small British presence in India could hardly have had the dramatic consequences imputed to it. Peter Marshall, for example, noted that "British merchants, especially when they were armed with political power, could win handsome profits for themselves, but it is hard to see how they could have laid Bengal waste in the space of a few decades."[22] Like other imperial historians with this belief, Marshall domesticates the Company's civil and military expenses as Indian rather than European, in part because he also believes that the British presence stimulated some aspects of production and circulation. And yet he concedes that there was little in the way of capital investment, and even less to suggest that Indian merchants were better off after the Company established itself than they had been before. Marshall reverts to the managerial and financial problems confronting the Company in the years after the granting of the Diwani (rights to collect revenue directly in Bengal), invoking Furber's canonic observation that the actual "costs" confronted by the imperial state were rising steadily during the last decades of the eighteenth century. Accepting the parliamentary view that the Company never recovered from the financial woes that afflicted it after the granting of the Diwani, Furber wrote that the importance of the profits from the China trade during the critical decade from 1783 to 1793 was in part to serve as a "screen for deficits incurred on Indian account," suggesting disingenuously that the China trade was in fact entirely independent. As for the Indian account, "the Company was already bankrupt and was certainly not moving toward solvency in this decade." He then concluded that given these financial challenges, "The Company's governors could only solve their problems by marching on down the road of empire."[23]

What Furber meant by this statement is in some ways obscure, since—averse as he was to any structural argument—he hardly conceded any inevitability to imperial expansion. On the one hand, he observed that "no amount of evidence that British India was a wasting asset to Britain could have brought the process of European expansion in India to a halt." On the other hand, he held that imperialism grew both from some Europeans' desire to participate in the profits of foreign trade, and the "weaknesses and diversities of Indian society, and in particular out of Indian powerlessness at sea." Yet he averred that "nothing in these pages gives the slightest warrant for thinking that . . . [the] hypothesis as to the all-important role played by Indian wealth or 'Plassey Plunder' in stimulating the industrial revolution should continue to be viewed with anything but skepticism." In short, while empire was the result of the interests of the few being substituted for those of the many, it did not harm the many in India, or benefit the many in Britain, in any significant way. Furber concludes his study by noting, "The drive behind these events which took place between the American and French Revolutions sprang from forces within eighteenth-century capitalism, which transcended national boundaries, but which could not help but leave Britain mistress of India. Britain alone possessed the sea power to conquer this empire and the strength to withstand the deleterious effects of imperialism when they came."[24] Here we read that the negative effects of imperialism were on Britain rather than India, in a reversal that seems staggering, especially given Furber's claims for historical neutrality.[25] Indeed, the only way to understand this apparent leap of faith is to appreciate the extent to which imperial historians such as Furber accepted so uncritically that British trade, however extractive or inequitable, represented the bequest of capitalism—and in particular the stimulating and important effect that the opening up of Indian markets availed—to a feudal and stagnant India. From such a perspective, empire could hardly be seen as such a bad thing. That empire was a losing proposition—at least in terms of Company finances narrowly conceived—provided proof positive for this view.

The relationship of empire to the Industrial Revolution in Britain has been yet another bone of contention. Furber wrote: "During the last half of the eighteenth century, European enterprise acted as a powerful catalyst on the economic life of the East."[26] But he saw no evidence that the India trade acted similarly on the economic life of the West. Likewise, Peter Marshall, in his careful study of East India "fortunes," discounted both the notion that there was a significant drain on Bengal and the idea that either public or private expropriation of Indian resources benefited Britain in any significant way. Instead, he wrote, "It seems generally to be accepted by economic historians that relatively abundant resources of capital existed in eighteenth-century Britain and that an over-all increase in capital accumulation was not a major factor in the development of industry late in the century. What was needed was the diversion of comparatively small sums into manufacturing or communications. There is little to suggest that money made in Bengal was directly used in these ways, except by isolated individuals." Whatever wealth did accrue was invested in land and conspicuous consumption, but even this would have been of minimal importance in Britain, where Furber asserted that the national income as a whole in 1770 was £140 million.[27]

This last assertion is nothing short of imperial sleight of hand. Given the ways in which economic historians of all ideological camps have come to consider the economic significance even of relatively small numbers, or rather percentages, it is no longer possible to dismiss the economic consequences of the India trade for British industrial growth, whether one approves of those consequences or not. There is of course considerable room for debate over the precise relationship between the supply of cheap raw materials from, and the emergence of expanding markets in, the colonies, on the one side, and the success and scale of the Industrial Revolution in

Britain, on the other, but that there was a strong connection seems now beyond debate.[28] Recent work in the economic history of empire amply supports the views of Burke and Dutt, if in more measured and dispassionate ways. For example, one plausible and extremely careful estimate of net transfers between India and Britain for the years between 1772 and 1820 confirms, "once again, that seemingly negligible magnitudes in terms of national income can reveal their significance when placed in a meaningful context."[29] Among other factors, it is necessary to consider the importance of Britain's national debt, in particular the relationship between this debt and national credit. Transfers from empire had enormous significance for Britain when it was confronted by the need to raise funds for its "massive expense abroad during the French wars" of the early nineteenth century. As one economic historian has recently observed, the very complexity in the course of industrial change followed by Great Britain between 1750 and 1850 has made the relationship between imperial trade and domestic prosperity as difficult to specify as it is impossible to dismiss. The Industrial Revolution was not just "an affair of steam powered cotton mills and iron works, built on technologies that only came to maturity in the nineteenth century, after the key colonial acquisitions had been made."[30] Rather, the Industrial Revolution was itself the result of other political and economic transformations, from the financial revolution in the eighteenth century—which as we have seen was significantly facilitated by the role of the Company—to the way in which imperial markets provided steady opportunities for expansion in key industries as various as the manufacture of woolens, silk, lead, tin, copper, and watches during the last half of the eighteenth century. Broadly based industrial progress not only gave Britain a new cutting edge

overseas during this period; it also made empire all the more significant, at every possible level, for the structural development of the
Industrial Revolution.[31]

Imperial historians such as Marshall have also traditionally
doubted that imperial policy was ever driven by either real or perceived economic interests associated with Britain's Industrial Revolution. Marshall has written: "It is extremely difficult to identify diverse and sometimes conflicting elements in the British presence in
eighteenth-century India with economic forces at home. The East
India Company's monopoly was still intact. It was under pressure
from other interests, and such pressures might be given some support by the national government, but in general its pattern of trading
remained very conservative . . . Nor can the British private traders
resident in India, for all the vigour of their enterprise, be regarded as
outriders for the new British industries." Significantly, Marshall ad-
duces the importance of the monopoly as having reduced the probability that British economic interests drove colonial policy in any
significant way. But Marshall has also argued in more specific
terms against the notion that developing British interest in the raw
materials of cotton and indigo either reflected the importance of
this colonial market for industrial expansion or dictated the importance of colonial expansion in areas such as Awadh. Marshall disparaged any structural relationship between empire and economy in
part by turning to the individual perceptions and motivations of British imperial figures. About Wellesley, for example, Marshall noted
that this expansive imperialist "indeed needed no prompting to
pursue an aggressive forward policy, but commercial calculations
were alien to him. He despised 'commercial prejudice and the eager
desire of temporary mercantile advantage.' 'Duties of sovereignty

must,' in his view, 'be deemed paramount to . . . mercantile interests, prejudices and profits.'" As Marshall went on to note, he might
have worked within an economic context, but there were no economic "imperatives."[32]

Wellesley was doubtless an imperialist for predominantly political
reasons, and indeed his capacity to run up debts for his aggressive
military policies often seemed the reflex of his uneconomic cast of
mind.[33] But this biographical observation, itself reflecting the generic disavowal of commercial motives behind the "high minded"
sentiments and aristocratic perspectives of Britain's political leaders,
hardly tells us anything about the force of economic interests. Nor
does it seriously address the economic effects of imperial expansion
on the wide variety of contexts that defined, interpreted, and mobi-
lized the strands of interest and policy that made up the "imperatives" that provided increasing support for empire during Wellesley's
period of rule. Wellesley was no less aware than Hastings and Cornwallis before him of the Company's need for cash and the economic
effects of political policies. Indeed, Wellesley himself wrote that providing the China investment with cotton from Awadh was "an object
of the greatest consequence," at the same time he was making more
and more political inroads in Awadh.[34] While emphasizing "the
many political advantages as would be derived to the Company
from the possession of the Doab," Wellesley also was clear that "no
country can afford a more fair promise than the ceded Provinces . . .
The revenue will greatly exceed all my calculations of its amount;
and the commerce will be a mine of wealth hitherto unexplored."[35]

The story of indigo made even clearer the direct economic incen-
tives at work in the expansion into Awadh.[36] Indigo production began as a convenient channel for the remittance of fortunes made by

Company servants and merchants, but it soon became one of the most profitable crops of empire, second perhaps only to opium, both of which were produced in steadily larger quantities in the regions that Wellesley absorbed in the annexation of 1801 (and that set the stage for Dalhousie's subsequent annexation of all of Awadh in 1856). That opium and indigo hardly benefited the local cultivators is an understatement. Not only did these two crops end up financing the lucrative China trade and thus funneling enormous profits to Britain; they also brought monopoly conditions to the Indian countryside that lasted well after the formal end of the Company monopoly for India trade (excluding China) in 1813. Indigo also devastated the soil in ways that provided a ready and all too accurate symbol of the economic effects of imperial rule on the Indian countryside itself. And the effects of the opium trade on China of course went far beyond the damage caused to agriculture in India.

Burke had argued eloquently that the Company had designed modes of collusion between its sovereign powers and its commercial functions that had worked to enrich its servants at the expense both of the British national interest and the Indian population. Indian merchants were forced out of business by monopoly practices, while artisans and cultivators were squeezed by the draconian lowering of prices and raising of rents. At the same time, he had believed— in this sense anticipating the conclusions of Furber and Marshall rather than Dutt and Habib—that the goods that were produced at artificial prices did not sell for a profit in Britain, at least not for a profit that benefited anyone other than the nabobs themselves. Burke advocated the end of force and the opening up of a free market, using language consistent with the arguments of Adam Smith, although he did not go so far as to recommend an end to the Company's monopoly itself. He believed that the Company should cease interfering in the country's trade and allow genuine competition and participation among native merchants. Of course, neither Burke nor Smith could properly appreciate the extent to which the language of free trade, which increasingly permeated Company regulations and began to take some effect after the regulations of 1784, failed to address the unequal terms of exchange that only became worse as Company political power expanded through the century and into the next.[37] Indeed, Burke accepted the general premise that trade was both necessary and good. But his principal concern was less the Indian peasant than the British polity, for he was worried that commerce, especially in an imperial setting, would lead to revolutionary change, not least because of the close connections between trade, credit, speculation, and peculation.

We have seen how corruption provided an easy way to blame the excesses of early capitalism on the greed of a few unscrupulous rogues. For Burke, corruption became a way of describing the liabilities of commerce without charging that commerce itself was the culprit. If personal corruption was a problem, it was in some ways one that was inextricably linked to the forms of imperial power that were an inherent part of Britain's commercial expansion. Within rural Bengal, it was manifestly clear that both Company commerce and private trade by Company merchants began to prosper through the use of the dubious monopoly of the *dastak* granted by the Mughal emperor—but in many ways the *dastak* only symbolized the range of ways in which the Company's political expansion into India was critical to the success of British commerce. British commerce was neither inherently superior to nor more competitive than

Indian commerce. And British commerce was certainly not conducted independently of its political claims, entitlements, pro-
tections, and powers. Sudipta Sen has ably demonstrated that

> Merchants and rulers of the East India Company were able to
> achieve their profitable aims precisely because they were able
> to defend their chartered monopoly in the marketplaces of east-
> ern India and a dubious agreement wheedled from a short-lived
> Mughal emperor. Long before the formal dates of conquest (1757
> or 1763), small exercises in the application of the law of contract
> with military support around factories and sites of manufacture
> anticipated a fiscal-military state that would guarantee favorable
> conditions of trade.[38]

Not unsurprisingly, even efforts to reform country trade and re-
strict the use of special privileges and local monopolies, whether enacted by Clive or Hastings, had only limited effects on the ways in
which European trade continued to assault local commercial practices and structures. British political expansion into northern India
during the late eighteenth and early nineteenth centuries not only
went hand in hand with economic expansion; the two kinds of expansion were mutually enabling. Meanwhile, the establishment of
political control and revenue responsibility also entailed the steady
depoliticization and demilitarization of the local political authorities—princes, *zamindars*, and *talukdars*—which had the inevitable
effect of providing additional scope for European commerce.

As stirring as were Burke's denunciations of corruption in India,
we can also see the ways in which Burke himself paved the way for
the normalization of the political economy of empire. Burke had

said, "It is well known that great wealth has poured into this country from India," though he went on to note, in a reflexive turn that gave away his greatest fear, "It is no derogation to us to suppose the possibility of being corrupted by that by which great Empires have been corrupted, and by which assemblies almost as respectable and as venerable as your Lordships' have been known to be indirectly shaken."[39] Burke had not called for the end of the Company monopoly, but he gave ample support to the growing concern that the Company be reformed in ways that would both calm moral panic about Company excess and open up the spoils of empire to the greater good of competitive trade. Bureaucratic reform was not enough, especially given the continuation of the Company monopoly along with Company commerce as usual. The impeachment trial appears in retrospect as a necessary political accompaniment to the Pitt Act of 1784. The trial served as a platform for the national exorcism of the excess of early empire, and did far more than the reforms alone could have done in restoring moral authority for Britain's imperial ambitions both in commerce and in rule. The issue of Company monopoly, however, continued to rankle, and the Company itself continued to be the victim of the contradictory forces that drove Britain's political and economic interests in imperial expansion.

By the time the impeachment trial ended in 1795, Cornwallis's enactment of the Pitt reforms and his initiation of the permanent settlement in Bengal appeared to have resolved the financial problems that had plagued the Company for the previous decades. And yet in many respects the Company was no better off. Private trade continued to be as expansive as it was unregulated, and the Company itself, especially under Wellesley's leadership, continued its earlier—and earlier condemned—policies of expansion and conquest. As Philip Lawson observed, "Though the economic picture projected in the 1790s looked rosy, misconceptions about India and military spending sucked all the investments and profits in trade dry. Only borrowing and deficit-financing, as it is known today, could fund the demands of the Company's needs in India, driven, as they were, by militaristic endeavour and unregulated Company trade."[40] Strictly speaking, the Company was a losing proposition, and this was not just because agricultural production failed to respond to the stimulus of private property as had been promised by Cornwallis's physiocratic justifications for the permanent settlement. The Company was still losing money because it was only one small part of the imperial operation. In some respects, the reforms of 1784 had done far more than to secure the position of the Board of Control, for they had effectively moved the Company to a peripheral role vis-à-vis the British state and its armed forces. The continuation of the Company monopoly concealed the ways in which the Company itself was the front for a wide range of interests and imperatives.

By the end of the first decade of the nineteenth century, however, these same interests and imperatives no longer were needed to sustain the fiction of the Company's economic autonomy. The three years of parliamentary inquiry and debate that began in 1810 to consider the renewal of the Company charter ultimately reflected the total transformation in the Company's position. India was now the base for global trade by British merchants, stretching from the Red Sea to Hong Kong. And India was also the seat of British imperial power in ways that no longer depended on the particular fortunes of the Company, one way or the other. The renewal of the Company charter in 1813 removed the Company monopoly for everything except the China trade, an irony considering that this trade had been added to the Company charter years before as a kind of addendum. By 1813, the cultivation of opium in India sustained a hugely profitable business that the Company ran with uncharacteristic efficiency, although in large part this was due to, on the one side, the use of monopolies for opium production by Britain, and on the other, control over the tea trade in China by the Hong Kong merchants and the Chinese authorities. Within India, however, political policy was driven by administrative and military interests, and economic policy by the private traders who "ran fast and loose over the sub-continent now."[41] Not coincidentally, empire in India had also become an extension of nationalism in Britain, even as the demise of monopoly gave way to the demands of private capital and produced a new fiction of a free market economy. Indeed, Adam Smith would have had few worries at this point, and even Burke's concerns about the unregulated character of commercial propensity would have been allayed by his own confidence in the new sanctity of the imperial mission.

Empire, in short, only succeeded as a national project when it could fulfill the economic demands of modern capitalism, even as in its early phases it was vital to the initial creation of modern capitalism. The monopoly idea could finally be discarded when the political conditions for the control of market forces had at last been established in the imperial theater. The construction of a sovereign mandate for the British presence in India was a necessary prerequisite for the abandonment of the Company monopoly, for imperial legitimacy could now do the larger work of asserting and supporting British commerce in India. Smith and Burke would doubtless have seen their combined legacies reflected in the ideological underpinnings of the new imperial economy that was established in the early decades of the nineteenth century, had they lived so long. They would have applauded the fact that this new economy, by their reckoning at least, was free, open, and progressive, a natural catalyst of good for Britain as well as for India. That is certainly how their imperial successors saw it. But they could only have been fully satisfied if they were convinced that Britain had assumed a legitimate sovereign mantle for its role in the East. Ultimately, the story of the emergence of the modern global economy depended on the emergence of political conditions that, in effect, allowed trade to be free for the colonizer and unfree for the colonized, and these conditions were inseparable from the growth and consolidation of European empire in the nineteenth century.

Warren Hastings painted in Mughal style,
gouache, ca. 1782.

⇥ 5 ⇤

Sovereignty

There is a secret veil to be drawn over the beginnings of
all governments. They had their origin, as the beginning
of all such things have had, in some matters that had as
good be covered by obscurity. Time in the origin of most
governments has thrown this mysterious veil over them.
Prudence and discretion make it necessary to throw some-
thing of that veil over a business in which otherwise the
fortune, the genius, the talents and military virtue of this
Nation never shone more conspicuously.

—EDMUND BURKE, "SPEECH ON OPENING

OF IMPEACHMENT," 1788

What did it mean for the Company to "possess" India, whether by Parliamentary right, sheer force, or local treaty? Burke was far from alone in questioning the right of a trading company to act like a state, even though he took care not to "condemn those who argue a priori against the propriety of leaving such extensive political powers in the hands of a company of merchants."[1] But there were many reasons to be concerned. The East India Company over time had acquired many features of the early modern state, waging war, making peace, assessing taxes, minting coin, and administering justice in territories that were growing by leaps and bounds. When Burke questioned the record of the Company in India, it is hardly surprising that he reserved great scorn for the Company's egregious commercialization of sovereignty. As he put it, the Company had "sold" the Mughal emperor: "The first potentate sold by the Company for money was the Great Mogul,—the descendant of Tamerlane. This high personage, as high as human veneration can look at, is by every account amiable in his manners, respectable for his piety, according to his mode, and accomplished in all the Oriental literature. All this, and the title derived under his charter to all that we hold in India, could not save him from the general sale. Money is coined in his name; in his name justice is administered; he is prayed for in every temple through the countries we possess;—but he was sold."[2] We can hear Burke's contempt for this iniquitous admixture of commerce and political right.

However contemporaries defined the sovereignty of the Mughal emperor or the charter of the Company, it was an irreducible fiction of early colonial rule that the East India Company held its various rights and privileges in full acknowledgment of its dependence both on the Mughals and on Parliament. The Company consistently ceded ultimate sovereignty in India to the Mughals, even when in Bengal in 1765 it was granted Diwani rights—allowing it to collect revenue directly. That this concession was increasingly seen as a lie, a necessary fiction more than a political reality, was another matter. Neither Clive nor Hastings worried excessively about the sovereign claims of any Indian power. Most British, in India and at home, shared the conviction that even the Mughal emperor ruled by the will of the Company, under a rhetorical arrangement that allowed it to control most of India at the same time it could directly take on the Marathas and the Mysoreans, the only two remaining obstacles in the way of complete possession of the subcontinent. At the same time, neither Clive nor Hastings labored under any real day-to-day control by Parliament either, let alone by the board of proprietors, and not just because it frequently took a year for correspondence to go back and forth between India and England. In both respects, the Company acted frequently as if it were an independent entity, a fully functioning state that was sovereign and autonomous, for all practical and some symbolic purposes too. In this context, it is not surprising that in 1784 a rumor spread that Hastings was about to declare formal independence for the Company state.

Macaulay captured the matter succinctly:

> When Hastings took his seat at the head of the council-board, Bengal was still governed according to the system which Clive had devised, a system which was, perhaps, skillfully contrived for the purpose of facilitating and concealing a great revolution . . . There were two governments, the real and the ostensible. The su- preme power belonged to the Company, and was in truth the most despotic power that can be conceived . . . But, though thus absolute in reality, the English had not yet assumed the style of sovereignty. They held their territories as vassals of the throne of Delhi; they raised their revenues as collectors appointed by the imperial commission; their public seal was inscribed with the im- perial titles; and their mint struck only the imperial coin.[3]

Although wrong in some details, Macaulay described a system pred- icated on a massive deception. Burke had railed against the ways in which the Company merchants had acted as if they were sovereign in their own right, buying and selling (often by bribery) the very titles, privileges, and rights that were part of India's sovereign system of rule. Hastings had been sent to India with explicit instructions to end Clive's system of dual rule and bring some semblance of order, decorum, and honesty to the political dealings of the Company. Perhaps this is why Burke found Hastings so much more troubling than Clive, whose actions were shrouded in part by the early history of conquest over which Burke was so keen to draw a veil. But even Clive cannot be given all the credit for initiating the deceptions that played so important a role in the British conquest of India.

Most imperial historians have argued that the East India Company was drawn reluctantly into political and military conflict in India, only taking an interest in territorial power and revenue as a last-ditch effort to protect its trading activities. In fact, however, from the mid-seventeenth century the Company had the legal right and the military will to wage war in aggressive ways, securing greater and greater territorial and political claims within the subcontinent. Through intermittent negotiations with the Mughal state as well as by means of a host of "subsidiary alliances" with regional powers, the Company increasingly asserted its own sovereign position. As early as 1686, Josia Child, the Company governor who found himself at war with the emperor Aurangzeb in 1688, wrote, "[Without territorial revenue] it is impossible to make the English nation's station sure and firm in India upon a sound political basis, and without which we shall always continue in the state of mere merchants subject to be turned out at the pleasure of the Dutch and abused at the discretion of the natives."[4] From 1668, the Company in Bombay saw itself as sovereign insofar as it represented the English Crown. The Company minted coins in Bombay in the name of the British crown, even though their own coinage acquired limited currency outside the British settlement. It also established courts of judicature over both European and Indian subjects, a practice that in other parts of India usually had to await the formal grant of *nizamat* rights. According to dominant official views from the late seventeenth century, Mughal sovereignty, where it applied, was absolute, and Oriental despots owned all land, so that the right to collect revenue was an entitlement to the land itself. But in fact this official discourse came up against two other trajectories in Company ideology concerning British status in India. First, the British were loath to concede any sovereignty to others, either to the Mughals or to other European powers. As C. A. Bayly has noted, "The presumption in the Laws of England that 'Turkes and other infidels were not only excluded from being witnesses against Christians, but are deemed also to be perpetual enemys and capable of no property' was toned down but never entirely forgotten."[5] Indeed, the British systematically (and far more frequently than other European groups) refused to pay forced levies to Indian powers wherever they could get away with it, despite their formal rhetoric of subservience to Mughal sovereignty. Second, the British construed every privilege they received from Indian powers, whether rights to territory, to revenue collection, or to use certain honorary titles, as the transfer of full sovereign rights. Perhaps the first major example of this came in 1717, when the Emperor Farrukhsiyar granted the right to trade freely within Bengal and its dependencies, providing the Company with various tax exemptions as well. As K. N. Chaudhuri has written, "In all future disputes with the local governors, the point was repeatedly made that the company traded in India by right and not by any favour of the imperial officers."[6] When the nawab of Arcot, ally of the

British but officially the governor of the Mughal emperor in Madras, relinquished in 1752 the quitrent (fixed rent) he had been paid by the Company for its Madras *jaghire* (land grant), the British saw themselves as having shed the "last fragment of dependence upon an Indian prince at Madras."[7] And yet, when the British claimed sovereignty over the myriad chiefs and warlords of the southern countryside, many of whom had never either ceded sovereign rights nor made tributary payments to the Mughals, they used a formal interpretation of Mughal sovereignty to give themselves the right of general conquest. Time after time, the British refused to accept that rights in India—like sovereignty itself—were not conceived in terms of simple, uniform, or exclusive proprietary dominion.[8] This refusal, of course, was far less about cultural misunderstanding than it was about the strategic use of cultural forms to explain and legitimate a relentless pattern of political and territorial conquest.

The contradictions in Company discourse were manifold. When the Company exercised the right of landlord *(zamindar)* or local lord *(jagirdar)*, it took upon itself powers that were hardly conceded to any of the other *zamindars* or *jagirdars* whose revenues it regularly assumed, lands it appropriated, or rights it absorbed. Even as the British saw fiscal dependency, taxation, and judicial rights of territoriality as incidents of sovereignty, they in fact adjudicated all questions of right in relation to a straightforward calculus of self-interest. Through the use of subsidiary alliances, the British were further able to expand their territorial power through taxing the lands of allies, requiring these allies to support garrisons of their own troops, and ultimately—as we have seen in the case of Hastings—forcing them to bail the Company out of debt for unrelated military engagements or financial encumbrances of their own. When, for example, the Company in Madras encouraged the nawab of Arcot to wage war against the raja of Tanjore in the early 1770s (in large part to gain lucrative assignments for Company servants who had lent large sums of money at usurious rates of interest to the nawab for his own obligations to support Company military engagements), its officers argued that the raja was a mere *zamindar* who was entirely dependent on a Mughal grant. Mughal sovereignty thus applied for the raja of Tanjore in ways that had been entirely circumvented for the nawab, let alone the Company itself.

It was within this larger context that Clive believed he was finally bringing some real political clarity to the unwieldy and often contradictory character of the Company's political position as well as its self-representation. The Battle of Plassey was in fact the outcome of Company assurance that it had been granted rights over Calcutta and its environs that made it independent of the nizam of Bengal, Siraj-ud-Daula. From the perspective of the nizam, however, the Company's refusal to acknowledge his accession by giving customary presents, as well as the Company's increasing fortifications of its settlements, no doubt seemed like open acts of rebellion.[9] Although subsequently justified by the Black Hole "incident," British hostilities in 1756 and 1757 were crude and opportunistic efforts to gain greater power in Bengal. Even Clive represented his famous alliance with Mir Jafar cynically, when he noted that "Mussulmans are so little influenced by gratitude that, should he ever think it his interest to break with us, the obligations he owes us would prove no restraint."[10] Some years later, when justifying his policies before the House of Commons in 1772, Clive spoke in what thereafter has become the standard disavowal of imperial conquest. He observed: "Ever since the year 1757 when we were roused to an offensive by the unprovoked injuries of the Tyrant Nabob Serajah Dowlah, an almost uninterrupted series of success has attended us. Perhaps it was not so much our choice as necessity that drove us progressively into the possessions we presently enjoy. One thing however is certain, that aggrandized as we are, we can never be less without ceasing to be at all."[11] But in the immediate aftermath of Plassey he had advocated a far less cautious, or for that matter defensive, approach to empire. He noted: "So large a sovereignty may possibly be an object too extensive for a mercantile company; and it is to be feared they are not of themselves able, without the nation's assistance, to maintain so wide a dominion . . . [But] I flatter myself I have made it pretty clear to you that there will be little or no difficulty in obtaining the absolute possession of these rich kingdoms."[12] Six years later, when he finally accepted the Diwani, Clive effectively bribed Parliament into accepting his territorial ambitions with extravagant promises of endless riches.

When Clive arrived in Madras in April 1765, he learned of the British success in Baksar and the occupation of Awadh. In a long letter to Company Chairman Thomas Rous, he wrote, "We have at last arrived at that critical Conjuncture, which I have long foreseen, I mean that Conjuncture which renders it necessary for us to determine, whether we can, or shall take the whole to ourselves." With the defeat of Shuja-ud-Daula, the Company had taken possession of his dominions, "and it is scarcely a Hyperbole to say that the whole Mogul Empire is in our hands."[13] He argued that the local inhabitants had no particular attachment to any nabob, and that in any case Company troops were superior in every way to Mughal ones. And he asserted that the "Princes of Indostan must conclude our Views to be boundless . . . We must indeed become the Nabobs ourselves in Fact, if not in Name, perhaps totally without Disguise, but on this subject I cannot be positive until my arrival in Bengal."[14]

In August 1765, having promised a huge financial windfall for the Company, Clive negotiated the grant of Diwani rights from the Mughal emperor, Shah Alam. The agreement formally recognized the emperor's authority over Bengal in return for an annual tribute of £325,000 to the Mughals. But the recognition was made in a larger context in which Clive succeeded in appointing Najaf Khan as Shah Alam's own Diwan in Kora and Allahabad, over the emperor's initial objections.[15] Shuja ud-Daula was restored to Awadh, though with a garrison of British soldiers he would have to support in addition to other obligations to the Company. Clive did not pursue his ambition to become the nabob in name, preferring instead to inaugurate what came to be known as his dual system.[16] But the dual system was not merely the split between Mughal imperial authority and British administrative control, as contemporaries understood it, for Clive himself saw it as the apotheosis of dual sovereignty. As he wrote to the court of directors of the East India Company when he informed them of the assumption of the Diwani, the Company "now became the Sovereigns of a rich and potent kingdom," not only the "collectors but the proprietors of the nawab's revenues."[17] He spelled out this distinction very clearly in his opening speech to the House of Commons in 1769, when he said: "The great Mogul (*de jure* Mogul, *de facto* nobody at all) . . . The Nabob (*de jure* Nabob, *de facto* the East India Company's most obedient humble servant)."[18]

The grant of Diwani not only alienated the right to collect all land revenue in Bengal; it also confirmed to the Company their other positions in Bengal, as well as all the grants the Company had obtained from the nawab of Arcot. Clive was careful as well to secure confirmation of the grant of his own *jaghire*. In becoming Diwan of Bengal, the Company was formally changing the nature of its relationship to the Mughal empire, though it was hardly becoming the proprietor of the nawab's revenues, as Clive claimed. Burke provided a broad interpretation of the meaning of the Diwani in his opening speech on Hastings when he said, "This is the great act of the constitutional entrance of the Company into the body politic of India. It gave to the settlement of Bengal a fixed constitutional form, with a legal title, acknowledged and recognized now for the first time by all the natural powers of the country, because it arose from the charter of the undoubted sovereign."[19] But he went on to make clear his understanding of the dual system: "This scheme had all the real power, without any invidious appearance of it; it gave [the Company] the revenue, without the parade of sovereignty. On this double foundation the government was happily settled." But by the end of the trial, Burke's nuance seems to have lost its force. When James Mill described the event in his history, he wrote, "The phirmaun of the dewannee, which marks one of the most conspicuous eras in the history of the Company, constitut[ed] them masters of so great an empire, in name and responsibility, as well as in power."[20] Mill based his interpretation of the Diwani on the response to it made by the select committee, which had described the Company as having "come into the place of the country government, by his Majesty's royal grant of the dewannee." Clearly, the meaning of "country government" changed considerably between 1765 and 1818.

What the dual system in fact meant, however, was that real structural change was slow. The nawab continued to exercise civil administration in Bengal, putting Muhammed Reza Khan in charge of all policing and judicial affairs. And the nawab continued to collect the revenue, giving the management of that task too to Reza Khan. Revenue collection continued to be conducted through settlements with local *zamindars* and chiefs. In 1767, Muhammed Reza Khan, along with several other officials in the nawab's court, was put on the Company payroll, in an effort to exert more direct control. But the Company played only a minor role in the whole process of revenue collection, overseeing it through a resident position first held by Francis Sykes. As represented to the Company's directors in London, the arrangements around revenue and justice deliberately preserved the "ancient form of government." This was perhaps the first example of British indirect rule. The British always seemed ambivalent when they were not directly in charge. In post-Diwani Bengal, there was significant tension between a preference to intrude as little as possible in local administration, and the growing conviction that the Company was far too dependent on Indian officials and intermediaries. Yet many of the directors in London feared that if Company officials became directly involved in local affairs, they would become as corrupt—and in some views "Asiatic"—as they had been in their private trading. In any case, Clive had presented London with a fait accompli, and for a time at least the directors were content to believe that Clive knew best how to implement the momentous accomplishments of the Diwani.

If the grant of Diwani changed the nature of the relationship between the Company and the Mughal empire, it also changed the Company's relations with the British state. It could hardly do otherwise. As Clive had said in his speech to the House of Commons in 1769, "I was in India when the Company was established for the purposes of trade only, when their fortifications scarce deserved that name, when their possessions were within very narrow bounds . . . The East India Company are at this time sovereigns of a rich, populous, fruitful country in extent beyond France and Spain united; they are in possession of the labour, industry, and manufactures of twenty million of subjects; they are in actual receipt of between five and six millions a year. They have an army of fifty thousand men."[21] In a dispatch of January 1767, the select committee declared that "the armies [the Company] maintained, the alliances they formed and the revenues they possessed procured them consideration as a sovereign and politic, as well as a commercial body."[22] Thomas Pownall put it bluntly when he analyzed Indian affairs in 1773: "The merchant is become the sovereign."[23] This transformation was viewed sympathetically, at least at first, because of Clive's estimates as to what the Diwani would be worth. Clive promised that the Diwani would yield close to four million pounds a year, suggesting initially that the amount would increase dramatically once under Company supervision. After the assumption of the Diwani, Company servants certainly thought differently about the Company's priorities and mandate. The Bengal Council noted to the directors in 1769: "Your trade from hence may be considered more as a channel for conveying your revenues to Britain than as only a mercantile system."[24] The only problem was that Company debts kept mounting, and Clive's optimistic picture was not in fact borne out by subsequent events.

Parliament had already bailed the Company out of massive debts, in return for which—and in expectation of the Diwani revenues—it negotiated an annual payment from the Company to the government of £400,000 beginning in 1767. The negotiations commenced when Lord Chatham (William Pitt the elder) claimed that the legal right to the Company's recently acquired territories and rights in Bengal lay with the Crown rather than the Company. Although the Crown's ultimate sovereignty over Company "forts, places, and plantations" had specifically been guaranteed in Company charters dating back at least to 1698, the new territorial acquisitions represented by the transfer of Diwani right raised new questions. The Company argued that it held the Diwani by a direct grant from the Mughal emperor that reserved de jure sovereignty. Chatham claimed, however, that the grant had been the result of a protracted, and successful, war of conquest, fought with substantial support from the British state. The Diwani belonged to the spoils of war, and the Crown should therefore be given a substantial share. In 1767, Parliament appointed a committee of inquiry to look into the matter, and examined such important Company servants as Henry Vansittart, John Z. Holwell, and Warren Hastings about the nature of the Company's possessions, the manner of their acquisition, and their estimated value. Edmund Burke was at the time an adamant supporter of the Company, asserting that the committee ran "a blind muck at the Company's right to their acquisitions, without knowing the practicability or regarding the justice of the measure."[25] Like other Company supporters, he was concerned that the ministry was attempting to infringe on the Company's basic chartered privileges. The debate demonstrated, however, that the exact nature of the Company's basic privileges under previous charters was unclear even before the new territorial acquisitions. The inquiry further suggested the extent to which the Company seemed deliberately ambiguous on the question of sovereignty, and not only its own. The Mughal emperor's sovereign authority was widely seen as a sham both in England and in India. As it turned out, the inquiry led to the negotiated settlement in which the Company agreed to pay Parliament £400,000 a year in lieu of any other claim on Diwani right or revenue. But the precise nature of the sovereignty—Crown, Company, or Mughal—was hardly clarified.

Clive's exuberance—and in turn that of many investors in Company stock—ran aground against a steadily worsening financial picture, both for the Company and for Bengal. The government quickly became aware that the Company seemed to be a growing liability, however sovereignty was defined. Not only did Diwani collections plunge precipitously, but the Bengalis also experienced a serious famine in 1769–1770, bringing collections in some areas to a virtual halt. When the ruthless means of collection were not judged to be at fault, the predatory character of British private trade provided a powerful explanation. Speculation in Company stock, leading to substantial increases in dividend payments, further eroded the Company's financial situation. And worst of all, increasing military expenditures put escalating pressure on Company revenues, continuing the crisis that had, in effect, begun with the ascendancy of Clive a decade before. As Holwell put it, "A trading and a fighting company is a two-headed monster in nature that cannot exist long, as the expense and inexperience of the latter must exceed, confound, and destroy every profit or advantage gained by the former. New temporary victories stimulate and push us on to grasp new acquisitions of territory."[26] This caution came from the man whose lurid, and fictional, account of the Black Hole had provided the charter myth for the Battle of Plassey and subsequent Company aggression. By 1772, after a world credit crisis in which East India Company misfortunes played a considerable role, there was a general perception that something had to be done. Clive's reputation fell with Company finances, because he was under sustained attack in publications by Bolts and Dow, and because he seemed more concerned about protecting his private *jaghire* than his rather precarious reputation. As mentioned earlier, Parliament constituted a select committee in April 1772 to inquire into the "nature, state, and condition of the East India Company and of British affairs in India." The inquiries of the select committee were followed by those of a secret committee, empowered in part to investigate issues around corruption, private trade, and Clive's *jaghire*.

The king's ministry pursued reform more because of the domestic political situation than because of an abiding concern to turn attention to Company management in India. Indeed, the Company's financial crisis was of major importance in British politics. It affected private investors—many of whom were members of Parliament—as well as the government finances. Not only was the Company subvention in abeyance, but it had also become clear that the Company would require another major loan. When the question of Britain's imperial status emerged again, it was once again because the question of sovereignty affected the British state, financially as well as politically. John Burgoyne, a Member of Parliament with serious India interests, lobbied hard that "all territorial acquisitions made by subjects belonged to the Crown." He also attacked Clive's *jaghire* when he added a provision that "to appropriate acquisitions so made to the private emolument of persons entrusted with any civil or military power is illegal."[27]

When Burgoyne's motion was brought to a vote, it passed by a wide margin. As Walpole described the event, "In so tumultuous manner was the sovereignty of three imperial vast provinces transferred from the East India company to the Crown!"[28] But in fact the situation remained ambiguous. Clive was soon exonerated of all criminal behavior, and was praised by Parliament instead for having rendered "great and meritorious service to this country."[29] He was also allowed to keep his *jaghire*. What did emerge out of the parliamentary fracas was the 1773 Regulating Act. Lord North intended for the act what Pitt had earlier wished and what Burgoyne had advocated as an issue of increasing importance. Rising to speak, North stated that he had a "direct, declared, open purpose of conveying the whole power [and] management of the East India Company either directly or indirectly to the Crown." This declaration fed the opposition's fears not only that the Company charter was being abrogated but also that Parliament would lose out to the throne. The reforms of the Regulating Act, however, were limited in both respects. Most daily business in India continued to be run by the governor—who was now elevated to the position of governor-general—and Parliament had to approve candidates for the top position and for the council board that was supposed to keep the governor-general in check.

Empire had become a matter of official state interest. If the Regulating Act was limited in its effects, it nevertheless set in place the principle, however abstract, that the Company was to be under the ultimate control of both Crown and Parliament. As Burke and others had recognized, this entailed an important structural shift for a trading company that had acted under a parliamentary charter as a monopoly firm. But the Company continued in many respects as a rogue state, in its relations both to the Mughal empire and the British Crown. It was the fate of Warren Hastings to be governor-general during the tumultuous decade during which these contradictions came to a head—even though the clearest evidence of the Company's corruption and sovereign excess for the years immediately after the Regulating Act emerges from Madras, over which Hastings had only nominal control.

The extraordinary levels of corruption attending the Company's relations with the nawab of Arcot and the raja of Tanjore in the 1770s dictated nawabi military policies and expeditions to raise ready cash and to pay back debts that were contracted in steadily escalating ways from Company officials. In the process, sovereignty became irrevocably connected to the scandals around the debts of the nawab. The great debate between advocates of the nawab and allies of the raja was cast in the currency of sovereignty, on occasion adducing the argument that only a Hindu king (the raja) could have legitimate sovereignty in a region of India that was predominantly Hindu (southern India).[30] Disregarding all their formal proclamations concerning the inviolability of Mughal legitimacy, many Company spokesmen not only suggested that the nawab of Arcot could not rule in the south; they also exempted him from the constraints of Mughal rule, manipulating the language of sovereignty with blatant contempt for local customs and conventions. A war against Mysore and two invasions of Tanjore had been specifically driven by the greed of Company servants, who were anxious to collect interest as well as collateral in relation to their transactions with the nawab. Burke himself had noted in stronger terms than most that the nawab of Arcot (in part because of his family's ties to Tanjore) was a puppet of the Company. "The Nabob," he said, "without military, without federal capacity, is extinguished as a potentate; but then he is carefully kept alive as an independent and sovereign power, for the purpose of rapine and extortion,—for the purpose of perpetuating the old intrigues, animosities, usuries, and corruptions."[31] Such sovereignty, for Burke, was not just hollow; it was cast in the service of scandal.

For Burke, as we have seen, India's dangers were much more powerfully evidenced by the life and career of Warren Hastings than by Paul Benfield, whose evident corruption and self-interest made him seem hardly a worthy target. Burke's condemnation of Benfield and of Benfield's collusion with the nawab of Arcot served only as the pretext for his assault on Hastings. But Hastings was a much more difficult target than either Clive or Benfield. Far more scrupulous than these nabobs, Hastings's ambitions were more political than financial, and he made clear his deep frustration with the limits and contradictions of Company authority in India. His specific mandate in 1772 was to end Clive's system of dual rule, taking direct charge for the collection of the Diwani revenue. Hastings was ordered to "render the accounts of the revenue simple and intelligible, to establish fixed rules for collection, to make the mode of them uniform in all parts of the province, and to provide for an equal administration of justice."[32] He established a revenue board in Calcutta—moving the establishment from the nawab's capital in Murshidabad to the Company headquarters—and empowered it to devise and supervise a new system of revenue collection. But he soon realized how ill-equipped the Company establishment was for its new responsibilities. In effect, he argued that the collection of revenue was the task of a state rather than a trading company, requiring greater executive authority and power. And his admitted goal was to devise a new state system, not to retreat to the Company's mercantilist origins. As he wrote to Lord North,

The vast change which has since taken place in the affairs of
the Company, especially since the acquisition of the Dewanny,
required the application of principles diametrically opposite to
the former practice for conducting them . . . it requires little argument to show the absurdity of promoting a man who had distinguished himself by his knowledge of the investment, or his
assiduity in the arrangement and distribution of stores, to the government of the country and the administration of justice . . . The
details of commerce are not fit objects of attention to the supreme administration of a state.[33]

In elevating the Company to the status of a state, Hastings was concerned to declare British sovereignty over all of the Company's possessions, and to assert that "the British sovereignty, through whatever
channels it may pass into these provinces, should be all in all."[34]

In assuming the responsibilities of sovereign rule, Hastings also
realized that "the due administration of justice had so intimate a
connexion with the revenue, that in the system which was adopted,
this formed a very considerable part."[35] Hastings set up two courts,
the diwani, which ruled on revenue and civil matters, and the
faujdari, which was to deal with internal order and criminal law.
Although he made clear the necessity of reform in concert with
the newly assumed responsibilities of the Company, he believed
that he was merely returning Indian law to its own "ancient constitution," invoking the idea that propelled Burke in his own assault on
Hastings and Company rule in India. As if anticipating Burke's
charge, and in effect suggesting far more agreement with Burke
on basic principles than later appeared to be the case in the trial,

Hastings wrote, "In this establishment no essential change was made in the ancient constitution of the province. It was only brought back to its original principles, and the line prescribed for the jurisdiction of each Court, which the looseness of the Mogul government for some years past had suffered to encroach upon each other."[36] The establishment of a supreme court in Calcutta under the terms of the 1773 Regulating Act was greeted by Hastings as the opportunity to devise a new system of justice that would preserve the ancient constitution and commence the process of legal codification. He began by commissioning his friend, Nathaniel Halhed, to translate and distill Indian law books to make this possible.

While Hastings achieved some success in the arena of law, he felt deeply frustrated in his larger ambition to reform Company governance and to rationalize Company sovereignty. In this, the 1773 Regulating Act was of little help, and in its establishment of the supreme council, a serious hindrance. Describing some of the problems of Company administration, Hastings wrote, "These are indeed the inevitable consequences of the ancient form of government, which was instituted for the provision of the Investment, the sale of the Company's exported cargoes, and the despatch of their ships being applied to the dominion of an extensive kingdom, the collection of a vast revenue . . . and the direction of a great political system . . . A system of affairs so new requires a new system of government to conduct it."[37] Although his immediate frustration had to do with the constant opposition of three of the four members of his council (led by Philip Francis), he was also hampered by the continuing lack of clarity in the relations of the Company to Indian authority as well as to British authority. When Hastings pursued aggressive military policies—whether they failed or succeeded—he ran into the limits of the Company's financial policy. When he declared that an Indian ruler was dependent on the Company, a mere landlord or bureaucratic functionary, he collided with the rhetorical sham of Company political theory, which was duplicitous both in sketching a formal feudal picture of Indian politics and in treating the Mughal emperor simultaneously as puppet and sovereign. And when Hastings argued that the Company should buttress its own authority through establishing clearer ties with the Crown, he alienated both the Whig faction in Parliament and the Company directors, who feared that he was willing to give up Company rights over its growing array of territories.

Hastings's interest in clarifying Company sovereignty was not unrelated to his political ambitions, even before the full flowering of his quarrel with Francis. In early 1773, he advocated that the "sovereignty of this country [be] wholly and absolutely vested in the Company," and that he be the sole "instrument" of this sovereignty.[38] Burke had read Hastings's ambition as personal megalomania rather than as the inevitable logic of empire. Even Francis agreed in principle with Hastings about most questions of governance (though he wanted to be the governor-general himself). Writing to Lord North in 1777, he observed that there could be no reform in India "as long as the Interests of the Company and those of Bengal are committed to the same hands . . . they are in fact incompatible. If the territorial Acquisitions are to be preserved, it must be under a System of Government which does not refer all its measures to the supposed Rights or Interests of a Body of Merchants."[39] No doubt he felt he was condemning Hastings when he argued that the authority of Company sovereignty should not be bound by the narrow interests of Company trade. But in fact, despite their differences about whether and how to engage the Marathas in warfare, Francis and Hastings were in fundamental agreement. Both of them understood the slippery relations between trade and sovereignty in India, where trade was only the ostensible object of imperial ambition. And they shared as well concerns that had been expressed so well in Adam Smith's critique of mercantilism.

Neither the regulating acts of 1773 or 1784, nor the steadily growing state apparatus, changed the Company's formal mandate. The Pitt Act of 1784 did clarify the Crown's formal control over the Company's political policies, in particular its power to wage war. A board of control was set up to supervise both the directors at home and the governor-general in India, and the board was specifically put under royal direction. Parliament, however, maintained its supervisory role—soon to be amply displayed in Hastings's trial—and the governor-general was given far greater powers than Hastings had ever had. And despite the recognition that the Company would be steadily involved in revenue collection and local administration, Company administrators were told that servants of the Company should concentrate more on the trading aspects of its operation. Pitt went so far as to insert a clause in the act stating that "to pursue schemes of conquest and extension of dominion in India, are measures repugnant to the wish, the honour, and the policy of this nation."[40]

Cornwallis, who went to India as governor-general in 1786, honored this stricture in formal terms, though his use of a political alliance with the Travancore raja to justify his war against Tipu Sultan in 1792 echoed Hastings's own manipulations of treaties and feudal theories. But in fulfilling the other mandates of the Pitt Act, both in stemming personal corruption and providing for a steady source of revenue, Cornwallis by no means followed his instructions to return to trade. On the one hand, he raised Company salaries in order to impose full restrictions on private trade, regularizing the bureaucratic character of Company service. On the other hand, he imposed the permanent revenue settlement on Bengal, largely following a plan by Philip Francis. The permanent settlement might have been designed to lessen the need for a regular British revenue establishment, but in fact it set the stage for ever greater Company involvement in local social and economic life. Cornwallis got away with all this not just because of his upright image in Britain, but also because he arranged for £500,000 to be sent annually to the exchequer in London, not just finally regularizing but increasing the earlier arrangement that had been made after the assumption of the Diwani. As significantly, Cornwallis set himself up as an imperial monarch, allowing himself to be represented with classical references as part of his own self-image of adhering to Roman civic virtue. And Lord Wellesley, when he became governor-general in 1798, not only abandoned the policy of nonexpansion—finishing off Tipu Sultan at Srirangapattinam in 1799—but also used the renewed warfare against France to justify his new policy of imperial aggression. In any case, by the 1790s there was an outpouring of patriotic and royal fervor and nationalist pride that was well suited to imperial expansion. Nevertheless, like all of his predecessors, Wellesley felt constrained to justify his conquests and politics in the complicated language of dual sovereignty. The fiction of sovereignty— once again both in regard to the Company's relationship to the Crown and its relationship to the Mughal emperor—continued unrevised.

As a productive fiction, dual sovereignty served multiple purposes, from disguising the extent and nature of imperial conquest to deferring British responsibility for imperial excesses. But while Burke was comfortable with the first set of purposes, he felt great anxiety about the second. He worried that the reality of empire would potentially undermine the convictions sustaining the ancient constitution in Britain itself. When Burke challenged his listeners to suspend their ideas of distance and difference in favor of sympathy for their fellow citizens of India, he implored them to realize that the crisis of legitimacy in India could lead to a crisis of legitimacy in Britain. In his speech on the Fox India Bill of 1783, he had said, "I am certain that every means, effectual to preserve India from oppression, is a guard to preserve the British constitution from its worst corruption."[41] And in his opening speech for the impeachment, he had warned that the "nature of our constitution itself" was at risk, so "deeply involved" was it "in the event of this cause."[42] Thus it was that the French Revolution only heightened Burke's concern to press for Hastings's conviction. The upending of tradition and order in France was deeply threatening, taking place as it did just across a narrow channel of water. But the relentless duplicity, venality, and corruption of India was in some ways even more threatening, because it implicated the British imperial idea, and as a consequence British sovereignty itself. Perhaps most troubling of all, the actions of Hastings, who as governor-general was the sole representative of British authority in India (however the sovereignty of Company or Mughal was conceived), threatened to draw back the veil over the beginning of imperial government. Hastings's support for the vicious attack on the Rohillas paid no heed to prudence and discretion. Hastings's lack of concern for honoring treaties with either the raja of Banares or the nawab of Awadh could undo the shining fortune, genius, talent, and military virtue of Britain in India. What Hastings defended as necessary for the maintenance of Company rule in India was seen by Burke as likely to topple that very rule, if not cleansed and exorcised. In an age of metropolitan crisis—one that was exacerbated by domestic political scandals, growing popular unrest, and the rapid influx of new money from imperial ventures—it seemed unwise to shine too penetrating a light on the beginnings of empire. In that context, Hastings's indiscretions threatened to call far too much attention to the scandal of imperial conquest.

Burke was perhaps correct to worry that Hastings's immediate legacy would be destabilizing for the expansion of empire, with the increased scrutiny concerning political as well as personal corruption in the years between the loss of America and the fall of old France. But in calling attention to Hastings's contradictions—his missteps as well as his achievements—Burke sought explicitly to separate the person of Hastings from the real project of empire. The personalization of imperial excess was a deliberate effort to exorcise the evil from the imperial idea. When Burke made his first great speech in the impeachment trial of Warren Hastings, he made it clear that he was not condemning the idea of empire. In demonizing Hastings, Burke instead paved the way for the nationalist heroes who would follow Hastings. While Cornwallis and Wellesley both continued Hastings's policies and inconsistencies, they were better placed in Britain to maintain their domestic reputations, even as they rode the wave of a rising nationalist tide that, in the wake of the trial, increasingly took empire as a badge of Britain's honor. But by this time, the contradictions of sovereignty had ceased to cause much concern. On the one side, the sovereignty of the Mughal was seen as a mere rhetorical convenience. On the other, the Company was now seen as performing the work of both Crown and Parliament (even if it still did so at great financial cost). Formally speaking, it was not until the "Great Rebellion" of 1857 (known in British history as the Sepoy Mutiny), and the final deposing of the Mughal king, that sovereignty in India was clarified. In one fell swoop, both the Mughal and the Company were dethroned, and the British Crown became paramount.[43] Burke would have been proud. He had made possible the apotheosis of British imperial sovereignty in India, when the veil was finally drawn securely over the origins of empire there. His achievement, however, was no longer relevant. It was erased along with Hastings's ignominy, for by 1858 there were few in Britain concerned that empire would compromise British sovereignty and the ancient constitution on which it rested.

Burke had been most deeply concerned with the ancient constitution of Britain. His anxious desire to purify the imperial idea was not primarily related to his concern about India. Indeed, imperial and metropolitan claims to sovereignty were inseparable, making the trial of Warren Hastings a test not only of the ideal of empire but of state sovereignty at home as well. Empire could work to enhance the glory of the ancient constitution, even as it could cruelly undermine it. The story of sovereignty has always been told as a universal tale that had its origins (and frames of reference) in Europe. The modern idea of sovereignty emerged, so we are told, in the debates of European political theorists and activists—around the historical swirl of kings, revolutionaries, counterrevolutionaries, demagogues, inter alia—in the seventeenth, eighteenth, and nineteenth centuries. Modern ideas of empire required a slight modification of the fundamental premise of sovereignty, but empire was always justified by the absence of sovereign forms—identities as well as institutions—in colonized territories, and the ultimate export of these forms to them from the imperial metropole. Indeed, third world nationalism has been seen as the great testimony to the universal value of this European idea, the ultimate proof of the foundational originality of Europe and the intrinsic power of the nation-state. Successful entry into the world of nations has always reiterated what appears as a Western triumph, the birth of sovereignty out of the crucible of colonialism. Imperialism has justified itself over and again, in its heyday as well as in its shameful moments of demise, through the great narrative of sovereignty.

This is a narrative that extends even to critiques of colonial history. For example, a recent critical work that purports to make empire central to the history of global sovereignty repeats key passages of this narrative. Michael Hardt and Antonio Negri assert that modern sovereignty "was born and developed in large part through Europe's relationship with the outside, and particularly through its colonial project and the resistance of the colonized."[44] But they write as if third world nationalism only contributed the idea that sovereignty could be radicalized (and globalized) in the service of colonial resistance movements.[45] For them, as well as for most political theorists, "Modern sovereignty is a European concept in the sense that it developed primarily in Europe in coordination with the evolution of modernity itself."[46] Surely empire was of more consequence than this. Certainly when considering Burke's participation in the understanding of sovereignty, empire played a fundamental role.

In 1782, Burke wrote a speech in connection with a parliamentary inquiry into the "State of the Representation of the Commons in

Parliament." In this speech Burke made one of his clearest statements about the nature of the nation, the meaning of sovereignty, and the relationship of both to the ancient constitution. Following Locke, he noted that government was chartered to protect property, but, departing from Locke and other seventeenth-century theorists, he stressed even more the importance of the need to preserve a prescriptive constitution. Prescription is the claim that sovereignty has to the future, or what he termed presumption. "It is a presumption in favour of any settled scheme of government against any untried project, that a nation has long existed and flourished under it. It is a better presumption even of the choice of a nation, far better than any sudden and temporary arrangement by actual election."[47] The nation itself was "not an idea only of local extent, and individual momentary aggregation; but it is an idea of continuity, which extends in time as well as in numbers and in space." For Burke, national sovereignty was a contract only in an abstract sense, since it can hardly be based on a set of discrete, knowable, choices. "And this is a choice, not of one day, or one set of people, not a tumultuary and giddy choice; it is a deliberate election of ages and generations; it is a constitution made by what is ten thousand times better than choice, it is made by the peculiar circumstances, occasions, tempers, dispositions, and moral, civil and social habitudes of the people, which disclose themselves only in a long space of time. It is a vestment which accommodates itself to the body."[48] Sovereignty, or the ancient constitution itself, has thus become naturalized as the necessary cover for the body politic, accustomed to its specific shapes and changing character. The principle of sovereignty is universal, but the specific form of sovereignty—and by implication any national constitution—is highly particular, the outcome of a specific if ancient history. Sovereignty may be the outcome of choice, but it reflects the agencies and agreements of a community forged through a long and established history.

Burke's views in 1782 had in fact changed greatly from those he had held in younger years. In his first writings on law he had been much more concerned to trace the contextual histories of legal development, arguing as he did against the opinions of Sir Matthew Hale, the great historian of the common law who held that the history of law was necessarily inscrutable, an "immemorial custom in perpetual adaptation." Now Burke seemed to agree with Hale, conceding that history's silences had foundational status for the idea of law.[49] Common wisdom has it that Burke had become more conservative as he aged, and was giving vent here to the full traditionalism of his older reactionary years. But it cannot be accidental that in 1782 Burke was spending most of his time thinking about Company abuses in India, wondering whether Warren Hastings was undermining universal principles and national reputations in his actions as chief of the East India Company. And in his opening speech on Hastings, he seemed preoccupied with matters concerning law and sovereignty, as if the conduct of Hastings was calling into question fundamental understandings of both. He praised Clive for arranging the transfer of Diwani rights: "For the Mogul, the head of the Mussulman religion there and likewise of the Empire, a head honoured and esteemed even in its ruins, he obtained recognition by all the persons that were concerned. He got from him the Dewanee, which is the great grand period of the constitutional entrance of the Company into the affairs of India. He quieted the minds of the people. He gave to the settlement of Bengal a constitutional form, and a legal right, acknowledged and recognized now for the first time by all the Princes of the Country, because given by the Charter of the Sovereign."[50] In Burke's view, dual sovereignty was necessary in order to accommodate difference, which for him had to be named as the ancient constitution of India. Clive's duplicity is rewritten as morality because of its apparent respect for sovereignty and the constitution of India, though the narrative of morality in conquest would not have borne the weight of Burke's critical scrutiny, had he chosen that path.

Hastings, however, was a different matter. He was brought to trial under British law on the grounds that he had been a British governor.

> My Lords, we contend that Mr. Hastings, as a British Governor, ought to govern upon British principles, not by British forms, God forbid. For if ever there was a case in which the letter kills and the spirit gives life, it would be an attempt to introduce British forms and the substance of despotic principles together into any Country. No. We call for that spirit of equity, that spirit of justice, that spirit of safety, that spirit of protection, that spirit of lenity, which ought to characterise every British subject in power; and upon these and these principles only, he will be tried.[51]

The trial was thus an epic test of the ancient constitution of Britain, both because Hastings would be brought before justice in London and because he had been the agent of British justice in India. This is why Burke had railed against what he called a "geographical morality." In his oration he said, "We are to let your Lordships know that these Gentlemen have formed a plan of Geographic morality, by which the duties of men in public and in private situations are not to be governed by their relations to the Great Governor of the Universe, or by their relations to men, but by climates, degrees of longitude and latitude, parallels not of life but of latitudes." Burke was clear that relativism of this kind could be used in India to justify unparalleled corruption and abuse. Worse, however, this relativism cast the great law itself into doubt. Cultural relativism would in fact work to give an idea of choice, compact, or contract far too much importance, for the law had to rest on a more transcendental foundation. As he said in his speech on Hastings,

> This great law does not arise from our conventions or compacts. On the contrary, it gives to our conventions and compacts all the force and sanction they can have. It does not arise from our vain institutions. Every good gift is of God; all power is of God; and He who has given the power and from whom it alone originates, will never suffer the exercise of it to be practised upon any less solid foundation than the power itself. Therefore, will it be imagined, if this be true, that He will suffer this great gift of Government, the greatest, the best that was ever given by God to mankind, to be the play thing and the sport of the feeble will of a man, who, by a blasphemous, absurd, and petulant usurpation, would place his own feeble, contemptible, ridiculous will in the place of Divine wisdom and justice?[52]

By cheapening the idea of sovereignty through the use of arbitrary power and despotic action, and then justifying this through his account of India's history and culture, Hastings had undermined the ancient constitutions of Britain and India alike.

Burke's commitment to a universal understanding of law was no less than an article of absolute faith in the sacredness of the constitution itself. Only a divine principle could provide the force and the sanction for law and sovereignty, at home and abroad. History in the form of "tradition" would shape specific understandings and institutions of law, but the history of violent conquest had to be veiled. Conquest was for Burke the "state of exception," the term Carl Schmitt later coined to characterize the sovereign who was outside or above the very law he was charged to protect.[53]

Burke argued against Lockean commitments for a variety of reasons. He was worried that philosophical resort to contract would license popular revolution, as indeed it was intended to do by Locke in the context of seventeenth-century England. This worry became the source of particular anxiety around the events in France after 1789, but it was not a new concern for Burke, either in the English or the Indian contexts. Burke also argued against an emphasis on contract because he wanted to ground sovereignty in something other than natural right, a form of universal reason he soundly rejected in favor of history, law, and God. Burke's genius was to invoke the general culture of belief around English common law, especially its combination of ancient wisdom and contemporary custom, to construct his own theory of sovereignty. In this sense, the mandate of the divine was to simultaneously justify and transcend the historical actions of men, to purge the law of the stain of its historical origins. Clive was a hero because he acted out the charade of dual sovereignty, and indeed because the level of his own corruption was best forgotten if Britain was to maintain its imperial mission. And yet Hastings was to be held accountable to Britain's own ancient constitution. At the very point that Burke came to hold that a prescriptive constitution had to be "immemorial," Hastings was to be judged wanting so that both England and empire might survive.[54]

Burke's contemptuous condemnation of Hastings's invocation of cultural difference was thus in the service of an absolute idea of truth that slid, however uneasily, from the particularity of England's historical formation to the universality of an idea of law. But he did not leave his case at that, for he also argued that Hastings had misunderstood, and viciously violated, India's own ancient constitution. It was ironic that Hastings's own commitments to a rule of law—one that was in truth framed much like Burke's—would get him into such trouble, since it was widely believed that he had done himself particular harm when he used Halhed's defense of his record. In preparing Hastings's first defense against the impeachment charges, Halhed had invoked Sanskrit legal texts—the basis of both his own and Hastings's major contribution in the area of codifying Hindu law—as well as a medley of Indian understandings of kingly authority in order to suggest that Hastings had to assume an Oriental mantle of despotic authority. Clive had simply acted the despot, whereas Hastings, who at his worst was more considerate and more reasoned than Clive could ever be, sought to justify despotism. When Hastings, quoting Halhed, had said in his defense that "the whole history of Asia is nothing more than precedents to prove the invariable exercise of arbitrary power," he had meant to gesture to a larger historical context. He had spoken about the great variety of "tenures, rights, and claims, in all cases of landed property and feudal jurisdiction in India from the informality, invalidity, and instability of all engagements in so divided and unsettled a state of society . . . as Hindoostan has been constantly exposed to . . . ever since the Mohomedan conquests." When he said that "rebellion itself is the parent and the promoter of despotism," he meant to imply—echoing Burke's own earlier critique of "Muhammedan" government in a tract he wrote with his cousin William—that Hindus rebelled for justifiable reasons. But when he went on to say that "sovereignty in India implies nothing else [than despotism]," he fell straight into the trap that Burke had set.[55]

At the time of the great impeachment trial, Burke would hardly concede either the illegitimacy of Mughal rule or the essential rebelliousness of Hindus in the face of foreign rule. The stakes here had shifted far away from Tanjore and Arcot, let alone Bengal, and pertained to matters far more important than merely the future of imperial acquisitions in India. Burke's sense of the particularity of each historical formation of a prescriptive constitution could not countenance either arbitrary power or the language of despotism. The "mean and depraved state" said by Hastings to have been the fault of the Mughals was now turned to Hastings's own account. For Burke, the mandate of history was to transform necessarily iniquitous beginnings into something "better than choice," what he called "the peculiar circumstances . . . [and] habitudes of the people."[56] History, in short, was about tradition, and by implication, the sanctification of contingency. When contrasting Britain and India, Burke used this idea of history to create the space for a difference that did not compromise morality. In the case of Britain's role in India, conquest was not about the original formation of the law but rather its appropriation of India's own law—an appropriation that transferred responsibility for the maintenance of another law rather than Britain's own. "For by conquest which is a more immediate designation of the hand of God, the conqueror only succeeds to all the painful duties and subordination to the power of God which belonged to the Sovereign that held the country before."[57] But even here, cultural relativity labored under the burden of Burke's absolutism.

It was in this context that Burke provided a long analysis of Islamic political and legal theory, demonstrating the extent to which law in India had been seen as transcendent in much the way it was in Britain. But his argument's awkwardness, as well as the careless scholarship underpinning it, suggested that he was ambivalent about the need for empirical demonstration. He asserted simply that "in Asia as well as in Europe the same Law of Nations prevails, the same principles are continually resorted to, and the same maxims sacredly held and strenuously maintained."[58] Historical analysis thus confirms the universality of the legal ideal, but it cannot capture the force of it. Tamerlane was a better man than Hastings, but in the end, "All power is of God." This was the primary puzzle of sovereignty: the war between the universal and the particular in the formation of Burke's sense of sovereign right and civic virtue. Burke attempted to use Islamic legal and theological texts to sustain an idea of an ancient constitution that was formed not only out of the specific historical experience of the British nation, but also in relation to a decidedly Christian idea of God's generative relationship to the law. Burke's call for sympathy for the fellow citizens of India was predicated both on sameness (the universal province and claim of law) and on difference (the distance as well as the distinctness of place).[59]

Burke's conservatism is therefore hardly given the lie by his concern for India. Burke believed that the ancient constitution was both primordial and shaped by shared history, even as he was committed to the idea that the law was universal in its principle if singular in its form. His paradoxical formulations were made clearly in the service of Britain, rooted as they were in his sense that British justice was the most developed, and enlightened, in the world. His sympathy for India was the sympathy of a paternalist who believed his charge could only benefit from the relationship of dependency. And his sense of Indian sovereignty, and nationhood, was itself always dependent on his greater concern for the past and future of Britain itself. If he could draw the veil on Clive's conquest of India, he set the stage for the ultimate drawing of the veil on Hastings as well. In doing so, he played a vital role in the regeneration of the British imperial mission at a time of resurgent British nationalism and jingoism. Burke's attentiveness to place worked in the end to make one place sovereign and another place colonized. And this was a contradiction that would require a different kind of political vision to undo.

Still, Burke's contradictory insistence on universality and specificity in the context of India did make clear the extent to which his own sense of sovereignty was both brought into crisis and yet unchallenged by difference. On the one hand, he needed to resist the cultural relativism that would both justify Company despotism in India and call into question the absolute truth and universal provenance of England's own traditions. On the other hand, he needed to formulate a sense of history that was rooted in an ancient but still historical past that could provide the basis for a national claim to the ancient constitution. In this respect, India's alterity had to be simultaneously affirmed and disavowed. Ironically, imperial ideology made it possible for Burke to do this, though the thinly veiled fiction of dual sovereignty compromised the force of this complementary idea. For Burke, the contradictions of English, or British, sovereignty were highlighted by resort to empire, even if the greatest role of empire was to test the very transcendence of his commitment to the ancient constitution. Before Burke, most English political theorists had systematically denied or ignored the presence of empire in their understanding of sovereignty, despite the obvious fact that modern sovereignty was born in an age of empire. And yet, in the end, Burke's genius lay not in the recognition of difference but in the use of it to justify his own critique of the social contract.

Empire had always been denied or ignored because it came to constitute a crisis for modern theories of sovereignty. As Hobbes, Locke, and other theorists of the seventeenth century attempted to find ways to justify and anchor the rapidly changing claims of political leaders and institutions, they assumed that the people who would trade sovereignty for order and property would be members of a familiar, distinct, and shared political community. Although there was considerable debate, and widespread uncertainty, about who could legitimately be part of this community, there were always unspoken limits. The limits and conditions of nationality were formed by the same history that gave rise to modern ideas of sovereignty, along with the notions of society, geography, race, religion, class, and ethnicity that provided the ideological stakes for the formation of nations and empires alike. C. B. Macpherson has demonstrated the role of an emergent ideology of possessive individualism in the development of sovereign guarantees for both property and trade, and the limits of wealth and gender have been much written about.[60] But for theorists as various as Locke, Hobbes, and Burke, there were also limits that attended emergent ideas of community, nationality, and race. Nations might have been imagined, but they were imagined in relation to specific communities that were believed to be natural and primordial (however much they changed and grew over time). National imaginations might have been stretched as well as formed by print capitalism, state forms of government, and the growing sense that only the nation could both realize and protect social, religious, and political identities. But these same imaginations were produced as much by the encountering of limits as by expansion. From the late sixteenth century at least, English preoccupations with nationhood were largely reactive, vitally linked as they were to travel in and experience of other worlds beyond Europe.[61] Although the ideological origins of empire reveal the development of a consensus that empire was Protestant, free, and maritime, the racial and sectarian conditions of British nationality only became fixed once empire had brought the English up against the terrifying perils of difference.[62] British travelers, traders, adventurers, and colonists only discovered the importance of their own racial and national identities when they were threatened with being identified with the natives of the new lands where they began to claim rights to property and political determination.[63] If the American Revolution played out one contradiction of British sovereignty, it did so by using territory to distract attention from the far more significant contradictions of race, language, religion, and history. The fact that the British only recognized their Britishness when they were in danger of being mistaken for Native Americans or African slaves tells a rather different story. And when these same British settlers claimed full political rights for themselves, even the most enlightened seemed unconcerned about extending these same rights to other communities.

For many political theorists in eighteenth-century Britain, the foundational crisis of sovereignty was seen to have disappeared after the revolution and restoration of the seventeenth century. Debates over sovereignty after 1688 might still have focused on the relationship between the Crown and Parliament, but Sir Robert Filmer's famous defense of monarchy in the mid-seventeenth century steadily lost any real authority. More importantly, debates about sovereignty became caught up in arguments over political imperatives and civic obligations, private interests and public good, national loyalty and religious belief, and the increasing importance of trade and mercantilism in politics and social life.

Trade itself could be used to justify sovereignty even as sovereignty was used to protect and further trade, but convictions about national identity only collided with sovereignty in imperial domains. As a result, eighteenth-century concerns about sovereignty came to crisis because of empire. In colonial America, British settlers raised questions around representation, taxation, and local authority in ways that challenged the unquestioned reach of sovereignty at the same time they began to clarify some of the conditions of that sovereignty. Britain had claimed sovereignty over its own subjects wherever they traveled, but while these subjects had to accept other national sovereignties in Europe, they assumed a virtual extension of their territorial claims in all imperial ventures. The flip side of this extensive extraterritoriality was the unbreakable connection between British settlers in the Americas and the British nation, a connection that was broken by the American experience, and in such a way as to discourage settler colonization for the next hundred years. But if the American Revolution raised the question of the relationship of sovereignty and territory with a new sharpness, it also raised the stakes for imperial interests and acquisitions in other parts of the world.

For Britain, empire as an idea was only examined retrospectively. Empire began as a natural extension of sovereign ambitions that survived largely by willful forgetting and dissembling, well beyond the specific historical sham of dual sovereignty in India. The conceptual relations between empire and sovereignty could be left vague until they collided with the anxieties that grew around the expansionist activities of the East India Company and the recognition of racial and cultural difference. The underlying national consensus that was required to make the claims of sovereignty carry weight beyond the national border only gradually became clear. Empire was fundamental to the history of British sovereignty, but not in relation to the triumphal connection between British empire and American independence.[64] Instead, empire worked to crystallize the limits of national sovereignty even as it necessitated the extension of borders and the overcoming of limits under other kinds of imperial conditions. Empire might have exposed the serious contradictions that emerged when economic interest, military might, and political expansion failed to secure cultural legitimation, whether at home or abroad. But it found new vocabularies of legitimation and political right to overcome the scruples Burke so eloquently raised when dominion abroad had to be justified. Burke's rhetoric in the trial was thus of critical importance in the attainment of an imperial ideal.

Empire ultimately came to serve the expanding cult of nationality in England during the late eighteenth and early nineteenth centuries. The idea of Britishness was in the end triumphant in large part because of the growing collective sense of opposition to France (and the Continent more generally), and because it folded some Scots and Irish into a national project that highlighted differences between East and West, even as differences of class, gender, and race were given short shrift.[65] While in some respects the loss of America only made the crisis of empire more pressing—posing a new set of national exclusions as fundamental to the problem of sovereignty—it also made the idea of empire all the more compelling. By the time

Cornwallis had moved from the scene of his American failure in Yorktown to his Indian triumph, the contradictions of sovereignty were to be resolved by a new set of commitments around the importance of empire for Britain itself. The problems posed by imperial sovereignty became increasingly erased by the successful ambition of national sovereignty.

Burke's role in the trial of Warren Hastings highlights the contradictions that were part of late-eighteenth-century ideas of sovereignty. Yet it is ironic indeed that Burke's own understanding of sovereignty—given his commitment to the ancient constitution rather than the idea of contract—made empire ultimately less of a problem than it became for liberal theory, where contradictions outlived the trial.[66] For Burke, and indeed for most British historians of empire from at least the middle of the nineteenth century on, the trial brought closure to the crisis over sovereignty that empire in India had posed. Burke would himself have much preferred a successful prosecution, and he was deeply embittered by the failure of the trial. Yet he had made his argument in such a way that despite the outcome of the trial, Lord Cornwallis could effect the transformations envisioned by the passage of the 1784 Pitt Act. In bringing Hastings to scrutiny before the combined houses of Parliament, Burke had made empire safe for British sovereignty. By implication, British sovereignty was no longer threatened by empire. Sovereignty could now be seen as autonomous and encompassing through its justificatory logic that the good despotism it provided was much better than the bad despotism India had known before conquest. As a consequence, the great antagonists Burke and Hastings—not the millions of Indians in whose name Burke pretended to speak— could both become tragic heroes of their parliamentary duel.

*Lord Clive meeting Mir Jafar, soon to be the new nawab of Bengal,
on the battlefield of Plassey, 1757.*

⇥ 6 ⇤

State

*This bill [Fox's India Bill], and those connected with it,
are intended to form the Magna Charta of Hindostan.
Whatever the great charter, the statute of tallage, the pe-
tition of right, are to Great Britain, these bills are to the
people of India.*

—EDMUND BURKE, "SPEECH ON FOX'S

INDIA BILL," 1783

Robert Clive might have conquered Bengal, but it was Warren Hastings who first seriously began to rule it.[1] Hastings ascended to the position of governor, and soon thereafter governor-general, as a bureaucrat rather than a soldier. His first act was to end Clive's system of dual rule, undertaking direct management of revenue collection in Bengal rather than relying on the nawab. To do this, he had to devise an entirely new revenue system, establishing direct administration over local agencies and landlords. Hastings also instituted new systems of civil and criminal law, crafted on the basis of a thorough study of indigenous systems of justice. By the time Hastings returned to London in 1785, he had changed the fundamental nature

of Company rule in India. He had, in fact, established the foundations of the colonial state, setting up structures that were refined by
Cornwallis and then appropriated by Wellesley for the administration of the next phase of imperial conquest. Burke was wrong to suppose that any of the regulating acts could provide the basis for a
"Magna Charta for Hindostan," but Hastings had, in effect, used
them to provide a charter for the foundations of the colonial state
in India.

Hastings succeeded in his enterprise even though the regulations
of 1773 were intended to harness the Company far more securely to
the policies and control of the British state than ever before. The
Regulating Act had covertly overridden the clauses of the original
Company charters, reserving for the state "the right to interfere in
all aspects of the most powerful commercial enterprise in the
realm."[2] The act had succeeded because of the desperate financial
straits of the Company. And yet the centralization of powers under
the governor-general, even with explicit lines of authority vested in
the British state and the controlling influence of the governing
council, gave new power to the Company leader for the establishment of a state system in the colonies. The time lag of six to twelve
months for correspondence between England and India was only
part of the reason that local affairs continued to be largely autonomous. Empire had an inexorable logic of its own, and Hastings was
a model servant of empire. In reality, he could fulfill Company
mandates only by working steadfastly to secure greater authority for
a new kind of state form. Accordingly, Hastings created the basic
structures of a colonial state, a state that asserted its legitimacy far
more through its careful attention to the procedures and protocols
of rule than it did by concerning itself with principles of sovereignty
having to do with either rulers or people.

Michel Foucault has written that the modern state is character-ized by the preoccupations of "governmentality." By this he meant the full administrative apparatus of government, more an economy of rules and procedures than a politics of negotiation and conflict. As he wrote, "To govern a state will therefore mean to apply econ-omy, to set up an economy at the level of the entire state, which means exercising towards its inhabitants, and the wealth and behav-ior of each and all, a form of surveillance and control as attentive as that of the head of a family over his household and goods."[3] In point-ing toward the patrimonial origins of the modern state, Foucault could have been writing about the specific conditions of the colo-nial state, where the state was transplanted onto the ruins of patri-monial states through a complex transfer from economic and mili-tary power to a new set of political projects that used bureaucracy to distract attention from the myriad contradictions of imperial sover-eignty. Bureaucracy for Foucault entailed not just the control of in-habitants, but also the accumulation of empirical knowledge previ-ously unknown, which in the Indian case consisted of new state activities ranging from the surveying and mapping of new territories to the delineation and assessment of every manner of agricultural and rural activity.[4]

Hastings's most prosaic accomplishment was to devise, with the unlikely help of Francis, a rule of property: a system of agricultural tax collection based on the presumed right of the state to collect "rent" and to assess it on the basis of its own calculations of "sur-plus."[5] His most praised accomplishment was the establishment of a rule of law based on Islamic law and Hindu texts. These accomplish-ments were obscured by the continuing confusion over questions of sovereignty, not to mention Burke's representation of Hastings as a despot who used "arbitrary power."[6] Yet Hastings worked to establish a revenue administration largely on lines laid out by Francis and later canonized by Cornwallis in the famous "permanent settlement" of 1793. And despite the fact that Hastings betrayed the contradictions of his own commitment to the rule of law when he used his newly constituted supreme court to hang a Brahman—a dreadful violation of Hindu custom and a judgment that overtly contravened Islamic legal principle—Hastings is perhaps best remembered for the care he took to establish a colonial form of legal practice that appeared to be directly modeled on indigenous customs, texts, and practices.

The British state not only worked out many of the changing internal relations of Crown and Parliament during the time of Hastings's rule in India; it also amassed the resources—economic, military, and political—for its own attainment of relative dominance in Europe through its growing imperial foothold. At the same time, the development of colonial forms of governmentality, in the elaboration of an administrative bureaucracy that deployed direct political authority through its rights to manage revenue, judicial systems, and local welfare, became critical to the emerging colonial state precisely because this state did not offer even the possibility of popular sovereignty. Governmentality thus worked to extract massive amounts of revenue while respecting local landlords and cultivators—at the same time that it captured enormous power over local structures and networks of social, cultural, political, and economic life while promising British justice based on Indian principles. The state also transposed its military operations into policing systems, establishing direct relations with local police and connecting the rule of law to the project of maintaining order. As the colonial state developed and expanded during the nineteenth century, it took on various putative welfare functions and a wide variety of managerial tasks, but all of these elaborations depended on the initial innovations of Warren Hastings.

The Regulating Act of 1773 was not explicitly developed with this aim in mind. Still, it was generally assumed that the price for the bailout of the Company was steep, and that the Company would become, in effect, the monopoly agent of the British state in the East Indies. The act mandated that dividend payments on stocks and bonds would be limited to 6 and 7 percent respectively, until all debts were cleared. Conditions for representation, and voting power, on the board of directors as well as the general court of proprietors were made exacting and were strictly enforced. A supreme court was established, with its judges to be appointed in Britain by the Crown, to ensure judicial autonomy from and control over Company servants. And a governing council of four, with ultimate power to approve or reject the policies of the governor-general, was set up, with its members to be jointly approved by the directors and the cabinet. Despite concerns on the part of some that the regulations were not as extensive as they might have been, there was general agreement that they would lead to a sea change in relations between state and Company. In theory, at least, the regulations were extraordinary: private trade was prohibited; large salaries were to be paid to senior Company servants; the administration of justice was reformed; authority within the Company structure was streamlined and made responsible; and parliamentary and ministerial supervision of Company affairs was to be conducted on a regular basis.

In subsequent years, Hastings's military adventures and financial difficulties were seen as signs of the failure of the regulations. This is a view that accepts the assumptions of most imperial history, which has consistently viewed the Company as a problem for managerial reasons, asserting that (explicit instructions from home notwithstanding) greedy traders simply couldn't resist opportunities to go to war to expand their economic influence and control new markets. But Hastings was neither dancing absentmindedly into empire nor violating general imperatives for reasons having to do solely with the limitless greed of many Company servants. Company trade was in fact predicated on political advantage and control. Economic success was inexorably linked to military and political success. And none of these measures of success were designed to protect even the most careful Company servants from costly military expenditure and political calamity. They came, as it were, with the territory.

By this time, in fact, British interests required the deployment of large numbers of armed forces, naval squadrons, and administrators, for which profit from trade could hardly be expected to suffice. The Company was simply following the lead of the British state, which had developed as a military fiscal state during the late seventeenth and early eighteenth centuries on the basis of an active military presence and a high level of taxation.[7] Perhaps the single greatest innovation in the operations of the Company in India during the 1770s was its realization that profit from trade was insufficient to support its imperial operations. Trade was a source of major income, both for the nabobs who made their magnificent fortunes and for the British economy. But it was insufficient to establish the conditions of what in effect became the colonial version of Britain's own military fiscal state. As was the case in Britain itself, the cost of military as well as commercial ventures in the eighteenth century was always higher than anticipated, and required a secure tax base to provide regular funding. The problem, however, was that neither the British state, nor the Company, seemed able to represent its interests as legitimate when advanced either by an imperial state or a mercantilist trading concern. Instead, the Company was seen as egregious and irresponsible, in clear violation of the interests and instructions of the metropolitan state.

Since empire was not yet fully legitimate—either in its operations or its aspirations—the Company had to be represented in part as the outcome of the agency of illegitimate men and activities. During the 1770s, attacks on the Company increased, leading to continued regulatory concern. But by 1780 it was clear that at least some of the stated aims of the regulations had failed. Corruption had not altogether ceased (though the situation was far better in Bengal than in Madras), war and territorial expansion had not stopped, and, even more worrisome, the Company appeared to be headed toward bankruptcy once again. The American War of Independence had further complicated matters, bringing Britain into another global war, threatening the loss of their rich American colonies. And yet it was precisely the impending loss of the Americas that made Indian possessions even more precious. Despite all the hand-wringing, it was clear that India was not going to be abandoned. There were bound to be more reforms, but this time efforts to bring the Company under firmer state control became almost necessarily linked to a larger effort to legitimize the imperial theater of Asia in a more dramatic fashion than any single act of legislation could hope to accomplish.

The establishment of the colonial state during the time of Hastings might not have required the impeachment trial in order to transform public opinion regarding Britain's imperial ambitions.

But the early colonial state did provide the basis for empire's ultimate success, in every possible sense. Hastings not only abandoned the contradictions of Clive's dual rule; he also established the first colonial revenue system and made it clear that the primary energies of the mercantile state had now to be directed to agriculture rather than trade. In effect, Hastings inaugurated the revenue state in India that dominated the colonial establishment for the next century and more. Cornwallis might have introduced the formal settlement of proprietary rights, created the basis for fiscal responsibility, and reduced corruption by raising the emoluments of the civil service establishment, but in fact he was simply raising the stakes of what Hastings had already initiated. The rule of property legitimized itself through the claim that the colonial state was introducing the security of property rights, while it worked to extract an increasing share of revenue to fund both military and administrative costs. The rule of law vastly expanded the domain of legal judgment while protecting the local state from the charge that the law was driven by its own political concerns. Both property and law were protected by a local policing establishment that answered to the new state even as it embedded itself within newly configured regimes of power and wealth in the countryside.

In assuming direct control over revenue collection, Hastings was concerned both to assert Company sovereignty over land and to raise the level and reliability of revenue returns. Hastings replaced many of the nawab's revenue-collecting middlemen—*mutaseddis, diwans,* and *sheristadars*—with his own administrators, and attempted to develop new procedures to monitor collection practices. At the same time, he felt the need to rely on traditional methods and procedures. Following nawabi practice, he auctioned off revenue-collecting rights to *ijaradars* (revenue farmers, who bid in a competitive auction for the annual right to collect revenue), but rather than engage revenue commitments for one-year periods, he used five-year terms. While this assured a relatively robust revenue return, it also endowed the revenue farmers, whether local *zamindars* (landlords) or not, with longer-term interests in productivity and management than had been the case with one-year terms. Nevertheless, his plan yielded the escalating criticism of Philip Francis, who, following the lead of earlier critics of Clive, argued that revenue farming not only squeezed the cultivators with no chance of improvement, but violated indigenous notions of property.

Hastings responded to these criticisms by noting that he was neither interested in abstract notions of improvement nor convinced that he was doing anything other than recognizing the local variability of land tenures, customs, and revenue rights. Besides, he had inherited a financial ruin, and was keen to use land revenue to enable the Company to recover its fiscal health as well as enact various reforms. Francis was surely correct to worry about the short-term interests of revenue farmers, but Hastings had a point; his own understanding of the relationship of property relations and sovereignty was limited in much the same way that his proposals for a *zamindari* settlement were based on universal and abstract notions.

Francis's physiocratic convictions that property had to be stable and the revenue rate fixed in order for capitalist improvement to make inroads into agricultural production became the putative grounds for one of many long-standing quarrels between Francis and Hastings.[8] Francis was critical of Hastings not only for what he took to be his interest only in short-term goals, but also because

Francis felt that only the traditional landlord class, or *zamindars*, could develop any stakes in local conditions and work to improve agricultural production. In fact, Hastings made most of his settlements with *zamindars*, though because of his more grounded sense of Bengal he discriminated among them when assessing the final bids.[9] He too sought to establish "an *equal*, an *easy*, and a perpetual assessment of the public revenue; to collect it through the medium of zemindars, where they are capable of the charge."[10] Despite the obvious differences and disagreements between Francis and Hastings, it is clear that much more united than divided them in their fundamental understanding of the need for structural change.

Francis was even more critical of Hastings for his alleged—and allegedly mistaken—notion that all land belonged to the king. Indeed, Francis believed that Hastings not only mistook the king's right to collect revenue for an actual property right, but that he flagrantly violated Mughal sovereignty. While noting that "it has been the policy of Mr. Hastings to abolish the Sovereignty of the Mogul in fact, and to deny it in Argument," he observed that the Company continued to coin money in the name of Shah Alam and to collect revenues by virtue of his grant.[11] Echoing previous critiques of Clive, he wrote that "the People at present have either two Sovereigns or None."[12] Francis held that the British government should simply declare its sovereignty over Bengal, preferably by a formal surrender of these provinces by the Mughal emperor, but he was hardly realistic about whether, or for that matter how, this might be done. Instead, he simply attacked Hastings for the manifest contradictions inherent in Company rule after the acceptance of the Diwani.

Hastings responded by arguing—in terms that resonate with Burke's subsequent rhetoric—that he was in fact respecting the "ancient constitution" of Bengal and India by accommodating local practices and understandings to the "genius and principles of our own."[13] It is well established that Hastings was concerned to maintain certain older practices, in this as in other aspects of government. But Hastings was far more concerned with revenue than had been the case before. And Company concern with revenue did lead to significant changes in the local political economy. This overriding interest in the extraction of resources, whether on the part of Hastings or of Cornwallis, was progressively at odds with old-regime interests that had allowed revenue rates to fluctuate more readily, remissions to be given more often, and various kinds of ceremonial "gift" exchanges to remain important.[14] The colonial state was adamant in its conviction that a proper revenue system—by which it meant a system that did not incur opposition or resistance on the grounds that it appeared to be entirely foreign in its development and implementation—was necessary for its survival. And the permanent settlement of Cornwallis, however flawed it soon turned out to be in reality, was successful in the short term precisely because it gave the appearance of preserving the old regime at the same time it introduced the virtues of secure private property, all the while making possible the efficient extraction of revenue at a much higher and more regular rate than ever before.

That Hastings had more interest in respecting local practices and understandings than Francis was revealed far more clearly in their dispute over legal reforms than in the domain of revenue collection. As soon as Hastings assumed the governorship of Bengal in April 1772, he set to work on a plan to take over the administration of civil justice. In August of the same year he submitted his judicial plan, providing that "in all suits regarding inheritance, marriage, caste, and other religious usages, or institutions, the laws of the koran with respect to Mahometans and those of the Shaster with respect to Gentoos [Hindus] shall be invariably adhered to."[15] The most radical feature of the plan was the intention to take over the responsibility of administering and enforcing personal law; the nawabi courts had in effect allowed Hindus to observe their own legal codes, but neither oversaw the process nor enforced the resulting legal decisions. And even Muslim personal law was now to be conducted under the auspices of new civil courts called *Diwani adalats*, over which the revenue collectors were to preside. Hastings also established new criminal courts, called the *faujdari* courts, effectively appropriating authority over all criminal cases from the nizam's government. Hastings realized that in establishing direct rule, he needed to claim exclusive rights to judicial and punitive authority, for he saw these rights as fundamental to his efforts to reserve all sovereign authority for the Company. He justified his takeover with reasons having to do with the corruption of the nizam's court, an argument that held little sway in Bengal given the much higher levels of corruption in all Company affairs. As Hastings put it, "Our interfering in the courts of the Nezamut, or the criminal courts, is an usurpation, but we could not avoid it. Had we left them to the Nabob, they would have been made the sources of venality and oppression, and our collections would have been perpetually interrupted by their officers."[16]

Hastings also claimed that his reforms were merely enacted to uphold the "ancient constitution," intended as they were "to recur to the original principles and to give them that efficacy of which they were deprived by venal and arbitrary innovations."[17] In fact, Hastings's representation of the consistency of his reforms with prior practices was more rhetorical than real. Even his interest in applying Hindu or Muslim personal law to civil cases led to new and radically different systems of classification and codification. Additionally, his interest in personal law was an extension of the new importance played by revenue collection. As he observed, "In the execution of this commission [to take direct control over revenue collection], it was discovered that the due administration of justice had so intimate a connexion with the revenue, that in the system which was adopted, this formed a very considerable part." It was the profound interconnection of family and personal law with systems of inheritance that made the Company so interested in understanding the intricacies of Hindu and Muslim civil law in the first place. And his concern to appropriate all punitive rights as the necessary perquisites of state sovereignty led both to major revisions of Islamic law and to the development of radically new institutional forms. In relation to Islamic law, Hastings was concerned that government would have to intervene to ensure the implementation of punitive justice, since Islamic law was "founded on the most lenient principles and on an abhorrence of bloodshed."[18] And, like other European commentators, Hastings worried that legal practices of the old regime were irregular and arbitrary. He believed strongly in the necessity, and greater efficacy, of fixed and immutable penalties.[19] Yet the actual record of Company justice by no means indicates that arbitrary and discretionary powers were disavowed. British justice turned out to be far more draconian—in practice as well as in principle—than Islamic justice had been, resorting much more frequently to capital punishment, and much less often to community-based methods of enforcement and reconciliation. As it happened, the Company state was far more concerned with public order, and with the specific use of the law to protect its own trade and commerce as well as authority, than was the old regime.

Francis had argued against Hastings's judicial reforms less on the grounds of tradition than in relation to his own concern about the inconsistencies of Company sovereignty. It was not obvious how his own plan to confer most judicial authority to *zamindars* and other landlords would resolve contradictions in sovereignty, though it plainly would buttress the property rights of the landlords in ways consistent with his own desire to effect a permanent settlement. Even Lord Cornwallis, when he ultimately enacted the permanent settlement, was reluctant to do this, instead reforming the *faujdari* courts by substituting two covenanted servants of the Company for the *faujdar* and using *kazis* and *muftis* (lower-level judges) merely as court assistants. In retrospect, Hastings was by far the most Orientalist of all judicial reformers in colonial history, carefully introducing new legal procedures with the full justification—both for Indian and British constituencies—of the maintenance of Indian traditions. Nowhere was this clearer than in his efforts to draft a code of Hindu laws.

Hastings argued that he was following the ancient constitution in using pundits as legal experts rather than judges, though in many cases he substituted British civil servants for traditional Muslim judges. Although British suspicion of the alleged role of bribery and corruption in indigenous courts played no small part in his enthusiasm for codification, Hastings wrote merely that he was concerned to codify Hindu law in such a way as to expedite the task of the courts. As he put it,

> It has never been the practice of this country for the pundits or expounders of the Hindoo law, to sit as judges of it, but only to give their opinions in such cases as might be proposed to them, and as these perpetually occurring occasioned very great delays in

our proceedings, or were decided at once by the officers of the
Courts, without any reference, it was judged advisable for the
sake of giving confidence to the people, and of enabling the
Courts to decide with certainty and despatch, to form a compila-
tion of the Hindoo laws with the best authority which could be
obtained; and for that purpose ten of the most learned pundits
were invited to Calcutta from different parts of the province, who
cheerfully undertook this work.[20]

In fact, eleven pundits were hired by Hastings to compile a general
law code, and they worked together between May 1773 and March
1774 to produce a Sanskrit text that provided excerpts from a variety
of authoritative sources along with extensive commentaries.[21] A Persian translation was planned from the outset, although apparently
the text was composed on the basis of an oral Bengali translation by
one of the pundits. The Persian text was then translated into English
by Nathaniel Halhed, a young Company servant who had studied
Persian before going to India in 1772. Halhed's translation was used
by Hastings to justify his claim that personal law need not be angli-
cized, affording, as he said, "at least a proof that the people of this
country do not require our aid to furnish them with a rule for their
conduct, or a standard for their property."[22]

   When arguing for the preparation of a new digest of Hindu law,
the great Orientalist and jurist William Jones subsequently declared
the translation virtually worthless: "Whatever be the merit of the
original, the translation of it has no authority, and is of no other use
than to suggest inquiries on the many dark passages . . . properly
speaking, indeed, we cannot call it a translation; for, though Mr.
Halhed performed his part with fidelity, yet the Persian interpreter

had supplied him only with a loose injudicious epitome of the original Sanscrit, in which abstract many essential passages are omitted."[23] Nevertheless, the Hindu code of law was used for many years as a reliable index of Hindu law. In fact, the code was used even after the publication of Henry Colebrooke's digest (which Colebrooke completed after Jones, who had begun the project, died in 1796), itself published in 1797–1798.[24] The code proved more useful in some respects since the digest only dealt with contracts and inheritance, while the code covered many more points of law. Even its detractors were critical mostly of the translation, and in later years legal scholars held that the code was "the last production of traditional legal scholarship, unadulterated by British concepts."[25]

While the code might have been of greater lasting importance for Oriental studies than for the practice of law, it did set a precedent in which British judges and courts felt obliged to consult a range of Sanskrit texts and authorities when adjudicating a wide range of matters concerning property, the family, and inheritance. And commentators as various as Jeremy Bentham, James Mill, and Charles Grant used it to argue about the significance of Hindu law, even though it was used by Grant simply to dismiss the immorality, injustice, and cruelty of the "crafty and imperious priesthood."[26] As the final irony, the code was used by Burke in the impeachment trial to bring Hastings to account, precisely for failing to uphold the ancient constitution of India.

If Burke was mistaken to attack Hastings for his inattention to India's ancient constitution, he missed his biggest chance to bring Hastings down for his actual execution of the rule of law. For the most egre-

gious blemish in Hastings career was in his use—or at least his acceptance of the use—of the new legal institutions and procedures of
Calcutta to bring about what was later called the "judicial murder"
of one of his chief Indian enemies, Nandakumar. On August 5, 1775,
an important and wealthy member of Calcutta society, the Brahman
Nandakumar, was hung after a hastily convened hearing in the supreme court, where he was convicted on a charge of forgery that was
not just flimsy, but something that Islamic law would never have
used as the basis for a serious charge.

The execution of Nandakumar certainly gave ample indication of
the extent to which Hastings was willing to allow colonial law both
to depart from earlier procedures and to serve his own immediate
political interests. Hastings had known Nandakumar since 1764
when he was the diwan, or prime minister of Bengal, under Mir
Jafar. When in late 1771 Hastings was first entrusted with the task of
deposing Muhammed Reza Khan and taking direct control over
revenue collection in Bengal, he was asked to use Nandakumar's extensive knowledge of the local scene, as well as his rivalry with
the nawab, to the Company's benefit.[27] Neither Hastings nor most
other members of the Company had especially good relations with
Nandakumar, but he was of some assistance when Hastings finally
managed to arrest Muhammed Reza Khan in April 1772. It was only
because of his help that Hastings found sufficient pretext for assuming civil and military administration, as well as direct control over
revenue collection. Meanwhile, Hastings placed the young nawab
under the control of Munni Begam, one of Mir Jafar's widows, and
employed Nandakumar's son Guru Das as the "diwan" of the nawab's court.

Despite the public recognition of Nandakumar's "services" in the elevation of his son to an important position in the affairs of Bengal, Hastings covertly attempted to isolate Nandakumar himself, cutting off his correspondence with his son and blocking him from any real access to the nawab's old administrative operations. Hastings ignored Nandakumar in 1773 when he appealed for protection from a possible plot against him on the part of Sadr-ud-din and Jagat Chand, both of whom had remained loyal to Muhammed Reza Khan and various other supporters of the older regime. By the next year, Nandakumar was in touch with some of Hastings's enemies in Calcutta, promising to provide damaging information about him that could be used to gain advantage in the quarrels that had already begun to escalate between Hastings and the majority of council, led by Philip Francis.[28] On March 11, 1775, Francis presented the council with a letter from Nandakumar alleging that Hastings had taken "presents" worth close to £45,000 in exchange for appointing Munni Begam and Guru Das as the guardians of the nawab and his court, in addition to other presents arranged for Hastings's agent Krishna Kanta Nandi. When Francis attempted to hear the charges, bringing Nandakumar forward to the council, Hastings stormed out of the meeting, contending that his fellow councilors were parties to the charge and therefore unfit to adjudicate the matter. Although the council was therefore unable to hear the charges in any formal manner, the alleged presents included a gift of 150,000 rupees—or about £19,000—to Hastings, described as the customary allowance for entertainment made to a governor on a visit to the nawab's court rather than a present per se. In the impeachment trial, Hastings admitted that he had accepted this allowance, maintaining as well that the amount was indeed a customary allowance for expenses associated with a "state" visit. Strictly speaking, even this allowance constituted a breach of his covenant not to accept any "gift, reward, gratuity, allowance, donation, or compensation," although it was manifestly clear he was by no means alone in making occasional, and not insignificant, exceptions to this rule, especially on official visits.[29] But he denied the other charges that Nandakumar had made.

Nandakumar's downfall, however, was on a different charge. Less than two months after Nandakumar presented his accusations against Hastings, he was formally accused—by Sadr-ud-din and Jagat Chand, among others—of committing a forgery in 1769. While this case had been "kept alive for four years past on purpose to keep him in dependence," it was only brought to the supreme court once it was clear that Hastings had reason to get rid of Nandakumar once and for all.[30] Hastings's friend George Vansittart had apparently given concrete assurances to the accusers that they would be supported should the case be brought to trial, and even the most "balanced" of accounts make clear that Hastings could not have been innocent of involvement in the case.[31] Hastings by then felt desperate, and was convinced that the majority of council members—John Clavering, George Monson, and Philip Francis—were intent on using whatever means to bring about his downfall, the most readily available being charges of corruption.

No one seemed better placed than Nandakumar to provide evidence for these charges, given his involvement in most of Hastings's early dealings with Bengal administration. The chief justice of the supreme court, Elijah Impey, was a good friend and supporter of Hastings as well, and he presided over the case against Nandakumar in June of 1775. The jury, composed entirely of Englishmen, delivered a verdict of guilty, recommending death by hanging. It was bad enough that forgery had never been a capital offense in Mughal law, but in the hanging of Nandakumar, Hastings publicly and dramatically declared his indifference to the doctrinal (Shastric) injunction against the execution of Brahmans. Hastings followed what he took to be Hindu law when it suited him, but now he needed to rid himself of a native threat to his local power and authority. Nandakumar was no ordinary Brahman, and this was no ordinary case.

Under Mughal law forgery was a possible crime, but its punishment was very rare, always at the discretion of local judges, and usually involved nothing more than a public flogging. The case against Nandakumar, even leaving aside that it was brought to trial six years after the event, would never have reached a Mughal court. As soon as the British began to establish courts in India, they became deeply concerned with issues around forgery and perjury, in large part because of their growing conviction that objective truth was hard to find in India, especially in legal proceedings, where Indians were also judged not only to be extraordinarily litigious but completely unreliable as witnesses. The upright Lord Cornwallis, for example, had confidently proclaimed, "Every native of Hindustan, I verily believe, is corrupt."[32] And by the nineteenth century, statements about the cultural indisposition to truth telling became a colonial cliché. Although colonial law formally admitted that different kinds of oaths, reflecting local beliefs and religious practices, could be accepted as equivalent to proper Christian oaths in court, there was an underlying suspicion that natives lied and native religion carried no sanction against perjury.[33]

Forgery was seen as a symptom of the same fundamental problem, and the colonial state accordingly directed considerable attention to the issue. In 1803 the criminal "profession" of forgery was classified as a heinous crime, and in 1807 the punishment for forgery and perjury was accorded the extraordinary measure of *tashir*, or public exposure.[34] British concerns about Indian truth developed in line with a definite colonial logic: the usual problems of linguistic and cultural ignorance were invariably translated as the fault of the colonized, and the steadily emergent crises around the appropriation and codification of "Islamic" and "Hindu" legal provisions and procedures—and the constantly blurred lines between domains of public and private legal concern—were invariably blamed on Indian character rather than colonial procedure.

In the case of Nandakumar, however, forgery was simply used as a convenient pretext to protect Hastings. The case of forgery that brought Nandakumar down concerned a bond that had been executed by an old friend, Bulaki Das, who had sought to secure his legacy for his wife and several close friends against other weighty claims by declaring a debt to Nandakumar that would be used in effect to shelter his money. One of Nandakumar's major claimants, Mohan Prasad, discovered the fraud and brought the case to a lower court in 1771, two years after Bulaki Das had died. When Prasad brought the case to the supreme court in March of 1775, it had long been in stalemate in the lower courts, and seemed an unlikely tool to use given Nandakumar's lack of personal interest in what was neither a clear case of malevolent intent to defraud nor a politically motivated charge.

Nevertheless, the case arrived at the door of the supreme court at an opportune time given the charges against Hastings, and the timing could hardly have been accidental. Chief Justice Impey accepted the case and convened a jury of twelve Englishmen to begin the hearing on June 8. After the reading of the indictment, Justice Robert Chambers (who had just arrived, at Hastings's invitation, from a post as professor of law at Oxford) argued that forgery was an inappropriate charge in Indian law, having only been made a capital felony in England during the reign of George II for reasons that did not apply locally. Impey, and the other two justices hearing the case, overruled this objection. The defense rested its case on June 15, and after what was by all accounts a prejudicial summation by Impey, the jury determined that Nandakumar was guilty as charged.[35] He was sentenced to hang on August 5, and despite all the irregularities of the trial, and the residual influence that might have been exercised by Francis and his majority group, no appeal was made. One of the richest and most powerful men in Bengal was made the victim of what seemed to many, then and later, to be Hastings's private vendetta.[36] And while the prosecution of this vendetta hardly cleared the field of all his enemies, no senior Indian came forward again to accuse Hastings of corruption.

The supreme court had hardly been established to dispose of important Indians who made life difficult for senior Company officials, but it was instituted in large part to maintain the principle of extraterritoriality for all British subjects in India. The Company assumed that British subjects were only answerable to British justice, and the country *(mofussil)* courts that had been established outside the British presidencies were not empowered to try Englishmen. The presidency courts—called king's courts—were tribunals of English law presided over by English judges and barristers. The Company's courts in the *mofussil* administered Hindu and Muslim personal law, upheld Islamic criminal law, and enforced Company regulations against Indians. But any Indian who wished to sue an Englishman had to bring the case to Calcutta, and soon after the establishment of the supreme court it became the guaranteed arbiter of justice for Englishmen all over India. The assumption was that wherever Europeans settled in India, both they—and the natives with whom they had any dealings—were to be governed only by British laws adjudicated by Company courts. As Elizabeth Kolsky puts it, "According to this odd but characteristically colonial logic, Indians residing in territories occupied by the British could legally be considered aliens in their own land."[37] And the British made sure not only that they would be tried by British law, British judges, and British juries, but also that in any contest between British and Indian judicial interests, colonial interests would dominate from the start.

Hastings's legal innovations and reforms thus set significant colonial precedents for Britain's relationship with India. Law was to be used to legitimate British rule, and it was intended to be as weighty and fair in India as it was in Britain. It was also deeply compromised, in ways that directly reflected the racial and cultural dimensions of colonial domination. Colonial law was ostensibly supposed to be sensitive to the religious nature of personal matters such as marriage, inheritance, and family issues as well as property, subject only to the constraints of new property systems set in place by revenue settlements. Civil law was a matter of state and one of the first domains in which sovereignty would be exercised, even as it was assumed that the British themselves would be protected by British law wherever they settled, whatever the character of political rule. Hastings also inaugurated the British colonial interest in codification, a preoccupation that attained its highest point in the legal code proposed by Thomas Macaulay some fifty years later. Indeed, legal reformers, from Bentham and Mill to Macaulay and J. F. Stephen, were especially passionate about the possibility of codifying colonial law because they believed this would make possible the codification of law in England itself, a goal that in fact proved far more elusive. Law, in other words, from the experiment conducted by Hastings and Halhed (with their committee of Brahman pundits in the early 1770s to the Indian penal code of 1860 and the Code of Criminal Procedure in 1861), makes especially clear the extent to which colonial India was a kind of social laboratory for the forging of modern institutions and the development of modern ideas.

In his speech before Parliament defending his record in India, Hastings had taken special pride in his transformation of the administration of land revenue in Bengal and his institution of new codes and procedures for civil and criminal justice in compliance with Indian constitutional traditions and norms. But he also took credit for what he claimed to be the enormous military and political accomplishments of neutralizing the Maratha threat and establishing a new form of government in Benares, all the while cementing the Company's subsidiary alliance with the great province of Awadh.

In fact, these "accomplishments" were not unrelated, and they remind us that the colonial state, as much as it sought to secure its legitimacy from the principles of law, property, and order, had to rely in the end on military power. When Hastings took control of Bengal in 1772 the Company was in a desperate financial position, and the treasury in Bengal was almost depleted. The Regulating Act of 1773 relieved some of the immediate pressure, but political and military threats mounted nevertheless. The Marathas increasingly challenged the British, threatening Awadh and even at one point demanding tribute from Bengal. After the Battle of Baksar in 1764, Clive had arranged for a garrison of Company soldiers to be housed in Awadh, for which the nawab was to pay a significant subsidy. In June of 1773 Hastings journeyed to Awadh with two clear aims: to raise some additional cash for his exchequer, and to secure greater military support from Awadh to take on the Marathas. Hastings negotiated an agreement for the Awadh court that seemed to do both. The nawab agreed to pay 50 million rupees (about £6.25 million) for some territory that was restored to him, and to pay an additional subsidy for a brigade of the Bengal army to provide greater security in the region. In return, Hastings agreed that Company troops could be used rather more liberally than intended by the directors of the Company, who were ever opposed to what they construed as expensive and politically dangerous offensive wars. Specifically, Hastings had sanctioned the use of Company troops for a campaign against Rohilkhand, just to the west of Awadh. In February 1774, the nawab, arguing that the Marathas had already made inroads against the Company by establishing close relations with the Rohillas, made good on this promise and attacked Rohilkhand. Later, when Burke argued in Parliament for Hastings's impeachment, he condemned Company troops for what he called the "extermination" of the Rohillas.[38]

By 1781 Hastings was once again in great financial distress, and his worries about the Marathas were intensified by the possibility of an alliance between them and Haidar Ali from Mysore. Despite Hastings's dubious justifications and clear instances in which he went against treaty agreements, winked at the torture of key prisoners, and repeatedly violated the instructions of the directors to engage in no offensive actions for either financial or political reasons, he was convinced that he was serving both Company and British interests. The imperatives governing imperial actions during those years were considerably more complicated than those Hastings described in his defense at his impeachment trial. The idea of having an Indian ruler—in this case the second in command of the Mughal empire—simultaneously pay for Company troops and allow these troops to be garrisoned at the center of his polity made possible the steady appropriation of political control over Awadh at the same time that it compensated for some of the military costs of maintaining a standing army. As early as 1773, the directors had instructed Hastings to make sure that in his negotiations with the nawab he would ensure "a free intercourse of commerce with his Dominions . . . as you are acquainted with the earnest wishes of the Company on this head."[39]

Although the Company attempted to bring some of the private trade in salt, betel nut, and tobacco under control, a relationship between political and economic interests developed in the ensuing decades.[40] The more the Company succeeded in curtailing the abuses of some private trade, the more it also developed an interest in taking direct political control over regions where it could conduct its own trade ever more "freely."[41] Company investments across eastern India initially revolved around cotton and silk textiles as well as piece goods; increasingly, the Company relied on trade in betel nut, opium, and salt, all of which drew it inexorably into the webs of political and economic interests engaged across the Indo-Gangetic plain.

Whether intentionally or not, Hastings managed in effect to disguise the extent to which some Company policies were driven by these local, and often unofficial, economic interests through a justificatory language of statecraft, diplomacy, and military necessity. Although Francis was the proximate cause of Hastings's difficulties during the 1770s, at some level all Francis did was draw attention to the most contradictory features of Hastings's own imperial vision, including his repeated efforts to engage the Marathas and find Indian constitutional precedent to design a new regime based on law, revenue, and military rule. Accordingly, metropolitan attention could focus increasingly on the new issue of political corruption rather than the older forms of corruption associated with Clive and his regime.

Standard histories of the East India Company repeat the view that the Regulating Act of 1773 had been unable to stem the growing managerial crisis represented by the form of Company rule itself. Thus, for example, the government was forced to put Company affairs in order by the end of Hastings's rule. In part this situation developed because of the continued financial crisis of the Company: not only did the Company fail to recover quickly from the crash of the late 1760s, but its precarious revenue situation also threatened to undermine the financial stability of the government itself. In the words of Philip Lawson, the government "could not stand idly by" while the "immense value of the Company's activities to British tax and custom revenues . . . [were] jeopardized," nor while it watched "the demise of Company trade policy." As he further observed, "So much of the nation's financial health was caught up in the eastern trade, and whole domestic industries depended on the regular supply of such commodities as tea."[42] But even worse, "the government found the idea of a Company making and breaking alliances with various Indian rulers very disturbing. Such prerogatives belonged to sovereign states not trading Companies, and if not controlled, the Company could conceivably lead the nation into a ruinous war with the Mogul empire."[43] These anxieties, however, reflected even deeper concerns, since the British state had to find ways not just to control the Company but also to create another kind of state that could conduct its global business more discreetly. Even as Hastings was establishing the colonial state, and engaging it in necessary military actions, he was making it imperative that this state secure new forms of legitimacy from its various metropolitan constituencies.

The task of Pitt's reforms of 1784, therefore, was to develop the rudiments of this new colonial state, and to control at least some of the forces that made the contradictions inherent in this state appear so dangerous both at home in Britain and on the ground in India. Under the new board of control, itself under royal direction, the power of war and peace was confirmed and officially transferred to the metropolitan state. For Lawson as for many other imperial historians, "Pitt's India Bill brought a disastrous period in the Company's history to a close."[44] In fact, the Pitt bill was hardly sufficient to do this, because only the full withdrawal of Britain from Indian politics would have sufficed. Instead, Burke's aggressive prosecution of the impeachment trial did what no regulating act could, by exhorting the British state to take responsibility for its imperial ambitions, whether political or economic.

Burke was aware that the contradictions of early empire were far too antagonistic and deep to be solved by yet another institutional reform. The past had to be pilloried and exorcised in order for the new imperial regime to emerge. It is no accident that while the trial itself failed to indict Hastings in the end, it did provide the basis on which Cornwallis could enact the Pitt regulations—with the integrity and imperial authority that both Parliament and the Crown, however reluctantly, had been persuaded were necessary after the previous decades of scandal and ignominy. That Cornwallis secured a reputation of honesty and probity was an added benefit, of course, despite the extent to which he merely implemented reforms and innovations of which Hastings had been the primary architect. Indeed, Cornwallis became the figurehead for the new colonial state that Hastings had designed.

The colonial state was, not coincidentally, born at the same time as the modern metropolitan state in Britain. Even as new relationships were forged between Parliament and the Crown, Parliament itself was increasingly subject to new expectations about representation, accountability, and the demand to regulate and weed out "old" corruption. At the same time, and with many of the same concerns and imperatives uppermost in the minds of key actors such as Pitt and Burke, the colonial state was harnessed most securely to the metropolitan state itself. Ironically, however, it was precisely at this moment that the colonial state was allowed to develop on seemingly autonomous lines. Thus it was that the colonial state could simultaneously be seen as, on the one hand, incidental to the consolidation of modern state forms at home and, on the other, a laboratory for modern statecraft and the basis on which the British state could achieve such grandeur in the subsequent decades.

Indeed, it was not merely the provision of cheap raw materials and growing markets that enabled Britain's monumental status in the nineteenth and early twentieth centuries. India was where law could be colonized and codified; imperial armies supported, based, and deployed; property regimes concocted and then linked to revenue collection; new bureaucratic forms developed and elaborated; generations of senior civil servants trained and promoted to even more senior positions at home; and new networks spawning the gentlemanly capitalists—who commandeered the rise of London as the banking and commercial capital of the world by the late nineteenth century—could prosper. It was, in short, the subjugation of India that allowed Britain to emerge as the most powerful and modern nation-state of the new nineteenth-century world order.

If Hastings was the architect of the new Indian state, and Cornwallis the first legitimate symbol of it, the final irony was that Wellesley, who ruled India from 1798 to 1805, was the one who set the imperial state on its nineteenth-century course, using what by now was standard imperial practice: rampant militarism, political ambition, and budgetary irresponsibility. Yet despite his eventual differences with Henry Dundas at home, and his disastrous financial legacies for the Company more generally, Wellesley managed not only to escape without any of the ignominy of Hastings, but also to use his experiences in India to make him the first legitimate military hero of the new imperial regime. Unlike his predecessors—many of whom had conducted wars against both the French and a variety of local powers—Wellesley was able to make the case that empire was both necessary to establish a satisfactory defense against French power across the Channel and in some respects central to Britain's struggle for European domination (a legacy that with certain exceptions lasted until Germany became the main rival for continental power more than a century later). In any case, by the early nineteenth century, domination had to be achieved on a global level in order to translate efficiently into local power within Europe itself.

Wellesley was the beneficiary of a newly ascendant British nationalism. The 1790s was a time when the loss of America, the rivalry with and growing distrust of France, the consolidation of a united Britain through Scottish and later Irish inclusion in Parliament (and significantly, in key positions in the East India Company), the stoking of patriotic fervor by figures as various as William Pitt and William Wilberforce, the alignment of the royal court with popular patriotism through new ritual practices, and the commanding British presence in the world's seas all served to make the idea of empire a much worthier enterprise. Burke's role in transforming the imperial imaginary has already been noted, but Wellesley played an important part as well, though he had to negotiate the limits of his position as chief operating officer of the East India Company.

Wellesley was especially adept at using selective information to exaggerate the French threat to justify his own military and political ambitions in India. He was particularly skillful in persuading Dundas, who was concerned about the French threat to British interests in India but completely opposed to any further military activity in India against local rulers, to allow him to attack Mysore in 1799.[45] This he did by suggesting that the French expedition that sailed from Toulon on June 1, 1798, was only going to stop in Egypt on its way to India, and he made much of the fact that in mid-June the governor of Mauritius had publicly announced the offer of an alliance from Tipu Sultan. Throughout 1798 and 1799 Wellesley wrote home that he was about to be attacked by Tipu Sultan when in fact it was the other way round. Charging that Tipu Sultan had taken the name "Citoyen" while planting a republican "liberty tree" in his capital, Wellesley also promulgated rumors that Tipu had mistreated English prisoners of war and would be the agent of France's takeover of the Indian empire.

British forces assaulted Seringapatam in 1799 and killed the Indian leader, in what was subsequently represented as one of the great moments of British civilization in India. The drawing-room toy that Tipu had used to entertain his guests—a large wooden tiger that repeatedly devoured a hapless English soldier—was carted back to England to display Tipu's tyranny to the home audience.[46] Further, while bringing all of Mysore under British dominion, the assault also allowed a further consolidation of Company control in the south since it was claimed that letters had been found in Tipu's possession that proved the nawab of Arcot was conspiring with Mysore. Although later learned to be fraudulent, they provided the necessary justification to pension off the nawab and effectively take direct control of the whole southern swath of India. Imperial power was once again secured through forgeries and invented pretexts.

For Wellesley, Mysore was only one part of the puzzle. He was especially concerned to neutralize the Maratha "threat," which he did in part by working to set the five major Maratha powers at odds with each other. In the end, he was not allowed to engage the Marathas in direct military action, though he used their threat to make further inroads into Awadh and effectively annex half of his ally's territory—some of the choicest agricultural lands in the subcontinent. Meanwhile, Dundas was increasingly alarmed at Wellesley's rampant expenditure and seemingly limitless ambition; aware that only the curtailing of military establishments in India would allow him to recover some expenses and hope to make any profit for the Company, he agreed to Wellesley's efforts to make subsidiary alliances, but even these political efforts were only the thin end of the wedge, invariably designed as the first stage of conquest. In the end, Dundas wished he had never been talked into appointing Wellesley, and he resigned from his position on the board of control in 1801, well before Wellesley returned to England in 1805 as a military hero and major political figure. By now, the Company was increasingly incidental to Britain's own developing interests in India, interests that were in fact significantly furthered by Wellesley rather than by the old guard, who were concerned only about protecting shareholder investments.

It was no accident that Wellesley inspired the loyalty of a new generation of Company servants, men such as Thomas Munro, John Malcolm, Charles Metcalfe, and Mounstuart Elphinstone, all of whom were instrumental in redesigning the colonial state in the early nineteenth century. If Cornwallis had initiated the permanent settlement in Bengal as the first phase of Britain's revenue state in India, he did so in large part because Francis's physiocratic proposals had allowed the major responsibility for revenue collection to reside with local landlords rather than the agents of the colonial state itself. Wellesley's young men had different aspirations, and they represented a different kind of imperial project. Munro was the architect of a new system of revenue collection (the *ryotwari* system), in which the colonial state sought to assess lands directly and collect revenue from the cultivators themselves, and he rose from settling much of the Company's new lands in southern India to be Madras's governor. Malcolm and Elphinstone were critical to the expansion

State

of Company power in western and central India, managing the final dissolution of the great Maratha confederacy, establishing *ryotwari* settlements with village elders as well as cultivators, and instituting procedures for local government. Charles Metcalfe, who became the resident of the Delhi Territory, was the architect of village settlements across much of the northwest. All of these men believed in the capacity of the state to do far more than merely survey territories, measure land, and assess revenues, for the purpose of all of these settlements was to transform Indian society itself, while remaining true, in each case, to the presumptive history of each region of India.

Characterized by the historian Eric Stokes as paternalists as well as utilitarians, all of these leaders were committed to the establishment and spread of a colonial state that would reach deeply not just into the Indian heartland but into local institutions, modes of agrarian management, and forms of political authority.[47] Their imperial project was meant to reverse the influence of Cornwallis, but it was also meant to be progressive and emancipatory. In effect, however, they worked to provide the political and administrative infrastructure for an empire that grew more and more secure, seen by subsequent generations as a natural extension of the British state at home. And that it was. It served as a laboratory and a training ground for civil servants and military leaders who returned to top positions in Britain, even as it later served as the staging base for the extension of empire across Southeast Asia and Africa. As an extension of the British state, it could only find its political legitimacy in the same constituencies served by the British state at home. And yet the notion that modern Britain as we know it was the product of its imperial power—and specifically of its participation in and dependence on the colonial state—is still strangely absent from both British national and imperial historiography. This omission is not unrelated to the ways in which history itself was implicated in the conquest of India and the scandal of empire, before this history was effectively erased by the imperial absence of mind that emerged during the nineteenth century.

Portrait of the nawab of Arcot, "Muhammad" Ali Khan, ca. 1774.

⊰ 7 ⊱

History

This is the historical age and this the historical nation.
—DAVID HUME, *LETTERS*, 1770

Robert Orme, the official historiographer of the East India Company and author of works on Mughal history as well as the early military conquests of the Company, stopped his historical accounts in 1762 because of his growing alarm about writing the history of scandal.[1] Orme was a meticulous chronicler of midcentury events, and the primary source for the history of Clive. He imagined that his position as the bard of empire would rise along with the power and reputation of this empire. He collected an extraordinary archive of materials about the military and political rise of the English in connection with his three-volume work, *History of the Military Transactions of the British Nation in Indostan from the Year 1745*, compiling what remains one of the largest deposits of manuscripts and accounts for the history of European conquest of India in the eighteenth century.[2] His archive, one of the two great collections of historical materials concerning southern India in the eighteenth century (the other being the collection of Colin Mackenzie, amassed between 1780 and 1821), includes 336 volumes of letters, maps, journals, and accounts concerning military transactions between 1745 and 1768, as well as another twenty volumes of materials about the "government and people" of India.[3]

By all accounts a pompous man, Orme was widely seen as a syco-phant for Clive, at least in the early years of their association before they had a falling out. Not always well liked, he earned more than his usual share of detractors in Madras when he put his historical skills to work for the directors in London as a local "spy."[4] He earned the special loathing of Pigot, who, during his first governorship, ac-cused Orme of extorting large sums of money from the nawab of Arcot and put an end to his Madras career. In fact Orme never made much in the way of either fortune or fame (far less than Pigot to be sure), and despite his enormous historiographical accomplishment was little read. As Thomas Macaulay noted years later, Orme, "infe-rior to no English historian in style and power of painting, is min-ute even to tediousness. In one volume he allots, on an average, a closely printed quarto page to the events of every forty-eight hours. The consequence is that his narrative, though one of the most au-thentic and one of the most finely written in our language, has never been very popular, and is now scarcely ever read."[5] But Orme's account of Clive's early exploits was in fact extremely influential. Orme was largely responsible for granting Clive a far greater sig-nificance in the early battles in southern India than would otherwise ever have been accorded.

The first volume of Orme's *History* was published in 1763 at a high point in Clive's career, just two years before the Battle of Baksar and the acceptance of the Diwani. But he waited until well after Clive's death to publish the second volume in 1778, and never extended his formal history beyond the events of 1762, despite having collected myriad materials with which to do so. He came to the belief that the history of military events in Bengal around the Battle of Plassey did not in fact shed great credit on the English forces: "I have wrote one book which comprises the loss of Calcutta, and I have looked forward into the subject far enough to see that the Bengal transactions will not do my countrymen so much honour as they have received from the first volume."[6]

Beyond this, however, he had serious misgivings about the levels of corruption that attended the British presence in Bengal after Plassey, even as he had already personally experienced the problem of corruption in Madras. As he wrote in 1767, "Parliament in less than two years will ring with declamation against the Plunderers of the East . . . It is these cursed presents which stop my History. Why should I be doomed to commemorate the ignominy of my countrymen, and without giving the money story, that has accompanied every event since the first of April 1757, I shall not relate all the springs of action, that is I shall be a Jesuitical Historian, two terms which Voltaire says are incompatible, for no Jesuit could ever tell a true tale, much less write a true History."[7] In large part because of his realization that the epic events in India no longer lived up to his mythographer's zeal, he turned back in time to write a history of the Mughal empire rather than carry the story of British conquest forward. Clive had seemed the right choice for Orme, as someone to whom he could hitch his fortune and as someone who could provide unique access to the momentous events that surrounded the establishment of empire. In retrospect, with enough time for the veil to be drawn selectively over the exploits of Clive, this was of course the right choice. But after Plassey it seemed a dreadful mistake.

Orme had wanted to be empire's bard; he had no desire to go down in history as the chronicler of the "money story" behind the rise of the British empire in India.

If Orme provided the most detailed, and sympathetic, historical account of Clive—at least of Clive's early years—he was the first of many historians for whom Clive was the founder of the British empire. He was also one among a number of contemporaneous writers who used Clive's story to assess issues of politics and policy around the British presence in India. Not all of them defended Clive, and there were those who were hardly reticent to judge Clive guilty not just of taking presents but also of engaging in massive levels of corruption. The year 1772 was an important one both for Indian history and for Indian historiography. It was the year that Parliament established a select and then a secret committee to examine the affairs of the East India Company in preparation for the drafting of the Fox Act, the first of a series of reforms of Company activities. It was also the year that three books were published concerning the history of India, two of which were severely critical of Clive. One of these was the third volume of the popular translation of (and commentary on) Ferishtah's *History of Hindustan* by Alexander Dow, a lieutenant colonel in the Company army who had studied Persian. In his introduction to the first volume of the *History*, published in 1768, Dow had written a general essay about matters ranging from the nature of Mughal government to the character of Hindu customs, manners, and beliefs. But in his introduction to the final volume, which carried the story of the Mughals from the reign of Jehangir through to that of Aurangzeb, he turned his pen to contemporary affairs. First he wrote a brief "Dissertation on the Origin of Despotism in Indostan," in which he blamed both Mughal rule and the

Brahmanic religion of the Hindus for despotic forms of rule. He wrote, "The faith of Mahommmed is peculiarly calculated for despotism; and it is one of the greatest causes which must fix for ever the duration of that species of government in the East."[8] He went on proclaim that the Brahman system of religion produced mildness, industriousness, and obedience: "They are of all nations on earth the most easily conquered and governed."[9]

After adducing the many reasons for despotism in the East, he went on to use his harshest language for his own nation, in his famous "Enquiry into the State of Bengal: With a Plan for Restoring that Province to Its Former Prosperity and Splendor." Dow wrote that despite its despotic form, Mughal rule was respectful of local rulers and practices in Bengal, where in fact, "we are more rigid than the Moguls: we have encroached on their privileges, and annihilated their power." He was especially critical of the British use of monopolies and exclusive trade to control commerce in Bengal, as well as of its lack of moderation in its demands for revenue, a failing that exacerbated the insecurity of property and land rights. He wrote with flourish, observing that "a barbarous enemy may slay a prostrate foe; but a civilized conqueror can only ruin nations without the sword." Dating the commencement of Bengal's decline "from the day on which Bengal fell under the dominion of foreigners," he calculated that Bengal lost approximately £1.5 million each year through its extraction of specie and its use of monopolies in inland trade, especially in basic commodities such as salt, betel nut, and tobacco. He then claimed that the levels of taxation had risen to unprecedented levels, and that "seven entire battalions were added to our military establishment to enforce the collections . . . [that] carried terror and ruin through the country." As he expostulated,

"Though they exported the specie, though they checked commerce by monopoly, they heaped oppression upon additional taxes, as if rigour were necessary to power."[10]

British justice protected natives less than despots, and property lost any security it previously had. Dow recommended an end to monopoly, a reduction in revenue demand, the enhancement of the security of property, the establishment of British courts, and the observance of general toleration in matters of religious faith and custom. Although he did not mention Clive by name, his critique of British avarice and indifference was directed specifically at Clive and his circle. And many of his concerns were soon echoed in the halls of Parliament in the deliberations of the select and secret committees.

Even more influential perhaps, at least in part because of its relative intemperance, was William Bolts's *Considerations on India Affairs*, also published in 1772. Born in Holland in 1735, Bolts managed to secure an appointment as a factor of the Company in Calcutta in 1760. He wasted no time before becoming heavily invested in private trade, collaborating with the more senior John Johnstone and trading in woolens, saltpeter, opium, cotton, and diamonds. Bolts openly flaunted Company regulations, as when he directly threatened the nawab of Purnea in an effort to provide additional privileges for his agents, and when he spent much of his time outside Company territory in places such as Benares in order to pursue his private interests.

Later, after losing the local protection of Johnstone when Clive ousted Johnstone from the Governor's Council, Bolts engaged in even more egregious behavior. First he did business with the Dutch in direct competition with the Company, and then he used a French agent to approach the nawab of Awadh on behalf of his own business interests. Because he had managed to secure an appointment as alderman of the mayor's court he was hard to control, but Governor Verelst finally managed to deport him from India in 1768. Upon his return to England, however, Bolts joined Johnstone's faction in its campaign against Clive and Verelst, aided by the beginning of famine in Bengal and the impending fiscal crisis of the Company. The faction produced a number of pamphlets and broadsides against Clive, but the culmination of all the attacks came in Bolts's more lengthy text. Not only did it come out at just the right time; it played up the abuses of Clive much more directly than did Dow's writings. According to Ralph Leycester, another Company servant who had been forced out of Company service by Clive, Bolts's book was "swallowed very greedily by the public whose eyes are fixed on the correction of these abuses by the interposition of parliament."[11] Scandal was always a good way to garner attention, and the story of Clive and India was by far the biggest scandal of the day.

Like Dow, Bolts was seriously exercised about the Company monopoly over inland trade, though less because of the sufferings of local merchants than because of his own disadvantage. Still, he dressed his private concerns in eloquent language, as when he anticipated Adam Smith's critique of Company monopoly in his dictum that "the different interests of the Company as sovereigns of Bengal and at the same time as monopolizers of all the trade and commerce of those countries, operate in direct opposition, and are mutually destructive of each other."[12] He was especially concerned about the way Clive had sought to curtail the operations of private traders (who had used the putative tax exemption to extend the privileges of the Company monopoly to their own use) when he attempted to set up his ill-fated Society of Trade after accepting the Diwani. Under Clive's new regime, trade in commodities such as salt, saltpeter, betel nut, and tobacco was either controlled by the Company or by private traders who were direct recipients of his patronage.

Bolts was correct to note that Clive was disingenuous when he claimed that he was concerned about the use of the Company exemption because of its dire consequences for local merchants, none of whom benefited at all from Clive's reforms. And he made a compelling case when he used the language of free trade to buttress his criticism of the way the Company asserted its monopolistic right to expropriate goods from merchants at set prices to make its annual "investment" rather than bid competitively for goods against other private traders. The terrible Bengal famine of 1769 was caused as much by the breakdown of local markets as it was by the extortionate increase of revenue demand. But Bolts's text secured the influence it did in large part because he was able to hide the extent to which the end of the Company monopoly would directly benefit his own private trading operations, including his collaborations with Dutch and French agents.

Perhaps Bolts's most ingenious argument was not about markets but rather about the meaning of the Diwani itself, given the extent to which Clive's reputation was dependent on his claims about the unparalleled significance of the transfer of authority over Bengal in 1765. Bolts noted that the Company had repeatedly refused the transfer of the Diwani for reasons that seemed cogent and compelling. But he also argued that the office of Diwani was in fact a fiction that was fabricated as much by Clive as it was by the Mughal emperor. As he wrote,

> From what has already been said, we presume it will appear evident to every impartial person, that the DEWANNEE, whatever it had been, was an office which, when assumed, had no existence; the grant of it being received, or pretended to be received, from a Prince who, in fact, never had it in his gift; whose authority, on other similar occasions, had been publicly and wholly disavowed by the present receivers of the grant, and that the whole was a mere fiction, invented for the private purposes of the Company or Directors, and their servants or confederates: and to screen their seizing on the sovereignty of the country, by imposing upon and deceiving, if they could, not only the inhabitants of India and foreigners, but even the British nation.[13]

Bolts was right to call attention to the contradictions in British claims about sovereignty in India. At one level, the Diwani was exactly what Bolts said: a fiction invented to mask the conquest of eastern India by the Company—a conquest that had been in part military but that had also been conducted by strategic if corrupt alliances, economic extortion, and massive private enrichment. And yet the Diwani was a fictional account that lost credibility, at least in England, only because of the failure of the grant to raise the revenues Clive had promised, not because it exposed the contradictions of sovereignty and rule. At this stage, even Edmund Burke was convinced that some kind of contemporaneous fiction was necessary precisely to produce the conditions for imperial authority. Serious historical debate about the meaning of Diwani was deferred until much later, only surfacing again in relation to debates over the nature of a revenue scheme for Bengal in the wake of the Pitt reforms and then over Cornwallis's plans to increase the salaries of Company servants to distract them from their interest in private trade.

Rarely did historical writing have such immediate high stakes. Shortly before the publication of his *Considerations on India Affairs*, Bolts was ordered to pay 30 percent tax on the whole of his commercial profits from his illegal participation in the inland trade of Bengal, which was estimated to be around £100,000. Bolts claimed that he had only been able to remit £30,000, but he lost his appeal. Soon after he finished his book, he initiated a suit against the Company for damages incurred when he was arrested in and deported from India. He lost this case as well, and he was forced into bankruptcy in September 1773.

Although Bolts's book had clearly generated no small measure of the concern that had led to the parliamentary inquiries, Clive's eventual victory left Bolts little quarter in his efforts to protect either his reputation or his fortune. After his bankruptcy he left England, never recovering his fortune despite a picaresque career in a number of commercial enterprises: he died impoverished in Paris in 1808. But if he lost his struggle with Clive, he took Clive's successor and supporter, Harry Verelst, down with him. Verelst had succeeded Clive as governor of Bengal, but despite his bad fortune of inheriting the mess Clive left behind and presiding over the collapse of the Diwani, he remained loyal. After returning to England he prepared a defense of Clive and the Company, publishing *A View of the Rise, Progress and Present State of the English Government in Bengal* a few months after Bolts's work came out. Verelst provided a broad survey of the Company's system of trade, revenue, and jurisdiction, and attempted to vindicate both Clive and himself from the charge of using trading privileges to their own advantage. Referring directly to Bolts, he wrote that "the evils complained of in Bengal have arisen rather from the inability of the Governor and Council to restrain the daring and pernicious projects of private interest in others, than from a rapacious spirit in themselves," and accused Bolts of "distinguish[ing] himself as a great leader of sedition."[14] But his book was not widely circulated and never achieved the influence of Bolts's work. Verelst was also subsequently ruined by a series of legal attacks from Bolts's associates. Although he returned to England as a successful nabob, with a good wife and a beautiful home in St. James's Square, by 1778 he had lost most of his fortune, dying in debt and exile on the Continent in 1785, long before Bolts met the same fate.

Whatever the personal stakes of Dow's implicit and Bolt's explicit critiques of Clive and the Company, and however much these and other critiques might have been read as interested briefs, the level of vitriol in the attacks on the Company seems extraordinary in retrospect. What comes across in these historical writings is the extent to which the Company was seen as steeped in scandal, barely legitimate, and governed primarily by greed and self-interest. Verelst's defense of Clive was sober and systematic, but as we have already noted, even Clive's reputation as an imperial hero was only sustained in parliamentary debate due to a temporary combination of heady rhetoric and powerful friends. Orme's Boswellian efforts to project Clive's early years as extraordinarily heroic were stifled by his escalating embarrassment about Company activities, not to mention the parliamentary inquiries of 1772 that documented Clive's many abuses of power and position, despite the ultimate reprieve they gave. Empire was not yet anything like a noble activity, and even when the Company was defended by noble figures such as Burke, there was a clear sense that the political perils of old corruption at home paled before the excesses of what Britons were doing in the East.

In the 1770s Burke had defended the Company, in part because he towed the political line of the Rockingham faction, and in part because he believed that state interference with the Company would produce even greater problems of corruption. But it is still curious that he defended Clive with an eloquence that would soon be pitched against a man whose crimes seem minor in comparison, and especially curious that he did so in the actual sessions that considered the charges drawn in 1772 and 1773. That there were personal reasons for Burke's early involvement in Company affairs only compounds the curiosity and the contradictions of Burke's political history. For the moment, however, it is enough to say that even Burke's early relationship to the Company had a taint of scandal, and that the taint extended to Burke's own participation in the production of historical accounts concerning India and Company affairs in those years.

Ultimately, the reason that "these cursed presents" brought Orme's history to a crashing end, and more generally the reason for the overwhelming role that scandal played in the early writing of the history of Clive and the conquest of India, was that history was all about sovereignty. History, especially as it emerged in the eighteenth century as a modern genre, scripting the genealogy of nations through the lives of political leaders (whether monarchs, parliamentarians, pretenders, revolutionaries, or political officials), had to relate stories that not only conferred legitimacy on these leaders but also gave narrative justification to political sovereignty. Earlier histories had been necessarily preoccupied with the legitimacy of sovereign claims on the part of individuals (vis-à-vis their heroism, their political relations and exchanges with other rulers, their relations with divine powers and even divinity itself, and their genealogical relations with earlier political authorities), but increasingly the obligation of history was to substantiate the legitimacy of the nation, and in India's case, the legitimacy of England's imperial role. The histories written about the conquest of India had thus to narrate the military heroics of Clive and others at the same time they had to find ways to assert the legitimacy of the Company's position in India, in relation both to the established sovereign powers and to the English state. Scandal became a way of insinuating that political and economic power had been advanced on behalf of the private greed of individuals rather than the public interest of nations. And the public interest of nations was both the expression for sovereignty and its primary justification.

Scandal thus worked to call sovereignty into question. Sovereignty was still about kings, dynastic lines of succession, and even conquest, but it placed all of these traditional markers of politics in the service of an idea of right that could be based solely neither on divine right nor on might, linking monarchical understandings of political authority increasingly to modern concerns about representation. Whether representation referred to the demands of the American colonists or the concerns of British parliamentarians about scandal in India, it became a significant category for questioning the extent to which political authority even in imperial domains had to operate under new kinds of controls with stated limits and rules.

By the nineteenth century, liberal political theory had developed its own justifications for the distinction between democratic rule in the metropole and despotic rule in the colony. In the eighteenth century, however, when sovereignty was still emerging from its earlier dependence on beliefs in transcendence that were steeped in theological concerns about the relations of kings and the divine, history had the task of creating these very distinctions, as well as their forms of narration. Only with thinkers such as Thomas Hobbes in the seventeenth century was the concept of modern sovereignty born anew, the divine right of kings transubstantiated as the logic of contract. And while Jean-Jacques Rousseau attempted to propose methods for direct representation to overcome the distortions of Hobbes's own cynical relationship to the popular revolt against monarchy, Burke's continued allegiance to the ancient constitution suggests the unresolved nature of the place of representation even after the transformations of eighteenth-century political life in England.

It was thus no accident that history had to struggle to find different narrative forms to capture the changing demands of new ideas of sovereignty, but it has seldom been recognized that much of this struggle took place in histories written about colonial contexts, where sovereign relations and rights were even more fluid and contested. Scandal was of special importance in calling dramatic attention to histories where sovereignty itself was up for grabs. This is why it has been necessary to appreciate the extent to which histories of scandal and sovereignty merge in the history of empire. Nowhere, perhaps, do the histories of scandal and sovereignty merge so completely as in the events, and especially in the histories, set in southern India in the 1770s.

These historical works can be placed in somewhat broader context by browsing in the library of Colin Mackenzie, the great surveyor—and the highly regarded collector and archivist of precolonial south Indian history. On March 26, 1800, Colin Mackenzie scribbled an account of his historical library. This account was no random list, nor the occasion for his own account of India's history, about which he was in any case quite reticent. It tells us what he read and collected for his own personal library, and what he recommended that any serious student of Indian history read. Characteristically, Mackenzie starts by suggesting that "previous to entering on the study of its History a competent knowledge of Asiatic Geography should be obtained chiefly from the modern systems of de Lisle, D'Anville, Bernouiller, but particularly the writings of maps of Rennell regarding India." Rennell was Mackenzie's most distinguished cartographic forebear, and his maps of Bengal had provided the model for Mackenzie's own work in the south.[15]

After attaining some basic familiarity with Asian geography, the student should then proceed to basic reference works, such as D'Herbelote's *Biblioteque Orientale*, the *Encyclopedia Britannica*, and the *Modern Universal History*. After Stevens's *History of Persia* and White's translation of the *Institutes of Timur*, Mackenzie listed Gibbon's *History of the Decline and Fall of the Roman Empire*, in order to "furnish some interesting relations in a rapid but beautiful stile [*sic*] of the origin of the Muhamedan Religion and some other parts connected with modern oriental history." Gibbon, whose historical preoccupation with the threat that both barbarism and religion constituted for imperial survival set the terms for his own history of Islam, could only provide general background, since he neither wrote about the present nor carried his history to the East. But he clearly served as an important model for Mackenzie, who suggested that one move directly from Gibbon to the commentaries of Babur, the memoirs of Akbar, Jehangir, and Aurangzeb, and the comprehensive government manual of Abul Faz'l (Akbar's prime minister). Mackenzie then recommended that his ideal student read Sir Thomas Roe's account of his embassy to the court of Jehangir, followed by Alexander Dow's translation of Ferishtah's *History of Hindustan,* "to be read in this succession . . . from the General History of the Mogul Emperors in India to Auranzeb's succession." These books comprehended "what may be called the first portion of modern British Asiatic history so far as has been published to the European World." Mackenzie's only further comment—a lament— was that unfortunately no history for the period before the Mughals had so far been published, aside from a few accounts of religion, mythology, and antiquities, none of which by themselves counted as histories.[16]

Mackenzie suggested a few other books by European travelers and geographers, whose accounts of India during this period would "be useful at intervals with these to consult." These included John Churchill's *Collection of Voyages, Purchas Pilgrims, The Travels of Marco Polo, The Lusiads of Camaons,* as well as the memoirs of François Bernier and Bertrand Tavernier. He also noted the importance of Orme's *Historical Fragments of the Mogul Empire,* and mentions the apparent authenticity of a modern history written "by a native, the 'Seyer Matacherin.'" But by now his library had entered the second half of the eighteenth century, and the presence of Britain begins to emerge in the form of not just authoritative memoirs, translations, and editions, but also military and mercantile activities. Orme's three-volume *History of the Military Transactions in India* is mentioned next to Jonathan Holwell's *Interesting Events in India*. Henry Vansittart's history is listed alongside the proceedings of the secret committee in 1772. Mackenzie's library now traverses the documentation of imperial conquest: he lists the *Parliamentary Debates on Indian Affairs*, written primarily by Edmund Burke, *The Tanjore Papers* (containing the documents relative to the two sieges of Tanjore and the revolution in the government of Madras, and the nabob's debt), John MacPherson's *History of the East India Company*, Hastings's *Memoir on the State of India* when he left it, and, last but certainly not least, the documents from the impeachment trial of Hastings. In short, Mackenzie confirms the contemporary importance of these histories.[17]

Perhaps Mackenzie's embarrassment about the imperial scandals associated with Clive and Hastings as well as with the events surrounding the nawab of Arcot conspired to make this last part of his inventory the least annotated section. Mackenzie himself had no problems accepting the wisdom of colonial conquest; he had gone to India first as a military surveyor and he played a key role in the siege of Srirangapattinam and the defeat of Tipu Sultan in 1792. And yet Mackenzie was a historical purist, and he liked to believe that the history of India before—and independent of—British conquest and rule was not just desirable, but possible.

Although Mackenzie came to be profoundly aware of the politics of historical knowledge in the process of compiling his own archival collection, he never seems to have reflected much about the problems these politics posed to the project of producing an authentic history of precolonial India. He certainly never commented on the scandals that surrounded the history of British empire in the second half of the eighteenth century, despite the prominence of parliamentary inquiries and trial transcripts in his list. Instead, he skipped quickly to the last part of his list. "In the foregoing lists I have chiefly confined its object to British India or the countries connected with it; to those desirous of extending their reading in a more extensive scale, much information of the modern authentic kind may be derived from, Pocock, Norden, Niebuhr, Shaw, Russel, Savary, Volney, Irvine, Clapper, Hamilton, Forster, and Pennant." And then, as if anticipating the Orientalist and anthropological turns in colonial knowledge, he concluded his list with a set of books, "exclusive of the Historical Branch," which concerned the manners, customs, and laws: "a separate class of reading [that] might be read in the following order." The list began with Baldeus's *Account of the Hindu Religion*, included the letters of Jesuit missionaries, the ethnographic commentaries of Holwell and Dow, Sir William Jones's recent translation of the laws of Manu, the *Proceedings of the Asiatic Society* (particularly the annual discourses of Sir William Jones), and finally the *Code of Mussalman Laws* by Hamilton and Sales's translation of the Qur'an.[18]

These last textual and ethnographic turns, however, are another story, dominating the first and second halves of the nineteenth century respectively. For now, we shall return to the scene of Mackenzie's embarrassment, the volumes that made up the most proximate, if also perhaps the most troubling, reminders that even his project of reading and collecting history was deeply implicated in British scandal. For despite Mackenzie's own purist convictions, his library clearly betrays that the historiography of empire was as mired in scandal as the history of empire itself. And given his special interest in the history of the south, the scandals that were most deeply disturbing to him were those contained in, and associated with, the histories of the Carnatic, especially Arcot and Tanjore, that were hurriedly penned in the years after the restoration of Tanjore in 1776 and the mission, and then imprisonment and death, of George Pigot, in 1777. These histories, though some were very grand, were usually little more than briefs prepared on behalf of two sides in what was one of the greatest quarrels of the time—that between the creditors and agents of the nawab of Arcot, and the creditors and agents of the raja of Tanjore. And of all the histories that were written in this dispute, the two most interesting had been composed by two famous sets of cousins, the Macphersons and the Burkes.

James Macpherson was well known for his notorious role in the history of Scotland. In 1763 he proclaimed himself the heroic discoverer of Scotland's great epic poem, publishing the Ossian epic of *Fingal* with much fanfare. While the text produced great excitement in Scotland, England, and the Continent (earning accolades from figures as various as David Hume and Johann Herder), it also soon began to excite suspicion concerning questions of authenticity. Samuel Johnson scorned the pretensions of both text and compiler, and published a broadside attack on Macpherson in 1775. But by then Macpherson had used his reputation to proclaim himself a historian of the stature of Hume, publishing that same year a follow-up volume to Hume's *History of Great Britain*, which he believed he could usefully bring up to the present on the basis of his new work as historical sleuth. Claiming to have discovered new records concerning James II, he simultaneously published his own edition of *Original Papers, Containing the Secret History of Great Britain from the Restoration to the Accession of the House of Hanover, with Memoirs of James II.* Shortly thereafter, he took up business with his cousin (by some accounts, half-brother) John Macpherson.

John had joined the East India Company in 1768, traveling during that year to Madras, where he had ingratiated himself with the nawab of Arcot, serving as his agent after he was expelled in the early 1770s from Company service—for reasons having to do with his own spectacularly corrupt dealings with the nawab. John was later reinstated by the Company, and in fact served as the successor to Warren Hastings as governor-general of India in 1785, though his tenure was short-lived and his reputation never free from the charge—correct, as it happened—that he was the paid agent of an Indian prince. After the restoration of the raja of Tanjore in 1776 (while he was in London attempting to clear his name), he enlisted James to help him mount a campaign on behalf of the nawab, who viewed the restoration as a violation of his sovereign authority over the Carnatic and an act of extraordinarily bad faith on the part of a Company of which he considered himself a principal ally and associate through complicated relations of indebtedness and credit.

In 1779 James accordingly published his next major work of history entitled *The History and Management of the East India Company, from Its Origin in 1600 to the Present Times.* This long book was published without attribution, though it was widely known that it had been primarily written by James, with some assistance from John who, less the historical stylist, had become well versed in the political history of southern India. The work itself was deliberately modeled on Edward Gibbon's *Decline and Fall,* beginning with explicit references to the decline of Rome. Macpherson was certainly not shy about his historical aspirations, but he also meant clearly to suggest that England's empire would only survive if it properly appreciated and supported the duly constituted and legitimate political authorities of India, among whom the nawab of Arcot figured most prominently.

Macpherson's principal objective was to narrate the history of sovereignty relating to the nawab of Arcot and the raja of Tanjore. He began with the "Muhammedan" invasions of India, from the early sultanate incursions to the establishment of Mughal rule. The province of Tanjore, he asserted, was an ancient part of the kingdom of Begenagur (Vijayanagara), ruled by a governor, or Naig (*nayaka*), who was under the full authority of the kingdom. Vijayanagara was subsequently defeated by a coalition of sultanate rulers, who themselves soon came under the centralizing authority of the Mughals. Meanwhile, the *nayaka* of Tanjore was conquered by Maratha rulers—Shivaji's cousin—who were themselves finally brought under the firm, feudal, control of the Mughal's duly constituted authority over the Carnatic, the nawab of Arcot. According to Macpherson, the nawab dignified the Tanjore ruler with the title of "raja" and granted him legal confirmation of the "Zemindary of Tanjore."[19] To summarize, "the Rajahs of Tanjore . . . were, in the strictest sense of the word, feudatories, liable to lose their territories to their sovereign, upon any breach of their duty, as subjects. It has been shewn, that the emperor of the Moguls was their undoubted sovereign, who governed them through the medium of his deputy, the Nabob of the Carnatic."[20]

Macpherson's historical assertions depended on the strict acceptance of a European feudal model for sovereignty, in which the Maratha rulers assumed the dependence of their predecessors, the *nayakas*, on the Vijayanagara rulers, whose authority had been taken over by the Mughal state. At the same time, the nawab of Arcot was

seen as the sole arbiter of Mughal authority in the southern penin-
sula, a historical proposition that had been complicated by the
demise of Mughal authority over the Deccan, especially after the
death of Aurangzeb in 1707. It was even more compromised by the
later rivalries between the nizam of Hyderabad—one of the Mughal
emperor's highest delegates by any account—and the nawab of
Arcot, rivalries that were in large part appropriated by their res-
pective alliances with the French and the English and the many
wars between them during the eighteenth century. Nevertheless,
Macpherson sought to demonstrate, through a reading of eighteenth-century treaties and warfare, that the nawab was the de jure
as well as de facto sovereign of the Carnatic, at least by 1755. And
Macpherson used a treaty of 1762, which settled a low annual tribute
on the raja of Tanjore to be paid to the nawab, as final proof of the
raja's violation of his feudal duties.

Macpherson heaped scorn on the rajas of Tanjore, implying that
the Maratha rulers had never secured full legitimacy beyond their
landlord (*zamindari*) status (an absurd proposal by anyone who accepted that conquest could confer sovereignty, as he did in every
other case), and chastised them for numerous perfidies. They did
not pay even their modestly assessed tribute, they entertained approaches from the French, they did not deliver provisions either to
the nawab's or the Company's armies when requested, and they engaged in direct political relationships with—and demanded tribute
from—the southern chiefs (*palaiyakarars*) who were themselves, according to Macpherson, in a clear feudal relationship of dependency on the nawab.

Characteristically, however, Macpherson was even more scornful
of the English, both the state at home and the Company. He began

his last chapter by asserting, "The East India Company, ever since their first institution, had industriously, and, till lately, very successfully, covered their transactions with a veil of secrecy; which few had the curiosity, and fewer still the means to penetrate." Anticipating Burke's acknowledgment of the role of the veil in the origins of British rule in India, he also sided with those, against Burke, who had sought to censure Clive and Company in the proceedings of 1772. Advocating universal commerce and decrying the Company monopoly, he wrote, "This maxim of mystery naturally sprung from the jealous principles of commerce, which hopes to preclude rivals, by a suppression of its profits." He went on to note that in recent years "some men of talents, who precipitately thought, that national indignation might produce national justice, unveiled some of the fountains of corruption in the East," only to encounter Parliament's failure of nerve, and the consequent response of the Court and its servants to "restore the transactions of the Company to their original obscurity" and rebound with renewed corruption and ill-intent. Small wonder, perhaps, given his view of the East India Company. The Company, he argued, had established its institution and management according to "narrow principles of mean traders," usurping "an absolute dominion over the stock-holders; and embezzling their property, "by unjust deductions, and iniquitous frauds."[21]

Even worse, Macpherson believed that the Company had wrongly asserted its sovereignty in Asia, neglecting its contractual relationships with local sovereign authorities on whom it depended to conduct commerce. As he wrote, "When the Company, by various revolutions in Asia, ascended from the condition of traders to that of Sovereigns, they multiplied their acts of injustice, in proportion to the extent of their power."[22] Macpherson was clear that he had demonstrated "that the Company's servants uniformly were considered and owned themselves the subjects of the Mogul, in all parts of that monarch's dominions, where they possessed settlements."[23] He asserted that since Muhammed Ali, the nawab of the Carnatic, was "the LAWFUL Nabob of that country, by the free and legal Saneds of the Mogul," any failure to serve and protect the interests of the nawab, let alone to favor the usurping raja of Tanjore against those interests, was a gross violation of sovereignty. Without sensing any contradiction, he thought to strengthen his argument by adding, "Mahommed Ali has adhered, without deviation, for more than thirty years, to the English interest, and the English cause." He further added that the nawab had paid a sum exceeding seven million pounds to the Company coffers between 1750 and 1773. For Macpherson, sovereignty was not to be confused with political loyalty and financial gain on the part of the Company; indeed, the protection of Mughal sovereignty was to be the very means for Company success in both its strategic and its pecuniary affairs. Macpherson concluded his history by condemning the breach of public virtue that had been occasioned by Lord Pigot's arbitrary and capricious actions in restoring the sovereignty of Tanjore, blaming Pigot for administering to the "most extravagant follies" of the raja, described in similar terms as others had applied to the nawab of Arcot when he was no longer their benefactor.[24] While local sovereignty was never taken all that seriously, it was still the principal currency of historical debate in the war between Arcot and Tanjore.

If any Briton had concerns about Indian sovereignty in the imperial eighteenth century, however, it was Edmund Burke. And Burke was the major author of the most important historical and political tract to be written in refutation of the Macpherson manuscript: "Policy of Making Conquests for the Mahometans."[25] This work was not only a defense of the raja of Tanjore, using a creative reading of the 1762 treaty, it was a full-scale attack on both the nawab of Arcot and Muslim rule in India. Edmund was recruited to this historiographical exercise by his cousin, William Burke, who had been engaged in extensive speculations in India stock from 1766 to 1769. Investing Edmund's as well as his own resources in Company activities, he was almost ruined when the stock market crash of 1769–1770 wiped out their investments. Afterwards, William had secured the opportunity to travel to Madras to work with George Pigot, though by the time he reached India in 1777 Pigot had already died in prison. Despite this setback, William was able to establish himself as an agent for the raja of Tanjore, whom he served for the next five years in India and England. It was just as he had taken on formal employment in the pay of the raja of Tanjore that William requested Edmund to help him write the rebuttal to Macpherson.

The Burkes argued that the sovereign rights of the raja of Tanjore had been iniquitously attacked by the Company when it licensed the nawab of Arcot to conquer Tanjore, an attack made even more egregious because it was done with Company arms. They asserted, "When the Company first began to interfere in the politics of India, they found the then King of Tanjore an hereditary sovereign Prince, in undisturbed possession of great splendor, power, and opulence, derived from a long line of royal ancestors." Quoting Orme as their authority, they maintained that "With Tanjore the Company formed the first regular alliance they made in India."[26] The nawab, by contrast, was in fact dependent on the British for his life and standing, having used his affiliation with the Company to overthrow Chanda Sahib and gain his throne.

The Burkes read the 1762 treaty as a general acknowledgment of Mughal sovereignty over all princes and principalities in India, but did not view it as in any way compromising Tanjore's authority or for that matter elevating the nawab beyond an ambiguous position. The nawab, they suggested, was precariously perched halfway between de facto dependence on the English and de jure dependence on a Mughal emperor who no longer had much real power or authority. Because it was so clear that the great empire was in the process of breaking up, sovereignty had to be recognized, and respected, in relation to possession:

> It was our business to respect *possession* as the only title that can be valid, where a great empire is broken up; and rather, as it is the title on which we ourselves stand. It was our business, that no antiquated claims should be revived; and no disturbances raised on such dangerous pretences. It was our duty, in order to make some sort of compensation for the mischiefs inseparable from a foreign and commercial superiority, to keep a balance of justice and proportion in the several powers that were subordinate to us.[27]

This assertion was a far cry from statements made later in connection with Hastings and the trial. Here Edmund clearly conceded the reality of English power, suggesting that the Company strive to maintain the balance of powers it encountered when it first interfered in local politics. He was resolutely opposed to participation in any local wars (disturbances) based on issues related to the complicated, and largely ceremonial, residues of Mughal authority. And he could not disguise his contempt for the nawab's claim to be the southern representative of Mughal power.

The nawab and the Company had justified their attack on Tanjore on two principal grounds, first that Tanjore had not remitted the full portion of the tribute exacted by the 1762 treaty, and second that Tanjore itself had invaded a neighboring chiefdom, the Maravar raja, for political and financial reasons. The Burkes were scathing about a Company assertion that it had been furnished with a "just pretext to accuse him of a breach of his engagements," revealing the base motives at work. In language that was clearly Edmund's, it was noted that "Justice had in fact as little connection with their actions, as the English language will suffer to exist between the words *just* and *pretexts.*" While the Burkes defended the raja of Tanjore's right to punish the Maravar for various sovereign reasons, they adamantly refused to concede any justice to the nawab's claims about Tanjore. Using arguments that anticipated later parliamentary speeches in their fiery rhetoric, Burke proclaimed, "To enter a country with fire and sword—to plunder it without mercy—to seize upon the person of a Prince—to confiscate his revenues—to despoil him of all his effects, and to imprison him and his family, are no light things; nor to be done but upon serious grounds, and the most urgent and evident necessity." Burke refuted the grounds that were given, noting that all Tanjore had required, under manifestly adverse conditions, was some modest tax relief. He further asserted that it was wrong to argue that the southern *palaiyakarars,* such as the Maravar raja, were dependents of the nawab. Quoting Company documents, Burke held that "the *independent authority* of the several Polygars in their several districts, was *ancient and hereditary,* and not derived from the Nabob or any one else."[28] That the Company had only asserted the independence of the *palaiyakarars* in relation to the nawab's authority in order to justify the Company's own relentless campaigns against them in the eighteenth century was conveniently omitted. But Burke professed himself to be as concerned to protect the just and hereditary rights of the rajas, *zamindars,* and other inhabitants from "our own government" as he was to protect them from each other.

Burke's severest critique of Company power was that it had been used to buttress the "ambition, pride, and tyranny" of Muhammed Ali, "this Potentate on sufference."[29] Although Burke passionately defended the sovereignty of the princes, in particular the raja of Tanjore and the many other *palaiyakarar* chiefs of the southern countryside, he could not bring himself to support the sovereign authority of the nawab. It was here that his early sense that the Company had actual sovereignty (and, to use the phrase he later made famous, arbitrary power) smuggled itself into his language and his argument. "If the Company, who under the name of alliance, or under even the name of subjection to a Mogul, are in reality now the actual Sovereigns and Lords paramount of India, still choose, as hitherto they have done, and as in wisdom perhaps they ought to do, to have a dependent government interposed between them and the native people, it is both their interest and duty that it should be such as is congenial to the native inhabitants, correspondent to the manners, and soothing to their prejudices." Burke clearly exposed his sense of the fiction of Mughal rule, even as he betrayed his own early prejudices, both about the horrors of "Mahometan rule" and about the imperial strategies of early indirect rule. Muhammed Ali was a "ferocious and insatiable Mahometan," his actions the most dramatic illustration of the "horrors of the Mahometan government in India." Burke had no apology to make about his support of the local rule of "native Indians," by which he meant Hindus such as the raja of Tanjore (who had of course invaded southern India from the Maratha country well to the north and west) and the other local *palaiyakarar* chiefs. "The native Indians, under their own native government, are, to speak without prejudice, a far better people than the Mahometans; or than those who by living under Mahometans, become the depressed subjects, or the corrupted instruments of their tyranny; they are of far milder manners, more industrious, more tractable, and less enterprising."[30] He held it self-evident that men "infinitely prefer a subjection to Princes of their own blood, manners, and religion, to any other"—especially in a situation such as India, "where there is no settled law or constitution, either to fix allegiance, or to restrain power." Here Burke not only endorsed a view of Asiatic despotism in sharp variance to his later parliamentary arguments; he also gave full vent to his distaste for Islam and his horror at Muslims, a race he held as "infinitely more fierce and cruel than the English," and a far greater threat to India.[31]

Even though Burke's critique of Company policies in India only grew more profound during the years between 1779 and 1786, his views about the ancient constitution and contemporary nobility of Mughal rule in India underwent a total transformation during the same period. By 1786, of course, Burke had become extremely anxious to argue that British sovereignty in India was limited, and that its success ultimately depended entirely on its respect for and recognition of Mughal sovereignty. Only a few years earlier, however, he had assumed that Mughal sovereignty in India was a fiction, and that the only sovereignty the Company had to respect and recognize was local. In his historical arguments about Tanjore and Arcot, Burke had held that sovereignty was about possession—and by implication hereditary rights—rather than about constitutions and ancient sovereign rights. Local sovereignty was conceived in anthropological terms, as the effective outcome of extant rights and contingent "on the ground" claims. To come to terms with this inconsistency, we must remember that Burke had earlier in his political career accepted the legitimacy of the Company monopoly and defended Clive in the face of serious and well-documented charges. It was only later that he began to worry about the legitimacy of British imperial aspirations and see the inextricable relationship between legitimacy abroad and at home. His latter realization flew in the face of accepted conventions of political assertion and historical argument concerning the character of sovereignty in India. The book Burke wrote to counter James Macpherson was an important move toward this realization, even if it also betrayed some of the fundamental contradictions in his own role as a critic of empire.

What is clear from both Burke's and Macpherson's texts, however, is the extent to which arguments about sovereignty were critical to early imperial histories of India. Even in the first contemporaneous histories of empire that were written in the late eighteenth century, the legitimacy of empire was itself largely contested and deeply compromised by scandal. Treaties were read both literally and univocally, usually in relation to two kinds of interpretations of European feudalism. The first was that all power was delegated from a single superior sovereign monarch, however decentralized the appearance of things. The second was that power might all have been delegated once upon a time by a single superior sovereign monarch, but that by a certain point, and for all practical purposes, power was held locally by the feudal chiefs controlling local domains. Even Macaulay was aware of the raw transparency of eighteenth-century British debate about imperial conquest and Indian society, although from an imperial perspective that held the decadence of eighteenth-century Indian politics responsible for inviting the Company to take charge. In his account of Clive, he had written:

> The situation of India was such that scarcely any aggression could be without a pretext, either in old laws or in recent practice. All rights were in a state of utter uncertainty; and the Europeans who took part in the disputes of the natives confounded the confusion, by applying to Asiatic politics the public law of the West and analogies drawn from the feudal system. If it was convenient to treat a Nabob as an independent prince, there was an excellent plea for doing so. He was independent in fact. If it was convenient to treat him as a mere deputy of the Court of Delhi, there was no difficulty; for he was so in theory. If it was convenient to consider his office as an hereditary dignity, or as a dignity held during life only, or as a dignity held only during the good pleasure of the Mogul, arguments and precedents might be found for every one of those views. The party who had the heir of Baber in their hands represented him as the undoubted, the legitimate, the absolute sovereign, whom all subordinate authorities were bound to obey. The party against whom his name was used did not want plausible pretexts for maintaining that the empire was de facto dissolved, and that, though it might be decent to treat the Mogul

with respect, as a venerable relic of an order of things which had passed away, it was absurd to regard him as the real master of Hindostan.[32]

Absurd though it might have seemed, both to Hastings and to Macaulay, this point of view is precisely what Burke staked his reputation on, and made as the centerpiece of his ethical assertion of the limits of imperial power.

That Indian sovereignty might be as historically variable as it was culturally distinctive was only considered in the most negative of terms, when Asiatic forms of rule were disparaged as despotic and unenlightened. That British sovereignty might have to confront other cultural formations, and even yield some of its own ground in the face of other sovereign claims, became the basis for a strategic politics that worked in very different ways depending on whether the audience was Indian or British.

Much has been made in the historical literature of cultural misunderstanding, but it seems clear that misunderstandings were strategic rather than the result of anthropological failure. When it suited, Clive was able to delineate the complex meanings of political gifting and court ceremonial, on several occasions using arguments about cultural difference to justify his corrupt acquisitions. Indeed, ideas of cultural difference were first articulated in serious ways precisely to provide alibis for behavior that seemed clearly to cross a line, even by mid-eighteenth-century standards of British corruption, peculation, and self-interest. And political and historical writings yield surprising insights about the complicated meanings of sovereignty, authority, and power in eighteenth-century India. It is now widely agreed, for example, that gifts, titles, privileges, and perquisites of rule were fundamental to the theory and practice of sovereignty.[33] These theories and practices, whether adopted by Mughal emperors, Maratha rajas, Rajput *zamindars*, or Tamil *palaiyakarars*, articulated a complex understanding of the fragile and contested character of power in a period of imperial decentralization.

In a peculiar sense, the historical analyses of the Macphersons on the one side and the Burkes on the other acknowledged these understandings, and can be read as texts that themselves reveal the contingent importance of exchanges, titles, revenue arrangements, and local rights in the delineation and articulation of sovereignty. And yet each set of authors attempted to sort, and distort, these complicated relations of sovereignty into straightforward accounts that only served their own imperial political interests, either elevating the nawab as a Mughal governor in total authority over a local *zamindar*, or converting a Maratha raja cut off from the rest of the Mughal political system into an independent royal figure with no need of establishing political relations with the Mughals, whether in northern India or simply in Arcot.

Imperial history thus began to assert imperial interests from the start, even if it accorded what in the next century already seemed unusual respect to the local world, and lexicon, of political integrity and meaning. It was this same strategic politics that made early empire even more scandalous, and that so clearly implicated historical accounts of Company actions in the self-interested rhetoric of different imperial actors. Burke's embarrassment at his early implication in imperial scandal—not to mention the fact that he was one of empire's losers rather than its winners—might well have led him to seek a higher ground for empire, and indeed to convert private gain into national wealth, but it most certainly did not lead him to turn his back on the imperial mission. Perhaps Burke's final transformation into imperial inquisitor was the result of his own recognition of the extent to which the taint of William's agency for Tanjore compromised his own capacity to claim historical objectivity and truth. By implication, perhaps a new universal theory of imperial sovereignty was critical for the development of history as a primary genre of Enlightenment thought precisely because of the imperial collision of metropolitan and colonial arguments about sovereignty.

If universality was in fact a condition of historical narrative, then histories could do no better than Macaulay's, exposing empire-making in those early years as the chaotic free-for-all it really was, while attempting to rescue the imperial idea against most of the evidence. As imperial history attained its own natural conventions and assumptions, notions of cultural and historical difference were used to explain why different standards and conditions became necessary features of the imperial world. Universality as a conviction of Enlightenment thought ironically anticipated the demand for the very exclusions made by nineteenth-century liberal thought, affording rights, citizenship, sovereignty, and history only to those who were seen to have attained the civilizational standing to act responsibly in the modern world. Increasingly, the ideal of universality became directly associated with the growing grandeur of empire, an ideal to be established by imperial power rather than a categorical limit to the exercise of that power. As the nineteenth century unfolded, the scandals that were at the heart of imperial beginnings—not to mention the scandal of empire itself—had to be laundered, converted into narratives of imperial, nationalist, and capitalist triumph by a new kind of imperial historiography. In this new historiography, British reforms were used to mask the scandalous origins of empire, either obliterating the early record or folding it into a narrative in which all abuses were blamed on the colonial other. The trial had to become something other than an embarrassment of empire, and empire had to become an idea that was sacred right from the start.

The great age of history itself—when European nations not only defined themselves but also asserted their civilizational privilege over those lands that were believed not to have any history of their own— was built on the most extraordinary abuses of historical consciousness and self-representation. David Hume was right, if a tad self-serving, to note that his own age was the age of history and that his was the historical nation. His massive *History of England* was a monumental achievement, an extraordinary narrative reflection on the history of monarchical institutions, civil society, and the nature of government. If he was England's most celebrated historian of the eighteenth century, his historical genius was in part the result of his capacity to see the history of England in relation to the evolution of complex institutions rather than simply as the inevitable triumph of the idea of constitutional monarchy. Hume's philosophical aspirations for universality had to confront not only his distrust of causal explanations but also his ultimate sense that everything was particular, that historicism was the necessary condition of any order of things. His suspicion about the ancient constitution—the basis for Burke's own effort to render empire sacred—was also the basis for his sense that civic humanism could only emerge and prosper once the arbitrariness of sovereign authority and legal institutions had been severely controlled by a new set of social understandings.[34]

But neither Hume's universal aspirations nor his skeptical sensibility concerning civil society could make sense of the new imperial world. Institutional change was still broadly evolutionary, and decidedly unilinear. In this respect, he was little different than Voltaire, who despite his considerations of Indian and Chinese forms of government, was very clear that universal history—by which he meant no less than the Enlightenment itself—could only be western, and for that matter Christian. Perhaps it was no accident that the man who brought Hume's history up to the troubling present—when England's unfolding imperial ambitions were first realized in the absorption of Scotland into the new multiethnic nation of Great Britain—was both an unabashed Scottish nationalist and a man who was deeply implicated in the early scandals of empire. Macpherson, whose position in Parliament was directly funded by the nawab of Arcot, understood clearly how imperial the foundations of British institutions of government and civil society really were.

Of the great eighteenth-century British historians, only Edward Gibbon was genuinely sensible of the longer-term importance of empire for the very nature of Britain's historical position. Gibbon was also the only real Englishman in the mix, though it is doubtless significant that he developed his own distinctive sensibility during his long years on the Continent. Gibbon decided not to write another history of England after reading Hume and Robertson, aware not only of the heroic achievements of his predecessors, but also of the contested terrain he had inherited from them. While Gibbon was reticent about drawing explicit parallels between the experience of Rome and the fate of England, he was certainly writing with a strong sense of the lessons of history for the present age. At one level, he believed that the reasons for the decline and fall of the Roman

Empire were simple and obvious—the result, he said, of "the natural and inevitable effect of immoderate greatness."[35] But as J. G. A.
Pocock has argued in great detail, Gibbon's history was far more
than a "simple narrative of the effects of corruption," an extension of
the Machiavellian concern about the impact on civic virtue of military autonomy and mercenary armies in the context of Rome's imperial aspirations.[36]

Like Burke, Gibbon was also deeply concerned with the effects of
the rise of commerce and the decline in virtue associated with the
loss of agriculture's primacy and with the increasing velocity, and
global extent, of exchange in a world that was becoming steadily
more interdependent. This concern was certainly reflected in his
speculations on the destructive potential of empire, though he was if
anything far more influenced by the writings of the Scottish Enlightenment than was Burke. Indeed, he was more preoccupied with the
threats of fanaticism and superstition that came from without than
he was with the rising importance of trade. For Gibbon, barbarism
was the flip side of religion. In the most controversial sections of his
history, he held Christianity itself accountable for many of Rome's
dire problems, though he attempted to blame most of the trouble on
the rise of monasticism and the dangers of the priesthood. His account of Islam was a more contemporary rendering of the problem-
atic relationship between barbarism and religion, making all too visible the indissoluble link between barbarism and superstition that
he had seen bedeviling the early history of Christianity.[37] Gibbon
was an exemplar of Enlightenment values in his strong belief in the
triumphant potential of civic virtue. At the same time, however, he
worried about the possibility that this virtue would be undermined

by imperial expansion, and he reacted to its revolutionary ascendancy much as Burke did in response to events in France, praising both Burke's eloquence and his politics in his "Reflections."[38]

In the histories that played such an important role in the Enlightenment, then, empire was always offstage, not a historical force that would dramatically change world history. Only Gibbon seemed aware that empire might become the ultimate test for the British state, despite the fact that Scotland's many gifted historians could have used their own recent history to question the costs and effects of Britain's imperial aspirations during the eighteenth century. Ironically, the more conservative the author, the more likely empire was to be taken into account. Enlightenment thought seemed preoccupied with itself, even in Scotland, and while accounts of foreign travel were critical to historical speculation about the stages of civilizational progress, they were only rarely used to challenge the self-assurance of those who saw themselves on the vanguard of this progress. Concerns about empire, whether Burke's or Gibbon's, hardly contested much of the Enlightenment narrative, the worry being instead that this narrative would be undermined by imperial excess. In surveying the historical writings of Hume's historical age, and his historical nation, it is noteworthy that empire plays so minor a role. Except, that is, in the proliferation of historical narratives that were themselves important players in the early scramble for imperial profit. It is hardly surprising that this caused considerable embarrassment at the time, as well as later.

The embarrassment of empire revealed itself in a number of ways. It could be seen in the empty gestures of Enlightenment universalism (whether by Hume or by Voltaire), even as it drove Burke first to develop a theory of local sovereignty and then to take on Warren

Hastings in the most dramatic parliamentary confrontation of the century. It could also be seen in the work (and library) of one of the great imperial historians of India, Colin Mackenzie. And yet the very openness of Mackenzie's archival interest to existing historical records and narratives in colonial India was in the end responsible both for his own desire to repress the imperial interest in, and influences on, that record, and its eventual suppression by the imperial establishment. What survived instead were only tributes to the glories of early empire, as well as historical testimonies to the chaos and decadence of a subcontinent that had—so the story went—virtually invited the British to stoop to conquer them. But for that to happen, historians such as Mill, Macaulay, and Seeley had to rewrite the history of British conquest for a new imperial age. The embarrassment of empire gave way to its naturalization and celebration, with no more blushing about either Clive or Hastings. They were now to become the great heroes of imperial history, the founder and the guardian, respectively. And in the imperial order of things past, Burke was to have an awkward, and uncertain, place, despite the critical role he played in making the new historical mythology of empire possible.

Portrait of Edmund Burke by Joshua Reynolds, ca. 1771.

⚞ 8 ⚟

Tradition

*If it could be truly said that a great gulf is fixed between
you and them, it is that gulf created by manners, opinions and laws, radicated in the very nature of the people,
and which you can never efface from them . . . we, if we
must govern such a Country, must govern them upon
their own principles and maxims and not upon ours, that
we must not think to force them to our narrow ideas, but
extend ours to take in theirs; . . . But in that Country the
laws of religion, the laws of the land and the laws of honour, are all united and consolidated in one, and bind a
man eternally to the rules of what is called his caste.*

—EDMUND BURKE, "SPEECH ON THE
OPENING OF THE IMPEACHMENT," 1788

Burke may not have used the word "tradition" a great deal, but it is
widely accepted that he was the great traditionalist of the eighteenth
century.[1] Tradition was conveyed by his frequent use of terms such
as custom, manners, laws, inheritance, ancestry, and prescription.[2]
Burke believed in the importance of history, but in a very different

sense than that held by many of the denizens of the Scottish En-lightenment, for whom history was fundamentally a story of change and progress. History for Burke was largely about the weight of the past, the significance of tradition and custom, and the working out of viable relationships between the particularity of specific politi-cal communities and the general force of natural law and higher morality.

Burke's idea of history was inextricable from his notion of tradi-tion, and invariably conjoined with the laws of society, a social order that subordinated individual will to a general good. By implication, Indian history was defined in relation to the geographically specific and civilizationally derived notions that Burke invoked when speak-ing of caste. Caste for Burke was the principle that bound men to the laws of land, religion, and honor, an eternal bond that was inherent to the nature of the Indian people. Burke had similar no-tions about the relationship between custom and history in Britain, but his delineation of the centrality of caste more than expressed his view that India is different: it also suggests the extent to which the difference was one of kind as well as substance. While British principles could be extended to encompass the customs of India, it is clear that Burke would not have allowed the opposite to be true as well. Once again, Europe could aspire to the condition of univer-sality, whereas India could only be represented in relation to the par-ticular.

Burke was insistent on respecting the integrity of India, its vari-ous laws as well as its constitution. But he was neither a cultural relativist nor, for that matter, an incipient Indian nationalist. Burke did make extraordinary statements, as he did when in the opening speech of the impeachment trial he asserted: "I must do justice to the East. I assert that their morality is equal to ours as regards the morality of Governors, fathers, superiors; and I challenge the world to shew, in any modern European book, more true morality and wisdom than is to be found in the writings of Asiatic men in high trusts." And yet at the same time Burke had no problem accepting the right of the British to rule in India. While Burke held that the British were bound to rule in accordance with the customary rights of their Indian subjects, he assumed that they had the right to rule these subjects. He claimed that the formal charter the Company was granted by the Mughals accorded it fundamental sovereignty. The Company ruled by virtue of "the great Charter by which they acquired the High Stewardship of the Kingdoms of Bengal, Bahar, and Orissa in 1765," a charter that he notes conferred sovereignty on the British whether or not "the power of the Sovereign from whom they derived these powers should be by any misfortune in human affairs annihilated or suspended." In other words, "When Great Britain assented to that grant virtually, and afterwards took advantage of it, Great Britain made a virtual act of union with that country, by which they bound themselves as securities for their subjects, to preserve the people in all rights, laws and liberties, which their natural original Sovereign was bound to enforce, if he had been in a condition to enforce it."[3]

Burke went on to explain that the authority vested in the Company by Crown and Parliament in England had thus merged with the authority vested by the Mughal, making the Company the virtual sovereign of a grand swath of India. While in principle this sovereignty was still "subordinate," it was in fact "sovereign with regard to the objects which it touched," and Burke's language throughout his orations on India made clear that he saw Mughal authority as significantly diminished by the fact that it was no longer capable of asserting the sovereignty it once had justly claimed as its own.

Much of Burke's attack on the nabobs and on Hastings was based on his contention that the British had failed to uphold their mandate, and instead had trampled on the traditional culture and society of India, neglecting to live up to the sovereign responsibilities it had inherited from the Mughals. He was especially irate with Hastings because he had defended himself on the grounds that he was simply practicing a form of Oriental despotism, a brand of "geographical morality" that Burke held to be an alibi for Hastings's monumental hubris and political ambition. But, as made clear in part by the vitriol of his attack on the idea of geographical morality, Burke did not concede his own ultimate sense of moral (or for that matter governmental) responsibility to Indian custom, however defined; instead he maintained throughout his speeches and writings on India that there were significant limits to moral or political relativism. While the British were bound by contract to preserve the customary rights of their Indian subjects, Burke was clear that they had even higher obligations. Burke conceded that there were despotic models in India that could be followed but rejected them in favor of his sense of the superiority of his vaguely defined constitutional government of the Mughals. Burke acknowledged that presents were given and hospitality for dignitaries afforded by rights of Indian custom but condemned Hastings for following customs of this sort; only "laudable customs" were in fact to be observed.[4]

Ultimately Burke believed that the final measure of morality was universal, "the eternal frame and constitution of things."[5] "We are all born in subjection," he said, "to one great immutable, pre-existent law, prior to all our devices and prior to all our contrivances." As he had said in his opening speech, "the laws of morality are the same everywhere, and . . . there is no action which would pass for an action of extortion, of peculation, of bribery and of oppression in England, that is not an act of extortion, of peculation, of bribery and of oppression in Europe, Asia, Africa, and all the world over."[6] Even if the East India Company had been accorded arbitrary power by some Indian emperor, it could not rightfully have exercised it. In one of his most rousing proclamations, Burke stated: "We have no arbitrary power to give, because Arbitrary power is a thing which neither any man can hold nor any man can give away." In the end, Burke believed in natural law, which mandated the necessity of the rule of law and the necessity of some form of constitutional governance. As he said, "The law is the security of the people of England; it is the security of the people of India; it is the security of every person that is governed, and of every person that governs. There is but one law for all, namely, that law which governs all law, the law of our Creator, the law of humanity, justice, equity,—the law of Nature and of Nations."[7]

Burke's resort to natural law was thus invariably the limit and measure of his interest in and deference to Indian tradition. Of course, Burke believed that genuine tradition, whether in Britain or India, was necessarily governed by natural law, so despite his serious engagement with Indian history and his deep respect for Indian culture, he was never unsure about how to make his final evaluations. Burke might have been able to think of India outside of empire, but it is impossible to read his speeches in their historical context without realizing the extent to which his imaginings of India were never independent of the context of empire and Britain. Burke's interest in India was therefore always an extension of his interest in Britain, and his respect for the idea of place was always motivated by a very clear attachment to his own particular place and the perspectives it required. His argument with Hastings was ultimately not over their different ways of defining Indian tradition, but rather over the effects these definitions had for the sovereign mandate of British rule in India.

In fact, Burke was in substantial agreement with Hastings on most issues relating to Indian tradition. They were both preoccupied with questions of the law, and they both agreed that law had to find ways to balance universal commitments to justice and the particular rights of different political communities. Hastings's use of Nathaniel Halhed to devise a Hindu code, and his careful establishment of judicial protocols to institute adherence to Hindu and Muslim personal law, were hardly motivated by views contrary to those of Burke. Hastings had made a strong case to the Company directors that local law had to be followed in Company courts since it was "consonant to the ideas, manners, and inclinations of the people for whose use it is intended." He therefore presumed that Indian law would be "preferable to any which ever a superior wisdom could substitute in its room . . . The people of this country do not require our aid to furnish them with a rule for their conduct, or a standard for their property."[8] This language could have been Burke's. Likewise, Hastings had patronized the study of Hinduism, including not just Halhed's code but also the translation of important Sanskrit works into English. While he noted that "every accumulation of knowledge . . . of people over whom we exercise a dominion founded on the right of conquest, is useful to the state," he also made clear his great admiration for the "sublimity" of many Hindu writings.[9] But despite these areas of agreement, Burke saw Hastings's invocations of Indian tradition as self-serving, and was repelled by Hastings's use of cultural arguments to justify immoral practices of statecraft.

Yet Burke himself was contradictory on the subject of statecraft. While he railed against Hastings on virtually every aspect of his rule, he exonerated Clive and drew a veil over the period of conquest in ways that appeared to justify the worst of Hastings's excesses as long as they could now be kept out of sight. In similarly contradictory fashion he appeared to uphold the traditional sovereignty and constitutional greatness of the Mughal empire as long as it was clear that this was only a thing of the past, now made obsolete by the decline and disintegration of Indian politics. Burke made no connection between British conquest and Indian decline, and instead sought single-mindedly to provide a moral as well as a historical charter for British rule. As he did so, he fashioned a space for Indian tradition that made the idea of caste especially attractive. Indian tradition would be respected, but that part of the tradition that would be respected most was the very part that consigned Indians to a place outside history, a sociological essence that dictated everything dear to "the very nature of the people." In a peculiar sense, Burke was ahead of his time in understanding that caste would be a convenient theory of political justification for imperial rule. He seemed to intuit the way in which an imperial sociological imaginary could be of great use to the imperial regime in India, focusing on the very "gulf created by manners, opinions and laws" that would later be used to predicate the basis of the ethnographic state in late imperial India.[10]

Despite Burke's condemnation of the Company for its excessive greed and its failure to understand and uphold Indian tradition, he would perhaps have been surprised and instructed by a history of India written by Ghulam Hussain during the last years of Hastings's rule. Ghulam Hussain (1727–1806) came from a family of high-level officials in the Mughal court, and he moved to Bengal in the years after the Battle of Plassey to seek service under Mir Jafar (unsuccessfully as it turned out). He did manage to secure employment from various Company officers, serving as one Colonel Goddard's agent in Lucknow in the years around 1770. From 1778 on he was based in Calcutta, where he was eventually offered employment by Hastings, though not in the capacity he desired. He wrote his history in Calcutta, completing it in 1781. Titled *Seir Mutaqherin (Review of Modern Times)*, it was grand in scope, covering the history of the Mughal empire from its earliest days until the present.

Hussain's history reflects the declining fortunes of his family; his father and grandfather had lived much grander lives and he doubtless attributed the uncertainties and setbacks in his own career and fortune to British conquest. But he provided extraordinarily detailed and insightful commentary on the nature of British rule, and while deeply concerned about the corruption of Company servants, he was most distressed about the unfriendliness, inaccessibility, and ignorance of the British. Hussain wrote that "as the gates of communication and intercourse are shut up betwixt the men of this land and those strangers, who are become their masters; and these latter constantly express an aversion to the society of Indians, and a disdain against conversing with them; hence both parties remain ignorant of each other's state and circumstances." As a result, he wrote, "no love, and no coalition can take root between the conquerors and the conquered." Additionally, the British understood little of the country they ruled: "Hence they know nothing of either the reason or intent of them, but by the absurd report of their own servants, who being all beardless and unexperienced, have no view but that of their own benefit, and think only of pleasing their English masters."[11]

Ghulam Hussain diagnosed the main problem as having to do with Britain's conquering India with no intention of staying on. As he noted, "The English have besides a custom of coming for a number of years, and then of going away to pay a visit to their native country, without any one of them shewing an inclination to fix himself in this land; hence ignorance and incapacity come to be transmitted from hand to hand."[12] With only a few exceptions (and Hastings was one of them), the British did not learn the local language and were decidedly ignorant of native life, custom, and opinion. They did not stay in their posts long enough to learn about local conditions or develop local concerns. And because they only wished to collect as much personal fortune as possible and return to England, they had no wish to change anything.

In this the British were very different from the Mughals before them, who had come to India as conquerors, but also to stay:

> There were others that thought in a quite different manner; and these intending to settle for ever, and to fix the foot of residence and permanency in these countries, had a mind of turning their conquest into a patrimony for themselves, and of making it their property and their inheritance . . . These bent the whole strength of their genius in securing the happiness of their new subjects; nor did they ever abate any thing from their efforts, until they had intermarried with the natives, and got children and families from them, and had become naturalized. Their immediate successors

having learned the language of the country, behaved to its inhabitants as brothers of one mother and one language.[13]

Ghulam Hussain noted further that despite the major differences in
customs and beliefs between Hindus and Muslims, the two groups
overcame their initial aversion, and over time became as one: "The
two nations have come to coalesce together into one whole, like
milk and sugar that have received a simmering."[14] Again and again
Ghulam Hussain complained that the British only sought their own
society, having nothing but aversion for the natives, and that they
made no effort to bridge the cultural and linguistic divides that kept
them from developing sympathetic relations with Indians. Unlike
the Mughal rulers before them, who held open court (durbar) for
long hours every day to make themselves fully accessible to their
subjects, the British were unconnected and unsociable. Even those
Indians who had initially welcomed the British soon turned against
them, feeling "nothing for them now, fully sensible that these new
rulers pay no regard or attention to the concerns of Hindostanies,
and that they suffer them to be mercilessly plundered, fleeced, oppressed, and tormented by those officers of their appointing, and by
their other dependants."[15]

From Ghulam Hussain's perspective, Hastings came off rather
well, despite his slow response to requests for patronage and employment. Although Ghulam Hussain was certainly aware that criticiz-
ing Hastings would not increase his own chances for success, he
was steadfastly loyal even after his fall, and wrote one of the most
glowing endorsements of his rule for Hastings's use during his impeachment trial. But whatever extenuating circumstances colored
Ghulam Hussain's account of the British, it is clear from this text

that they failed to win the hearts and minds of their new subjects because they refused to make fundamental concessions. Even in the best of cases, the British might have expressed admiration for the Mughal constitution or ancient Hindu texts, but they ultimately could only appreciate Indian traditions from a distance, in the abstract.

And here Burke, even more than Hastings, would hardly have been a consolation to Hussain, for whom the condescension of European empire meant that the British stayed irrevocably British, failing to follow the Mughal model of settlement and cultural assimilation. To be sure, Burke had argued for cultural and political respect, but he had also assumed that he could do so from the security of a cultural identity of his own that could be universal and local at the same time, while Indian culture could only be local. It was no accident that for Burke Indian culture was defined by the idea of caste: for this was an idea that (at least in British usage) was totalizing as well as eternal, and it resisted the entry of outsiders even as it made exit for those within its social grasp virtually unthinkable.

Indeed, Burke was one of the few eighteenth-century Englishmen to anticipate the colonial sociology that installed caste as the key to understanding India during the late nineteenth century. For caste, as it came to be known under later colonial rule, is not in fact some unchanged remnant of ancient India, not some single system that reflects a core civilizational value, not a basic expression of Indian tradition. It was only under British rule that "caste" became a single term capable of naming, expressing, and above all systematizing India's diverse and complex forms of social identity, community, and organization. In precolonial India, units of social identity were multiple, and their various relations and meanings part of a complex, conjunctural, and constantly changing political world. Social identity instead was embedded in contexts that had to do with temple communities, regional as well as local territorial affiliations, lineages, families, royal retinues and orders, warrior subgroups, kingdoms, occupations, sects, factions—to mention only a few examples—that only later became congealed around, and under, the single idea of caste. Under British rule, caste became the colonial form of civil society, justifying the denial of political rights to Indian subjects (never citizens) and explaining the necessity of colonial rule. But in the eighteenth century, caste was given little significance by most British commentators, who were far more likely to invoke questions of history or religion than of society itself.

From the start, however, European imperial power, as described by Burke and others, was predicated on the assumption of European universality. Nations such as India could be colonized not just because they lost battles, failed to develop the economic resilience and political unity necessary for independence, or were seen as underdeveloped in other respects, but also because they were local. Even when colonizers such as Hastings, or Burke, urged respect for local culture, they did so either to facilitate imperial power, as in the case of Hastings, or to ennoble the idea of empire, as in the case of Burke. Both Hastings and Burke, whatever their actual intentions, created the necessary conditions for the use of tradition to justify imperial power. Hastings might have patronized distinguished Orientalist scholars, and Burke might have spoken eloquently about the glories of the East, but they introduced the notion that tradition could be useful for rule. It is perhaps not a historical accident that the scandals of empire so condemned and excoriated by Burke gave way to other kinds of scandals in the years after the conclusion of the impeachment trial. By the late eighteenth century, empire, no longer steeped in European scandal, vindicated itself through its confrontation with Indian tradition. Increasingly, local custom became the principal site of corruption and vice, and by the early nineteenth century the notion of a civilizing mission began to be articulated in relation to rituals practiced in India.

This process did not happen immediately, nor was its outcome necessarily prefigured by the history of early empire. The utilitarian reformers who were cultivated by Wellesley and came to dominate the imperial establishment in the first few decades of the new century were not responsible for the elevation of custom as both the mission of and justification for the colonial state. Indeed, many of the young reformers who spent their full careers in the East lived and worked with Burke's zeal, sincerely believing that empire was a noble enterprise, and a temporary one at that. Nevertheless, the general tone of praise for Indian culture that had been adopted by many of the eighteenth-century colonizers gradually began to give way to the horrified description of rites of barbarism that were used to convey the civilizational corruption and scandal that was endemic in the East.

While the changed tone of cultural rhetoric was driven principally by the new crusading evangelicals, led by Charles Grant and William Wilberforce, these new cultural preoccupations also served to fill a gap that was left in the wake of Burke's cleansing of imperial excess. Where once scandal referred to the exploits of the colonizers, scandal now began to refer to the lives of the colonized. Tipu Sultan had been vilified in the British imaginary by Wellesley and his associates, in large part to vindicate a military campaign that was costly, dangerous, and opposed by the board of control. Colonel William Kirkpatrick, Wellesley's military secretary and member of the Mysore Commission, wrote that Tipu Sultan was "the intolerant bigot or furious fanatic; the oppressive and unjust ruler; the harsh and rigid master; the sanguinary tyrant"; and Mark Wilks, whom Wellesley installed as the British resident of Mysore in 1803, wrote that Tipu Sultan had "perpetually on his tongue the projects of jehad—holy war."[16] But barbarism was still associated primarily with political regimes and individuals rather than cultural practices, despite myriad graphic descriptions of torture and self-mortification that were associated with the religions of the East.

The most florid early examples of cultural scandal came with the dramatization of sati, the practice of burning widows written about in tones of horror well before Raja Rammohun Roy advocated its abolition in 1818. What magnified the significance of sati, and more broadly changed the character of British discourse on religion and culture, however, was not Roy's own personal concerns about the hideous abuse of women but rather the mobilization of missionary pressure to enter British India and Christianize the practice of empire. Missionaries had been kept out of British India for fear of offending Indian religious sensibilities, and throughout the late eighteenth century the East India Company followed local practice by endowing Hindu and Muslim religious institutions and festivals. The Company was preoccupied with the maintenance of order and the easy conduct of commerce, and under these conditions the Enlightenment commitment to religious toleration was easier to enact in India than at home.

When Charles Grant, a senior figure in the Indian Home Administration, returned from a long stint in India in 1790, he lobbied to include what became called the "Pious Clause" in the renewed Company Charter of 1793—but was rebuffed despite his high standing and considerable influence on Company affairs. The Pious Clause not only called for the Company to stop restricting the entry of missionaries into British India; it was designed to mandate that the Company support missionary activity: "Whereas such measures ought to be adopted for the interests and happiness of the native inhabitants of the British dominions in India, as may gradually tend to their advancement in useful knowledge, and to their religious and moral improvement; . . . the Court of Directors . . . are hereby empowered and required to send out, from time to time . . . fit and proper persons . . . as school masters, missionaries, or otherwise . . . The said Court of Directors are hereby empowered and required to give directions . . . to settle the destination and to provide for the necessary and decent maintenance of the persons so to be sent out."[17] Despite widespread support for the clause from the ascendant Clapham group, opposition was intense. Sir Stephen Lushington spoke for many old Company hands when he feared that missionary activity (and for that matter the extension of education more generally) would mean the end of British supremacy in India, for reasons that had readily been seen in the Americas, where the colonized had been all too aware of their own capacity for and right to self-rule.

Grant had made his case for missionization in his pamphlet "Observations on the State of Society among the Asiatic Subjects of Great Britain, Particularly with Respect to Morals, and on the Means of Improving It. Written Chiefly in the Year 1792." This text had an extraordinarily long and influential career; although it was first circulated to generate support for the inclusion of missionary activity in the Company charter renewal of 1793, it was actually printed for a much larger audience only in connection with the charter renewal of 1813, when at last it was successful. In his pamphlet, Grant argued that Britain had an obligation to attend to the happiness, general welfare, and moral improvement of the people under its rule in India, and that the only way to do this was to accept that empire must legitimate itself through Christian principles, and by seeking to promote those principles through education and conversion. Bengal had seriously deteriorated under British rule, but the causes for this were not, Grant suggested, merely political and economic. Rather, even as the Company would take on a moral character by accepting its Christian obligations and duties, the people of India would find genuine improvement only through Christianization.

Grant's diagnosis of Hindu character was severe, and out of keeping with the general admiration that had been expressed for Indian civilization by contemporaneous British commentators as diverse as Dow, Orme, Hastings, and Jones. Grant wrote, "We cannot avoid recognizing in the people of Hindostan, a race of men lamentably degenerate and base, retaining but a feeble sense of moral obligation, yet obstinate in their disregard of what they know to be right, governed by malevolent and licentious passions, strongly exemplifying the effects produced on society by great and general corruption of manners, and sunk in misery by their vices." Despite the language of racial condemnation, Grant sought to suggest that the problem was not in fact endemic to the people of Hindostan, but rather to their religion. In an extraordinary statement of displacement given the political context, he wrote that this religion was "a despotism, the most remarkable for its power and duration that the world had ever seen." He quoted from William Jones's recent translation of the *Manu Dharma Shastras* for proof that Hindu law enjoined fraud, lying, abuse, and oppression, and he provided graphic images of the popular worship of cruel and licentious gods, most especially Kali. Most troubling of all, however, was the institution of caste, itself the product of the fraud and imposture of the Brahman priests who used religion to enslave and oppress the rest of society.[18]

Grant's powerful tract anticipated the arguments that missionaries made—both when they joined the fight to be welcomed by the imperial venture in the years leading up to the Company's charter renewal of 1813 and after they finally gained access to Indian souls—about the depraved nature of Hinduism as a religion and the power of caste as an institution used to secure the place of Hinduism in Indian society. Indeed, missionaries had been the first to mount a systematic critique of caste—and by implication of the Brahman priesthood—during the first decades of the nineteenth century, in ways that later led many British officials to rue the day that missionaries had been allowed access to India, especially after the Great Rebellion of 1857.

Missionaries also followed Grant's lead in dramatizing the importance of customs or rituals deemed as barbaric, advocating government intervention in areas ranging from sati and human sacrifice to the rite of hook-swinging, and more generally seeking to clothe the British empire with the moral cloak of Christianity. In the early days of 1813, various missionary societies inaugurated a new paper, the *Missionary Register*, which published evocative accounts of the evils of Hinduism and the critical role of missionaries in bringing light to Asia.

Meanwhile, William Wilberforce arranged for the publication of

Grant's tract, and used his writings extensively in his stirring speeches in Parliament.[19] In assailing Indian society, he asserted that "both their civil and religious systems are radically and essentially the opposites of our own. Our religion is sublime, pure and beneficent. Theirs is mean, licentious, and cruel . . . the essential and universal pervading character [of their civil principles] is inequality; despotism in the higher classes, degradation and oppression in the lower." Wilberforce's speeches had echoes of Burke in their denunciation of the Company and their call for the moral regeneration of empire. As he had noted on another occasion, "The foulest blot [next to the slave trade] on the moral character of the country was the willingness of the Parliament and the people to permit our fellow-subjects . . . in the East Indies to remain . . . under the grossest, the darkest and most degrading system of idolatrous superstition that almost ever existed upon earth."[20] Wilberforce brought India and the Company to the popular imagination in Britain in a way that had not been the case since the days surrounding the opening of the Hastings impeachment a quarter-century before. Warren Hastings betrayed the difference of the new age when he noted with sad resignation that Grant's new attitude was finally triumphing over his own legacy of toleration and respect.

The *Missionary Register*, first published in January 1813, played an important role in generating widespread support for a missionary presence in India. During the debate over the charter, more than 837 petitions containing approximately half a million signatures supporting the entry of missionaries were submitted to Parliament.[21] The *Register* was designed precisely to mobilize this kind of campaign, and it did so most successfully by publishing articles on the society and culture of India, especially on themes such as "Hindoo Superstitions," "Hindoo Mythology and Deities," and "Human Sacrifices." The "Hindoo Superstition" in which the journal took a special interest was widow burning.

At the height of the charter debate in June 1813, the *Register* published an extract on sati from William Ward's *Account of the Writings, Religion and Manners of the Hindoos*, published in Serampore in 1811. An early source of authoritative information on Hindu religion and society in Britain, Ward's book went through eight editions between 1811 and 1822, serving as a major source for evangelical as well as ethnographic publications. Ward's text had begun as a careful and relatively dispassionate account of various customs, but it shifted dramatically after 1813 to the point where, in its final edition, it advocated the civilizing mission of empire.[22] When the book was quoted and paraphrased by the editors of the *Register*, its dry discussion of the different possible scriptural bases for sati was overlooked in favor of its more dramatic descriptions of actual events. The *Register* reprinted Ward's most horrific stories of widow burning, framing each extract with a call for sympathy and action—for example, when it noted: "Let every Christian Woman who reads the following Statement, pity the wretched thousands of her sex who are sacrificed every year in India to a cruel superstition, and thank God for her own light and privileges, and pray and labour earnestly for the salvation of these miserable fellow subjects."[23] The *Register* was remarkably successful in raising funds for mission work and support for missionary activity against the concerns of the Company. In working to make sati emblematic of Hindu practice and belief, it, and the larger missionary movement of the early century, made the compelling argument that empire had a sacred mission to protect the women of India from a barbaric culture and religion.

Late in his life, William Ward wrote that he wished he could "collect all the shrieks of these affrighted victims, all the innocent blood thus drunk up by the devouring element, and all the wailings of these ten thousand orphans, losing father and mother on the same time," in order to present them "at our missionary anniversaries, and carry them through every town of the United Kingdom."[24] As Ward and other missionaries carried the message of India's great need across Britain, it was no accident that missionaries increasingly provided the basis for the popular support of Britain's imperial presence in India. The Company government accordingly began to feel compelled to intervene in local affairs in ways that it had been careful not to do before.[25]

The Company, however, was extremely careful to enlist local support for the abolition of sati, as well as scriptural evidence to suggest that it was not violating the real religion of the Hindus. While pressure grew in England against sati in the years after 1813, it was not until 1829 that the governor-general, Lord Bentinck, finally felt he had sufficient grounds on which to enact the legislative prohibition of sati. In proclaiming the abolition of sati, Bentinck cautioned that abolition was to be in no way construed as part of an effort to convert Hindus to Christianity. Instead, he proclaimed, "I write and feel as a legislator for the Hindus, and as I believe many enlightened Hindus think and feel," and he was careful to point out that his primary concern was to "wash out a foul stain upon British rule."[26] Although the Company government was always circumspect in India about its dramatic intervention in Indian cultural customs, the abolition of sati became perhaps the most important moral justification for empire across Britain and the west in the years thereafter.[27]

If by 1829 sati became the central scandal of empire, it was joined soon thereafter by another religiously defined and validated "custom" that became almost as important a symbol of Britain's civilizing mission. Captain William Henry Sleeman, who served as chief agent under Bentinck, made his career by sensationalizing his campaign against the "Thugs," popularizing the notion that bands of ritual murderers roamed the Indian countryside committing terrorist crimes in the name of Hindu goddesses. He first alerted the British public to the barbarism of *thuggee* in an anonymously authored article published in the *Calcutta Literary Gazette* on October 3, 1830. The article asserted that Kali shrines across India accepted the offerings of ritual murderers as holy gifts to the goddess. Most gripping of all was the way in which this system of murder was religiously sanctioned and organized. Calling for the government to "put an end in some way or other to this dreadful system of murder, by which thousands of human beings are now annually sacrificed upon every great road throughout India," the article further suggested that under British India the Thugs were not just prospering but spreading their evil creed: "And, as hares are often found to choose their burrows in the immediate vicinity of the kennels, so may these men be found often most securely established in the very seats of our principal judicial establishments."[28]

Using the public outcry that followed the publication of his account, Sleeman secured support from Bentinck to wage a war against the Thugs, and over the next decade he claimed to have captured more than three thousand highway robbers and to have executed four hundred of the most hardened criminals. He also published a series of works, from his lexicon of the Thug language (*The Ramaseeana; or, Vocabulary of the Thug Language*, 1839) to his history of "that extraordinary fraternity of assassins" (*The Thugs or Phansigars of India*, 1839), as well as his long and popular work, *Rambles and Recollections of an Indian Official*, published in 1844. His extensive writings inspired a number of other works, perhaps most famously Philip Meadows Taylor's romantic fiction *The Confessions of a Thug*, published in 1837.

When describing the extent to which the Thugs had spread themselves and their evil deeds across the subcontinent, Sleeman wrote, "Every arrest brought to light new combinations and associations of these professed assassins, and discovered new scenes in which their dreadful trade was at work."[29] While he noted that it was astonishing that the horrendous problem had only been recognized recently, no previous government had been concerned to see random incidents of violence as connected: "The fact is, that until these five or six years, no one had any correct notion of its extent: all that was known up to that period was, that travelers were occasionally enticed and murdered by people called Thugs, who assumed the garb of inoffensive wayfarers." Indeed, it was hard to recognize Thugs, since they not only looked like ordinary villagers, but often were from different social groups. Just as a proper ethnographic eye was necessary to understand the intricate functioning of this cultic fraternity of murderers, Sleeman observed that the suppression of *thuggee* would require a major and coordinated assault. "It was obvious that nothing but a general system, undertaken by a paramount power, strong enough to bear down all opposition by interested native chiefs, could ever eradicate such well-organized villainy."[30]

Sleeman thus proposed a major initiative, which he promised would have a satisfactory payoff in the end:

> There can be no doubt that if the British government will pursue vigorous measures for a few years, the system will, with proper supervision on the part of the ordinary police, be completely eradicated, never again to rise; but if exertions are slackened, and any fully initiated Thugs left at large, they would infallibly raise new gangs, and Thuggee would again flourish all over India. It is certainly incumbent on a government which assumes to itself the character of enlightened, and which is now paramount in India, to exert itself for the suppression of such an atrocious system.[31]

Sleeman's work alone provided ample justification in some parts of British India for the investment of greater resources into an aggressive police force, as well as for expansionist military policies. His writings confirmed to a broad public in Britain that Hinduism was the cause of India's scandals, and that British rule would help good triumph over evil.

The Thuggee Act of 1836 ruled that "whoever shall be proved to have belonged, either before or after the passing of this Act, to any gang of Thugs, either within or without the Territories of the East India Company, shall be punished with imprisonment for life, with hard labor." This was a helpful change of procedure, since it was much easier to prosecute a prisoner on the charge of being a member of a particular community than it was to establish sufficient evidence about the commission of a crime, especially when the crime was associated with highway robbery. The *thuggee* ruling allowed the state to claim due process when convicting "criminals" who could not be proven to have actually committed the crime. Sleeman was successful in establishing the convenience of the *thuggee* campaign and then using the license it provided to classify a wide range of itinerant groups under a single criminal classification, but even he had to pull back from an escalation that had no natural boundary.[32] When certain objectives were achieved, he often declared that *thuggee* had indeed been eradicated, claiming success for his mission just at the point it might have begun to spin out of control.

The problem, of course, was that the various groups labeled as thugs were highly miscellaneous, including itinerant mendicants, soldiers disbanded from service by chiefs who had been either conquered or at least converted into landlords, migrant labor, as well as other gypsy-like groups such as the *banjaras*, who were always on the move. Many of the groups identified as thugs had been retainers in the Malwa kingdom, most of whom found themselves without employment after British conquest. *Thuggee* was even more diverse and unstructured in its origins and activities, many times reflecting nothing more than an underground economy of poverty and desperation, connected in many instances with the dislocations rendered by colonial conquest and rule.[33]

British concern about the lack of safety and stability on the roads of the subcontinent was not unrelated to the expansion of its country trade to the interior of India, and in particular the transport of opium to Calcutta for its use in the China tea trade. What gave the classificatory rubric of *thuggee* its ring and its power (and its ability to displace concerns over things like the opium trade) was the linking of an imagined religious cult committed to murderous activities with the legal and political logic of an expanding colonial state. Despite the fragile nature of both the diagnosis of *thuggee* as a "system" and then the general campaign against it, *thuggee* became an important symbol of the civilizing mission of British rule.

Indian tradition came to take on very different meanings for the British in the early decades of the nineteenth century. Increasingly, tradition became useful for a variety of colonial projects, from the evangelical ambitions of the Clapham group and various missionary organizations, to the law-and-order concerns of the Company state at a time when it had lost its trading monopoly and was seeking to establish itself as the most efficient means of colonial administration. While the British state was initially nervous to make too much of the scandal of sati, given the possible unrest (especially in the upper classes and castes) that any interference in local religious custom might cause, it soon found it convenient to use the abolition of sati to justify its mission. And no sooner did it do so than it launched an aggressive campaign to identify and eradicate the barbaric practice of religious robbery and murder (this time with fewer prominent adherents). The scandal of empire no longer evoked the names and legends of Clive, Benfield, Hastings, and the nouveaux riches nabobs, but rather the ritual practices of sati and *thuggee*. Although the outburst of the Great Rebellion of 1857 forced the colonial state to abandon its aggressive new policies of missionization and civilizational reform, the notion of Indian tradition developed in these earlier decades, and the obvious uses of different colonial characterizations of this tradition as a justification for and means of rule became the basis for the establishment of the ethnographic state in late-nineteenth-century British India. The ethnographic state was about social regulation rather than social reform, and it assumed its moral authority on the basis of its social superiority rather than its harmony with or transformation of another civilization, as had been the case for earlier generations of imperialists. Caste ceased to be an institution that was to be overcome in order to convert souls, and became instead the colonial version of civil society that could be ruled through caste at the same time it was to be ruled because of caste.[34]

The ironies of this situation should not surprise us, for modern empire always justifies itself through a peculiar mix of cultural condemnation and civilizing intention. Empire can only prosper where the subjects of empire are seen as backward, or dangerous, or both, because of their subjection to forms of tradition and modes of belief that can only benefit from the civilizational beneficence and intervention of a modern Western power. Even as the British justified their new imperium in India through their commitment to free women from the curse of sati and protect citizens from the threat of highway robbery, the United States has more recently represented its primary role in Afghanistan as the liberation of women from the oppression of the fundamentalist Taliban and the protection of all Afghanis from the ruthless warlords who controlled the highways and trading routes of the region. Of course, the British neglected to mention that their own presence had greatly exacerbated the importance of sati (not to mention that their general commitment to social reforms meaningful to women was consistently insincere), and that the ritual murder they worked so hard to suppress was in large part, where it wasn't entirely fabricated, the direct result of early imperial conquest and occupation. That the United States neglected as well to mention its own role in establishing the Taliban and arming the regional warlords in its Cold War struggle with the Soviet

Union thus had an important imperial precedent. The narratives of empire today continue to echo those of yesteryear in which scandal was displaced from the colonizer to the colonized. That empire is still seen as a burden, the consequence of the West's superiority rather than the principal reason for it, should be a source of enduring historical shame.

Portrait of Warren Hastings,
a few years before Hastings was appointed
governor of Bengal in 1772.

✥ 9 ✥

Empire

The attacks that were made upon the Company in Parlia-
ment, the vote of censure moved against Lord Clive, the
impeachment brought against Hastings, the successive
ministerial schemes for regulating the Company's affairs,
one of which in 1783 convulsed the whole political world
of England, all these interferences contributed to make
our Indian wars seem national wars, and to identify the
Company with the English nation.

—J. R. SEELEY, THE EXPANSION OF ENGLAND,

1883

Edmund Burke was an eloquent and powerful critic of empire. Few orators, then or now, have captured the excesses and abuses of impe-rial power in such ringing rhetorical registers. His speeches and writings were embarrassing to later generations of British imperial-ists for whom the history of empire had to be as glorious in its begin-nings as it was in its present and future, and for whom Hastings in-creasingly became a key icon of imperial greatness. Yet despite the force of Burke's critique and the years spent prosecuting the East India Company, he neither condemned empire altogether, nor held the East India Company responsible for the manifold abuses of its imperial conduct. In the end, Burke's real legacy was the transformation of Company rule into British imperium. Through his role in shaping the reforms and then in impeaching Hastings, he managed to rescue the imperial mission, transforming corruption into virtue, private malfeasance into public good, mercantile disgrace into national triumph.

J. R. Seeley, the renowned Cambridge historian of empire, was one of the first to note this transformation in his influential lectures of the late nineteenth century on "The Expansion of Empire." He wrote that the first chapter of the history of British India "embraces chronologically the first half of George III's reign, that stormy period of transition in English history when at the same time America was lost and India won . . . [and] covers the two great careers of Clive and Hastings . . . [T]he end of the struggle is marked by the reign of Lord Cornwallis, which began in 1785."[1] Seeley went on to observe,

> There was much unreasonable violence in the attacks made upon Hastings . . . But, taking a broad view, it must be said that the particular dangers feared were very successfully averted, that Lord Cornwallis established a title to gratitude and Edmund Burke to immortal glory. For the stain of immortality did pass away as by magic from the administration of the Company under the rule of Lord Cornwallis, a lesson never to be forgotten was taught to Governors General, and at the same time the political danger from the connexion with India passed away.[2]

Seeley understood that something dramatic happened in 1785, though in invoking magic as the means of legitimating empire he did not fully accord to Burke the important role he played in the trial, where the "unreasonable violence" of Burke's attacks provided the exculpatory rituals that blotted out the stains of conquest.

Seeley did, however, comprehend the nature of the great transformation, not just in lessening the dangers of empire, but also in making the Company the agent of a newly conceived national mission. As he writes in the passage just quoted, Burke's interventions, through the regulating acts but most spectacularly as a result of the impeachment trial, worked in the end to identify the Company in particular, and the Indian mission more generally, with the English nation.[3] The trial of Warren Hastings had been the final act in the efforts spanning the eighteenth century to harness imperial power—along with imperial wealth and prestige—securely to Britain, both as "nation" and as "state." Once Burke had succeeded in this endeavor, the stain of commercial origins could be removed, the special mix of economic and political interests realigned as the expression of national interest, the blot of scandal washed out as the moral mandate for a new kind of imperial project was launched. Burke did his work very well indeed.

Seeley was far more astute than many later imperial historians, for he complained that this very transformation had made possible a national amnesia about the significance of empire for the history of England itself. He began his lectures with a critique of the blinkers of English historiography: "They [our historians] make too much of the mere parliamentary wrangle and the agitations about liberty, in all which matters the eighteenth century of England was but a pale reflexion of the seventeenth. They do not perceive that in that century the history of England is not in England but in America and Asia."[4] Seeley realized acutely that "when we look at the present state of affairs, and still more at the future, we ought to beware of putting England alone in the foreground and suffering what we call the English possessions to escape our view in the background of the picture."[5] In his most famous remark, he noted, "There is something very characteristic in the indifference which we show towards this mighty phenomenon of the diffusion of our race and the expansion of our people. We seem as it were, to have conquered and peopled half the world in a fit of absence of mind."[6] And yet despite Seeley's evident sense that historians had failed to understand the full significance of empire for national history, he attributed the problem in part to the history of the eighteenth century itself. For he also wrote, "Our acquisition of India was made blindly. Nothing great that has ever been done by Englishmen has ever been done so unintentionally, so accidentally, as the conquest of India."[7]

Seeley's account of imperial conquest repeats the justifications and alibis made first by the conquerors themselves: that the sole objective of trade turned into political conquest by accident rather than by contrivance or calculation. Seeley noted, "Nothing like that what is strictly called a conquest took place, but that certain traders inhabiting certain seaport towns in India, were induced, almost forced, in the anarchy caused by the fall of the Mogul Empire, to give themselves a military character and employ troops, that by means of these troops they acquired territory and at last almost all the territory of India, and that these traders happened to be Englishmen, and to employ a certain, though not a large, proportion of English troops in their army."[8] This could happen because anarchy had already set in, and India "lay there waiting to be picked up by somebody." What happened in India in the late eighteenth century was therefore an "internal revolution" rather than a "foreign conquest."[9]

Seeley's extraordinary capacity to appreciate the constitutive significance of empire for modern Britain thus must regrettably be
seen as the flip side of his failure to accept the integrity of India's
own history.[10] In the end, Seeley's view of the history of empire was a
product of the same imperial hubris that erased the story of scandal
and corruption along with the entire history of the subcontinent.
Even the canonic historians of the early nineteenth century, James
Mill and Thomas Macaulay, were unable fully to repress their anxieties about imperial origins, as much as their work was critical for
the development of Seeley's own understanding of Britain's Indian
empire. Mill, a man deeply appreciative of Burke's role in the reform of the East India Company, was for example far more critical
of Clive than Burke had been. A lifelong employee of the East India
Company, Mill was the chief examiner of the Indian dispatches and
published his major historical work, *The History of British India*, in
1817, providing the first serious historical account of the rise of the
East India Company to imperial power in India.

Mill was seriously critical of Clive's use of the Diwani to fuel
speculation in and support for the Company, and scathing in his
characterizations of Clive's own propensities to corruption and deception. About the acceptance of the Diwani, and the dual system
of rule more generally, he observed,

> The double, or ambiguous administration; in name, and in ostent
> by the Nabob, in reality by the Company; which had been rec-
> ommended as ingenious policy by Clive, and admired as such by
> his employers and successors; had contributed greatly to enhance
> the difficulties in which, by the assumption of the government,
> the English were involved: All the vices of the ancient polity were

saved from reform: and all the evils of a divided authority were superinduced. The revenues were under a complicated, wasteful, and oppressive economy . . . and the people were given up to oppression.[11]

Mill believed that Clive was prone to "crooked artifice" both in his politics and his finances, but judged Clive most harshly for inflating the potential value accorded to the Diwani settlement.[12] As he wrote,

> It was the interest of the [Company] servants in India, diligently cultivated, perpetually to feast the Company with the most flattering accounts of the state of their affairs. The magnitude of the transactions, which had recently taken place; the vast riches with which the new acquisitions were said to abound; the general credulity on the subject of Indian opulence; and the great fortunes with which a few individuals had returned to Europe; inflamed the avarice of the proprietors of the East India Stock; and rendered them impatient for a share of treasures, which the imaginations of their countrymen, as well as their own, represented as not only vast, but unlimited.[13]

In this, Mill held Clive personally responsible, both for setting the most egregious example in the accumulation of fortune and for "misleading" the Company "that India overflowed with riches"—for raising "the expectations . . . on which the credulous Company so fondly relied, that a torrent of treasure was about to flow into their laps." Writing his history as a Company man, Mill was insistent on separating the interests of the Company from those of its servants, and in so doing to privilege the view from England. And he wrote his history of Clive to warn the public against repeating the same mistake: "Till the present moment incessant promises of treasure have never failed to deceive, without ceasing to delude."[14]

Mill was offended by Clive's relentless self-interest, and though he judged Hastings harshly as well, he saved his most venomous comments for the founder, who cared nothing for the Company, and whose extraordinary audacity was unmatched by any other salutary talent. Remarkably, Mill follows his accounting of the general level of corruption on the part of Company servants by noting that no political or military policy was pursued solely for venal purposes, and he falls victim to his own loyalty to the Company when he ultimately excuses Company servants for their actions. Despite Mill's harsh verdict—echoing Burke's rhetoric while shifting the burden of Company misrule onto the founder of empire—Clive's reputation was soon to rebound, doing so most robustly in the famous 1840 essay by Thomas Macaulay, which was ostensibly a review of the favorable, though relatively dull, biography of Clive by John Malcolm that had been published in 1836.

While Macaulay was dismissive of Malcolm ("whose love passes the love of biographers, and who can see nothing but wisdom and justice in the actions of his idol") and his hagiographic approach to Clive, he was equally critical of Mill. "But we are at least equally far from concurring in the severe judgment of Mr. Mill, who seems to us to show less discrimination in his account of Clive than in any other part of his valuable work." For Macaulay, a historian more interested in the characters of great men than in the fortunes of trading houses, it seemed self-evident that "every person who takes a fair and enlightened view of his whole career must admit that our island, so fertile in heroes and statesmen, has scarcely ever produced a man more truly great either in arms or in council." Indeed, Macaulay saw Clive as the man who made the Indian empire possible, and accordingly he felt it necessary to praise the historic beginnings of empire and to canonize its founder.[15]

Like Mill, Macaulay's life was intimately connected with India, where he served for three years, from 1834 to 1837, as the legal member of the chief council (which advised the governor-general, then Lord Bentinck, on all matters). While in India, Macaulay wrote his famous treatise on Indian education (in which he had decisively recommended the use of the English language for upper-level curricular development) and devised his extraordinary draft for the Indian penal code.[16] Macaulay began his account of Clive, in what became the standard litany of all imperial renditions of India's past, by describing the despotic character of Oriental rule. "There can be little doubt," he wrote, "that this great empire [the Mughals], powerful and prosperous as it appears on a superficial view, was yet, even in its best days, far worse governed than the worst governed parts of Europe now are." The reasons for this pronouncement required little in the way of serious historical, let alone reflexive, scrutiny. In Macaulay's words, "The administration was tainted with all the vices of Oriental despotism and with all the vices inseparable from the domination of race over race." Despite endemic and structural flaws, the empire only began to weaken in serious ways under Aurangzeb, collapsing under its own weight soon after his death, when "the ruin was fearfully rapid." Macaulay went on to observe that "violent shocks from without cooperated with an incurable decay which was fast proceeding within; and in a few years the empire had undergone utter decomposition." Macaulay wrote the litany with his characteristic hyperbolic prose: "A succession of nominal sovereigns, sunk in indolence and debauchery, sauntered away life in secluded palaces, chewing bang, fondling concubines, and listening to buffoons. A succession of ferocious invaders descended through the western passes, to prey on the defenceless wealth of Hindostan."[17]

The view of endemic Mughal decline was not new, though here it was stated in bold caricature, more forcefully than ever, and with the clear aim to absolve England of any role in the creation of the political vacuum of the eighteenth century. Macaulay credited the French, and the marquis Joseph-François Dupleix in particular, with first seeing "that it was possible to found an European empire on the ruins of the Mogul monarchy," and indeed with devising the system of indirect rule.[18] "He was perfectly aware that the most easy and convenient way in which an European adventurer could exercise sovereignty in India, was to govern the motions, and to speak through the mouth of some glittering puppet dignified by the title of Nabob or Nizam." Macaulay averred that by the middle of the century, "the empire was *de facto* dissolved." The French were about to capitalize on the opportunities created by this dissolution when "the valour and genius of an obscure English youth suddenly turned the tide of fortune."[19] When Clive entered into the military struggles of Madras, he almost single-handedly gave the English the upper hand.[20]

What the English needed now was an excuse for imperial expansion. This they achieved through "that great crime, memorable for its singular atrocity."[21] He meant the "Black Hole," which Mill had also recounted but passed over quickly, perhaps because he was aware of the extent to which Holwell had exaggerated his account for dramatic effect. For Macaulay, however, "Nothing in history or fiction, not even the story which Ugolino told in the sea of everlasting ice, after he had wiped his bloody lips on the scalp of his murderer, approaches the horrors which were recounted by the few survivors of that night."[22] Clive was given his moment in history, and when he won the Battle of Plassey he did so, in Macaulay's account, with little help from Mir Jafar, who joined him only at the last minute, when the outcome of the battle was already clear.

Despite the general tone of praise, even Macaulay could not overlook the growing hint of scandal, though his "very faults were those of a high and magnanimous spirit." Although Macaulay judged Clive wrong in forging a document for Amirchand, he understood the difficulties of "Oriental politics." "He knew," Macaulay wrote sympathetically, "that he had to deal with men destitute of what in Europe is called honour, with men who would give any promise without hesitation and break any promise without shame, and with men who would unscrupulously employ corruption, perjury, forgery, to compass their ends."[23] But while he condemned Clive for his forgery, he excused him for his greed. Echoing Clive's own defense of himself in Parliament, Macaulay noted that Clive took far less in presents and loot than he could have, and that his *jaghire* was a public reward for his manifold services. He dismissed the worries of contemporaries whose attacks had in any case not held sway before the "justice, moderation, and discernment of the Commons."[24]

Macaulay's putative liberalism might have upset many fellow Englishmen; for example, he argued against separate racial legal systems and proposed the possibility that, in time and once educated,

Indians would become consumers as well as citizens. But he effectively sealed an imperial historiography on the conquest of India. Most subsequent imperial historians followed his suit in praising Clive as the founder, neglecting the uneven record and contingent character of Clive's accomplishment while excusing his corruption in terms taken directly from his own parliamentary defense. James Mill's history, for instance, was criticized for its condemnation both of Indian civilization and of European Orientalist scholarship, but neglected by the colonial establishment when it came to his assessment of Clive; Macaulay's lyrical account of the history of British conquest, by contrast, was influential in part because of his liberal credentials.

Macaulay's account of Hastings was far more ambivalent than his measure of Clive.[25] Although he credited Hastings with preserving and extending an empire, and with founding a polity, he seriously questioned his judgment and his integrity. Hastings did end the disingenuous system of dual sovereignty that had been set up by Clive, but he did so by unjust and fraudulent means. Hastings did raise money for Company coffers when the financial situation was so dire in the years after the credit crash and the Bengal famine, but he did so again by using methods that were justifiably attacked by Philip Francis and Edmund Burke. Macaulay admired Hastings's intelligence, as well as his administrative acumen, his zeal on behalf of the state, and his personal generosity. And he recognized that without him all of Clive's accomplishments would have been for naught. But Hastings had been too consistently unprincipled to be a model hero for imperial history. Burke's indignation might have "acquired too much of the character of personal aversion," and he doubtless lost all sense of proportion and balance in his attack on Hastings, but his zeal was pure, his malice unaffected by political or personal interest. As Macaulay put it, "The plain truth is that Hastings had committed some great crimes."[26]

Mill too had been critical of Hastings. Apart from his conviction that "a failure in pecuniary obligation can never justify a war of extermination," he held Hastings accountable for increasing the level of Company debt, in large part because of the considerable expenses of warfare.[27] In his account of the trial, Mill was preoccupied with the problems and pitfalls of legal procedure, but he was largely sympathetic regarding Burke's case, and clearly found Hastings's conduct wanting on many counts. And yet even by the year that Mill's opus was first published, the general tide had turned on the subject of Hastings. By the time Mill's work was republished with the Orientalist H. H. Wilson's editorial revisions, in 1858, it would doubtless have seemed unexceptional to a British reading public to have Wilson interpolate his defense of Hastings with only cursory mention of possible misdeeds.

Wilson's editing of Mill's text has been commented on for his critique of Mill's disparaging sense of Indian civilization, but not for his softening of Mill's account of early British rule. Wilson accepted that Hastings had imperfections and faults, but made clear that he felt Hastings had committed no great crimes and misdemeanors. Even Hastings's minor faults paled before his accomplishments: "Clive acquired an empire; its perpetuation is due to Hastings." Wilson felt it to be "preposterous to tax Hastings with either tyranny or avarice," in his dealings with Chait Singh or even the begums of Awadh.[28] He wrote,

> Whether, therefore, we look to the origination of the systems
> which have prevailed in India since the days of Hastings, for the

collection of the revenue or the distribution of justice—to the
consolidation and durability of the political power of the Company, which he found feeble and tottering, and left impregna-
ble—or to the liberal spirit of inquiry and zeal for the public
service which he impressed indelibly upon the character of the
Company's servants, it cannot be denied that his administration has infinite claims upon the gratitude of the Company,
and if India be worth the having, upon the gratitude of Great
Britain.[29]

Macaulay's essay on Hastings was ostensibly a review of G. R.
Gleig's three-volume *Memoirs of the Right Honourable Warren
Hastings*, published in 1841.[30] Macaulay caricatured Gleig for having
outdone even the conventions of biographical hagiography when he
wrote of Hastings's generosity to the cuckolded husband of his future wife, but Gleig set the tone for subsequent considerations of
Hastings far more than Macaulay did. His unabashed approbation of
Hastings's Indian career ultimately rested on the now necessary understandings of imperial beginnings, concealed to protect the new
imperial mission of the British state. By the late nineteenth century,
any residual sense of embarrassment about imperial conquest had
virtually disappeared, as for example when Fitzjames Stephen wrote
two substantial volumes in which he tried to put to rest all of the
allegations concerning judicial malpractice in the execution of
Nandakumar.[31] Sir John Strachey proclaimed that the alleged "horrors" around the trial of Nandakumar, the "extermination" of the
Rohillas, and the spoliation of the begums of Awadh had "never occurred."[32] In such a context of imperial forgetting, even Macaulay's
bombastic prevarication about Hastings seemed dangerous. John
Morley, the secretary of state for India in the Liberal government

from 1906 to 1910, was seriously advised to ban both of Macaulay's essays on Clive and Hastings.[33]

The first *Cambridge History of India,* planned as a comprehensive six-volume history ranging from ancient India to the period of Indian empire, was published between 1922 and 1937. Edited by H. H. Dodwell, a respected professor of the history and culture of the British dominions in Asia at the University of London, it was a collaborative effort that gave voice to leading British academics' understanding of the dominant trends and trajectories of Indian history. Clive was cast very much as the hero of imperial origins, his military savvy and political genius critical for the years of early conquest between 1749 and 1765. Time after time, Clive's "resolute conduct," "insight," "swift mind," and "extraordinary gift of leadership" were judged as of foundational importance for empire. The deception of Amirchand and the taking of presents threw "an ugly air over the business," but Clive's motives were not corrupt ("they might have had more for the asking"), and "here our judgment must fall upon the age rather than upon the individuals."[34] Clive was given measured censure for setting a bad example; Hastings too was not blameless. And yet "the impeachment was a calamitous mistake and before it had gone very far it developed into something like a cruel wrong."[35] Parliament should have heard Burke's case and expressed a "temperate disapproval" of Hastings, but Hastings himself had confronted immense difficulties and in fact offered "magnificent services to his country."[36] Hastings should have been given a "grant of some high honour from the crown," and he could have been the prime architect of the reform of the whole system of the Indian government. Instead, "the impeachment of Hastings was an anachronism, a cumbrous method of inflicting most unmerited suffering on one of the greatest Englishmen of his time, something very like a travesty of justice."[37] Burke had surrendered to a "violent animosity against the accused," refusing to "accord him even those rights and facilities which it would have been unrighteous to deny to the worst of criminals." And so "perhaps the greatest Englishman who ever ruled India, a man who with some ethical defects possessed in superabundant measure the mobile and fertile brain, the tireless energy and the lofty fortitude which distinguishes only the supreme statesman, was left with his name cleared but his fortunes ruined, and every hope of future distinction and even employment taken from him."[38]

Dodwell's history thus reflects the kind of uncritical hagiography of the founders and the guardians of empire that came to characterize imperial historiography, even when cast in the relatively measured prose of official academic history.[39] If Hastings had seemed compromised to Macaulay, Burke was the one with the deepest flaws by the time British history had responded to the first serious nationalist mobilizations against imperial rule in India. What was already "unreasonable violence" for Seeley became, for Dodwell, "violent animosity," and in this basic denunciation Burke's serious questioning of empire was forgotten along with the violence of the conquest and occupation itself. The idea of empire's importance, as well as of its permanence, seemed increasingly to depend on a view in which both Clive and Hastings were to be seen as the uncontested heroes of Britain's imperial past.

Even Seeley had believed that since Britain's government of India was a good thing for both India and Britain, the legacy of Clive and Hastings had to be seen in a positive historical light. The only real

worry about Clive was that his actions had placed an immense burden on Britain's shoulders. Nevertheless, Seeley advised that the
burden of empire be accepted as the inheritance of the past, and
that for India's sake, if not for Britain's, it would be necessary "to govern her [India] as if we were to govern her for ever."[40] It is not, therefore, insignificant that Seeley is to the present day referred to as the
"founder of the field of Imperial history," and his work regarded as a
"lasting historiographical influence," not just for his claims about
the importance of empire, but also for his abiding commitment to
the principle of liberty over despotism.[41]

Seeley's continued importance is confirmed in the new five-volume *Oxford History of the British Empire* (1998–1999). In his introduction to the volume on "historiography," William Roger Louis,
the general editor of the *History*, chose three works that were "especially significant for the background of the volume": Gibbon's *Decline and Fall of the Roman Empire* (1776–1788), Macaulay's *History
of England* (1849–1855), and Seeley's *Expansion of England* (1883).
As Louis explained, the three works "have a central bearing on the
interpretation of Empire's end, its purpose as well as its beginning,
and they all continue to inspire debate."[42] Seeley's work was held to
be especially important, not least because he had the foresight to
note the contradiction between democracy in white settler colonies
and despotism in India. And yet despite this apparent criticism of
empire, Seeley viewed British rule as immeasurably better than Indian rule, and India as an imperial burden as well as a permanent responsibility.

In part, Seeley was prescient enough to understand that Britain
would not be able to maintain its world dominance without an empire to rival either the United States or Russia, but in his call for a

global "Greater Britain" he accorded no more political recognition to contemporary India than he gave it historical recognition in his view of the Indian context for conquest. In invoking Seeley as a progressive historical figure in relation both to his sense of imperial origins and his concern about imperial governance, Louis betrays the continued acceptance on the part of most imperial historians that empire—whether good or bad for either colonizers or colonized—was a legitimate political and economic form. Empire is written about as if it can be evaluated "neutrally" now that the passions (and the promises) of anticolonial nationalism have subsided. Somehow, despotism continues to be more acceptable when exercised in imperial contexts than in European ones, where the same kind of neutrality would be considered unseemly, as we see consistently in the historical evaluation of fascist regimes in Europe. Neither fascism nor slavery could ever be written about in the terms used for empire.

This conceit of historical "neutrality" has in fact characterized the writing of imperial history from the early nineteenth century to the present, whether in the hands of Mill, Macaulay, and Seeley, or more recently in the work of Holden Furber, Peter J. Marshall, and William Roger Louis. The *Oxford History of the British Empire* is a monument to the ideal of neutrality in which the costs and benefits of empire are still debated and the problems of empire are still understood almost exclusively from the vantage of Europe. More specifically, the history of the Company continues to be written as if the principal issues had to do with managerial incompetence and administrative failure, rather than its larger implications and effects. The devastations of imperial rule on the colonized, and the extent to which the struggles and challenges of postcolonial regimes are themselves critical legacies of imperial rule, are discounted even as these questions are subordinated to discussions about the effects of empire on Europe. Once again, imperial history undermines the significance of its own subject. Even where empire is the principal academic subject, it is accorded only a marginal historical role, for the claim that through its imperial history Europe itself was critically formed and launched into modernity—whether in economic, political, social, or cultural respects—is still hardly thinkable.

By ignoring these pressing postcolonial questions, imperial history of this kind ironically diminishes the importance of empire for both the metropole and the colony. If, as I have argued here, fundamental notions of European modernity—ideas of virtue, corruption, nationalism, sovereignty, economic freedom, governmentality, tradition, and history itself—derive in large part from the imperial encounter, then even Seeley's conviction that most of England's eighteenth-century history happened in the colonies must be taken far more literally. For openers, imperial history must engage the insularity and autonomy of the sovereign assumptions of national history. The British state only began to reform the power and privilege of old corruption once it had to respond to the public outcry over the corruption engaged in by English nabobs in India, who became disturbing symbols of the excesses of capitalism. The impeachment trial of Warren Hastings was a critical moment in the delineation of the relationship between the managerial constraints considered fundamental to early imperial trade and the final resolution of the imperial project as an extension of the national interest. The modern idea of sovereignty developed not just in tandem with the nation-state and the metropolitan struggle between contractual accountability and political right, but also in tension with the history of im-

perial expansion and the contradictions that emerged around different publics and constituencies for political rule. The foundational
significance of free trade and the idea of an open economy emerged
in relationship to a history of monopoly capital in the imperial theater, which facilitated the substitution of the extra-economic controls of a colonial state (and the political economy of empire more
generally) for the earlier monopoly guarantees made to a national
trading company. The modern state was born in part from distinct
colonial roots—from the specification of property rights in relation
to the revenue needs of an expansionist state, to the development of
legal and administrative means to compensate for the failure to provide even the promise of popular sovereignty (because an external
imperial regime, however representative the colonial state might be,
is always seen as despotic). Modern history in Britain emerged out
of an imperial mix in which the scandals of early conquest in India
were as important as Burke claimed they were, even though he left
out the earliest ones.

When these scandals were forgotten, they became the repressed
residue of empire, the necessary detritus of the consolidation of the
nationalist ideals of state and sovereignty. The idea of Europe itself
depended on the sealing off of its borders from the continued recognition of its implication in and dependence on the role of empire
in capital accumulation and the broad array of opportunities, influences, and resources from the greater world. The opposition of Europe and its other is the result of that denial, another artifact of
empire. Even more literally, Europe was built from the riches of
its global possessions. The commandeering of these resources ultimately required the mystifications of empire that had begun so
firmly to congeal in the last years of the eighteenth century. First

Europe "became" itself through imperial conquest; then it veiled its dependence on the world outside by legitimating and naturalizing empire, ultimately representing it as at best nothing more than a burden and a terrible responsibility.

The survival of the basic assumptions and perspectives in imperial history has continued to conceal the extent of Europe's dependence on empire, at the same time that it has eroded any serious recognition of the extent of its influence on the world it colonized. The critical sense of the imperial past that was once generally accepted among eighteenth-century historians as various as Alexander Dow, Robert Orme, and Ghulam Hussain during the early years of colonial conquest—and was revived and immeasurably enhanced by the writings of nationalist and now postcolonial historians—has been consistently downplayed in much imperial history. Recent historical works restate the imperial assurance that the economic rapacity of Company traders, whether in the form of official or private commerce, was unleashed on a level playing field with local commerce, and could hardly have been responsible for exacerbating local conditions. These views often purport to accord agency to the colonized but instead displace the structural conditions of imperialism onto a generalized conception of global capital that has lost any critical relationship to the history of empire.[43] Even when critical of the role of capital, these perspectives often end up tacitly accepting that empire really did succeed in expanding the economic vitality as well as the productivity of commerce in India, for India as well as Britain.

When imperial history loses any sense of what empire meant to those who were colonized, it becomes complicit in the history of empire itself.[44] It is one thing to argue that the experience and ideological presuppositions of the colonizers are deserving of historical attention; that has been my aim here. It is altogether different to assert that because there were perceived "affinities," say, between metropolitan and colonial elites, the fundamental notions of empire were not driven by racial and cultural prejudice.[45] Imperial weakness and vulnerability were notions that appealed to colonizers, but they were cruel misrepresentations of history to any among the vast population of the colonized—including most of the colonial elite—whose histories were so dominated by empire.[46] The frozen paradigms of imperial history, whether presented as revisions of imperial or of British history, have resurfaced with alarming ubiquity in recent years, in a wide range of earnest efforts to restore historical balance to the question of empire.[47]

But not even the most neutral or reactive assessments of empire's effects adequately prepare postcolonial readers for the recent publications by the historian Niall Ferguson, who has received considerable attention and acclaim in recent years.[48] For Ferguson, who deftly begins his account by mentioning a few of the most foul examples of imperial atrocity to signal the objectivity of his account, British empire played a necessary and even benevolent role in the modernization of the world. By modernization he refers both to the domain of politics—especially in the extension of the rule of law and the belief in the primacy of democratic political systems—and to culture, with the anglicization of the world having been, by his account, a most excellent accomplishment for all. He acknowledges with sadness, though little concern, that it was in fact this forced induction of traditional peoples to cultural modernity à la Anglaise that "provoked the most violent nineteenth-century revolt against imperial rule."[49] Imperial rule not only meant good rule (even as Ferguson never thinks to doubt imperial accounts of regimes it conquered or over-threw as examples of bad rule), but also ushered in an era of eco-nomic progress. Ferguson writes: "Without the spread of British rule around the world, it is hard to believe that the structures of liberal capitalism would have been so successfully established in so many different economies around the world . . . the nineteenth century Empire undeniably pioneered free trade, free capital movements, and, with the abolition of slavery, free labour."[50]

In particular, Ferguson argues that "there would certainly not have been so much free trade between the 1840s and the 1930s had it not been for the British Empire."[51] Not even he would contest that the economic benefits to the United Kingdom were huge—Fergu-son correctly notes that the benefit was as high as 6.5 percent of the gross national product—but the idea either that trade was free for India or that the benefits were distributed equally throughout the global economy is hardly, as Ferguson confidently asserts, "be-yond dispute." Ferguson even defends indentured labor, despite the great hardships suffered by laborers, on the grounds that the "mobilization of cheap and probably underemployed Asian labor" had significant "economic value."[52] For Ferguson, imperialism was the means for the inauguration and spread of global capitalism, and that was a very good thing indeed. It was certainly advantageous for Britain, but what economic value did all this have for cheap, under-employed Asian labor?

Accordingly, the book dresses up and resuscitates imperial views of the world. Lands and peoples that had been conquered and ab-sorbed into imperial regimes are likened unproblematically to rogue states and terrorist groups. The political and economic difficulties of nations as various as Bangladesh and Pakistan or Rwanda and Zaire are blamed on a precolonial past, with colonial rule's principal problem having been its failure to complete its civilizing mission. Despite the historical shortcomings of the account, it taps into a contemporary malaise with the critique both of the West in general and of the imperial past more specifically. And since Ferguson has taken on the burden of advising U.S. policy makers (and citizens more generally) about the lessons British empire can provide for current foreign policy, it also taps into a restless desire to make the historical burdens of empire especially relevant to (and positive influences on) the current war on terror and Islam. According to Ferguson's book, the burden the United States has inherited from the United Kingdom is to continue to spread the benefits of capitalism and democracy "overseas." Since "just like the British Empire before it, the American Empire unfailingly acts in the name of liberty, even when its own self-interest is manifestly uppermost," all this not only works to exempt empire from the historical burdens of domination and exploitation; it also serves to explain why empire continues to be a necessary form of rule and civilizational progress.[53]

Such history also neglects the myriad scandals that have been as much a part of the invasion and occupation of Iraq as they were part of the original conquest and occupation of India on the part of the British. It thus seems all the more critical to refocus our attention on the history of empire, cutting through the unquestioned assumptions of imperial history whenever it mistakes colonial ideology for balanced history, a litany of managerial crises for the political history of empire, the genuine perils of empire for its relentless historical imperatives. In our postcolonial world, it can surely no longer be acceptable to cast the racial policies of colonial rule in terms of a civilizing mission, even as we can no longer innocently describe im-

perial despotism as benevolent. If British empire is praised for introducing free trade into India, it is therefore necessary to remember
not just the economic history of corruption and extraction, but also
the ways in which the demise of monopolistic national trading companies hardly led the way for the creation of neutral market conditions, given the continuation of imperial control over markets in every possible sense.

Here the eighteenth century becomes especially critical, for it
was the time when both empire and nation were themselves being
formed in the crucible of a global history that could not yet conceal
its contradictions and conflicts any better than it could hide its rapacity and its scandal. Burke was clear about why he had to draw
the veil over the origins of empire even while shining a penetrating
and critical light on the atrocities and scandals of imperial conduct.
And Seeley was right to observe that England suffered from national
amnesia about its imperial past, though he was unable to see that
this amnesia was necessary if empire was to thrive. When we look
through the fog of absentmindedness, as Burke and Seeley in their
own ways invite us to do, we recover both a sense of the constitutive
importance of empire for modern Europe and the record of violence and scandal that mars all imperial encounters, especially for
the myriad populations who were subjected not just to imperial
rule, but also to the disingenuous imperial conceit that empire was a
burden for the colonizer. The burden of empire was placed squarely
on the shoulders of the colonized. The shrouding of this fact is the
scandal that should not be allowed to repeat itself, either in our historical interpretations of the past, or in present efforts to appropriate
this history for the use of new forms of global domination.

Notes

Illustration Credits

Index

⇥ *Notes* ⇤

Prologue

1. For the original account, see Jonathan Z. Holwell, *A Genuine Narrative of the Deplorable Deaths of the English Gentlemen and Others Who Were Suffocated in the Black-Hole in Fort William, at Calcutta, in the Kingdom of Bengal; in the Night Succeeding the 20th Day of June, 1756,* in Holwell, *India Tracts* (London: T. Becket, 1757), quotations on pp. 392, 387, 388.

2. Ibid, p. 392. In an analysis of the Black Hole incident, Partha Chatterjee demonstrates how one of Holwell's central concerns in his narrative is in fact the need for self-control on the part of the colonizing European, suggesting thereby that much of the text is written as a moral for the exercise of imperial power. While this is certainly so, he also reminds us that the first purpose, or at least use, of the text was to justify the exercise of imperial power itself, something Holwell intended to take full personal political advantage of as well. See Partha Chatterjee, "A Secret Veil," unpublished manuscript in the author's possession.

3. Holwell, *Genuine Narrative*, p. 398.

4. Ibid., pp. 398, 397. Perhaps one of the most intriguing of the contradictions here revolves around the figure of a Mrs. Carey, who accompanied her husband to the prison, and then was said by Holwell to have been kidnapped, with the implication of certain rape, by her captors. Subsequent accounts suggest that Mrs. Carey was not, as Holwell initially suggested, the only woman in the Black Hole, but in Holwell's own account, the scenes of men disrobing and dying are undisturbed by any sexual tension or embarrassment. And the implication of kidnap and rape has been shown to be false. See the discussion in Betty Joseph, *Reading the East India Company, 1720–1840: Colonial Currencies of Gender* (Chicago: University of Chicago Press, 2004), pp. 71–73.

5. Holwell, *Genuine Narrative*.

6. Iris MacFarlane has argued that even the few possible victims of the Black Hole in all probability either disappeared or died in the chaos of Calcutta's capture rather than in prison. See MacFarlane, *The Black Hole; or, The Makings of a Legend* (London: George Allen and Unwin, 1975).

7. For the most serious account of the legend and its context, see Brijen K. Gupta, *Sirajuddaullah and The East India Company, 1756–1757: Background to the Foundation of British Power in India* (Leiden, Neth.: E. J. Brill, 1966), pp. 70–80. Gupta has analyzed the multiple accounts and established clearly that the number of Europeans who might actually have died in the Black Hole incident is as low as 18, out of a group of 39 who were taken prisoner (a group that could not have been more than 64 persons, given the number of unaccounted-for Europeans in Calcutta at the time of the capture).

8. Captain Rennie, *Reflections on the Loss of Calcutta*, 1756 (India Office Records, British Library).

9. Ranajit Guha began a recent book with the claim, "There was one Indian battle that Britain never won. It was a battle for appropriation of the Indian past." See Guha, *Dominance without Hegemony: History and Power in Colonial India* (Cambridge, Mass.: Harvard University Press, 1997), p. 1. I am not contesting that claim directly here, though I have argued elsewhere that imperial history has had rather more influence than Guha would like to accept on the structures and categories of historical self-representation. See Dirks, *The Hollow Crown: Ethnohistory of an Indian Kingdom* (Cambridge: Cambridge University Press, 1987), and *Castes of Mind: Colonialism and the Making of Modern India* (Princeton, N.J.: Princeton University Press, 2001). My argument here, however, is about the constitutive significance of imperial history for world history, and it is in fact in accord with Guha's own writing about the categories and assumptions of world history. Guha treats Hegel as the founding text of world history in his even more recent book *History at the Limit of World History* (New York: Columbia University Press, 2002).

1. Scandal

1. Edmund Burke, "Speech on Mr. Fox's East India Bill," December 1, 1783, in Peter Marshall, ed., *The Writings and Speeches of Edmund Burke*, vol. 5: *India: Madras and Bengal, 1774–85* (Oxford: Clarendon Press, 2000), p. 403.

2. Peter Marshall, *East India Fortunes: The British in Bengal in the Eighteenth Century* (Oxford: Clarendon Press, 1976), p. 179.

3. For the speech vilifying Benfield, see Burke, "Speech on the Debts of the Nawab of Arcot," *The Works of the Right Honorable Edmund Burke*, 8th ed., vol. 11 (Boston: Little, Brown, 1884).

4. See Lucy Sutherland, *The East India Company in Eighteenth Century Politics* (Oxford: Clarendon Press, 1952).

5. See Samuel Foote, *The Nabobs: A Comedy in Three Acts* (New York: D. Longworth, 1813).

6. Quoted in Philip Lawson, *The East India Company: A History* (New York: Longman, 1993), p. 120.

7. Philip Harling, *The Waning of "Old Corruption": The Politics of Economical Reform in Britain, 1779–1846* (Oxford: Clarendon Press, 1996), p. 18.

8. For a discussion of sovereign rights in this case, see H. V. Bowen, *Revenue and Reform: The Indian Problem in British Politics, 1757–1773* (Cambridge: Cambridge University Press, 1991), pp. 64–66.

9. News of Haidar Ali's success in the south was especially worrisome. See ibid., pp. 76–77.

10. Lawson, *East India Company*, p. 121.

11. A. Francis Stuart, H. Walpole, J. Doran, et al., *The Last Journals of Horace Walpole during the Reign of George III, from 1771–1783* (London: J. Lane, 1910), pp. i, 72.

12. Egerton Manuscripts, vol. 218, ff. 149–151 (India Office Records, British Library).

13. Clive Manuscripts, G.37/4 (India Office Records, British Library).

14. Ibid.

15. Ibid.

16. There are conflicting stories, some saying Clive shot himself, others that he slit his own throat, and others insisting that the suicide had only to do with his bad health. But it seems clear that the precipitous fall in his political fortunes contributed to his distaste for life.

17. Peter J. Marshall, *The Impeachment of Warren Hastings* (Oxford: Oxford University Press, 1965), pp. 14–15.

18. On curtailing territorial expansion, see Lawson, *East India Company*, p. 128.

19. See Ranajit Guha, *A Rule of Property for Bengal: An Essay on the Idea of Permanent Settlement* (Durham, N.C.: Duke University Press, 1996).

20. For the financial figures, see C. H. Phillips, *The East India Company, 1784–1834* (Manchester, Eng.: Manchester University Press, 1961), p. 124.

21. See my argument in *Castes of Mind: Colonialism and the Making of Modern India* (Princeton, N.J.: Princeton University Press, 2001).

22. Quoted in Lawson, *East India Company*, p. 146.

23. For an example of the reach of indirect rule, see my *The Hollow Crown: Ethnohistory of an Indian Kingdom* (Cambridge: Cambridge University Press, 1987). For a general account of the history of the British annexation of India before 1857, see Michael Fisher, ed., *The Politics of the British Annexation of India: 1757–1857* (Delhi: Oxford University Press, 1993).

24. This perspective is found in even some of the best works in the field, including Bowen, *Revenue and Reform*, and Lawson, *East India Company*.

25. For one such notable effort, see Sudipta Sen, *Distant Sovereignty: Na-*

tional Imperialism and the Origins of British India (New York: Routledge, 2002). Also see Michael Fisher, *Counterflows to Colonialism: Indians in Britain, c. 1600–1857* (New Delhi: Permanent Black, 2003).

26. See my critique in the coda to *Castes of Mind.*

27. Even important exceptions, such as Linda Colley's *The Britons: Forging the Nation, 1707–1837* (New Haven, Conn.: Yale University Press, 1992), betray the problem here. While Colley has been innovative in suggesting the importance of the East India Company as a force contributing to the integration of Scots into Britain, she has downplayed the constitutive significance of imperial activities in other respects. In a review essay, she has elaborated on her historical suspicion of Edward Said's suggestion that empire had major or determining importance in early modern British history—see Colley, "The Imperial Embrace," *Yale Review* 81, no. 4 (October 1993). More typical is Peter Marshall's skepticism about the effects of empire on Britain's history, as in his article "No Fatal Impact? The Elusive History of Imperial Britain," *London Times Literary Supplement*, March 12, 1993, pp. 8–10. Even new and revisionist work in British history continues to ignore the imperial context, as for example in Philip Harling's recent monograph *Waning of "Old Corruption,"* which despite its critical engagement with questions of corruption in eighteenth-century Britain has no mention of Warren Hastings, and only one of India. Even in works where concerns about empire play an important role, India and the East India Company are often little mentioned, as for example in Kathleen Wilson's *The Sense of the People: Politics, Culture, and Imperialism in England, 1715–1785* (Cambridge: Cambridge University Press, 1995).

28. This is a different kind of imperial history to be sure, one that has dramatically, and critically, expanded the historiographic borders of British history. See, as perhaps the best representative example of these works, Kathleen Wilson, *A New Imperial History: Culture, Identity, and Modernity in Britain and the Empire, 1660–1840* (Cambridge: Cambridge University Press, 2004). See in particular her introduction, where she notes, "The new imperial history presented here is very much a work in progress, but its conditions of possibility are grounded in the willingness of scholars from different disciplines to take seriously questions of cultural difference and their imperial frames in the long eighteenth century" (p. 26). For a general argument about the significance of empire to the history of Britain in the seventeenth and eighteenth centuries, see David Armitage, *The Ideological Origins of the British Empire* (Cambridge: Cambridge University Press, 2000). For a discussion of the relationship of history and nation, see my "History as a Sign of the Modern," *Public Culture* 2, no. 2 (Spring 1990).

29. Kathleen Wilson, *An Island Race: Englishness, Empire, and Gender in the Eighteenth Century* (New York: Routledge, 2003), p. 17.

30. For an early example, see the preface to Marshall, *Impeachment of Warren Hastings*: "Since 1947, however, the incentive to pass judgement on British India by acquitting or condemning Hastings is obviously much reduced, and the historian can concentrate on explanations rather than verdicts . . . Detachment also makes it possible to do justice to the intentions of both Burke and Hastings and to appreciate the suffering inflicted by the impeachment on both of them" (p. xiv). My interest here is not in dismissing either the intentions or the suffering of Burke and Hastings—I will in fact consider both—but rather in suggesting that this kind of detachment has not always been productive for historical inquiry; indeed, in many cases it has merely renormalized empire in the historiographical literature. The implications for general views can be readily seen in a recent debate between Rudrangshu Mukherjee and Peter J. Marshall, in Patrick Tuck, ed., *The East India Company: 1600–1858*, vol. 4: *Trade, Finance and Power* (New York: Routledge, 1998), pp. 195–245.

31. W. R. Louis, A. M. Low, et al., *The Oxford History of the British Empire*, vol. 1 (Oxford: Oxford University Press, 1998). W. R. Louis is general editor of the five-volume series, published from 1998 to 2000.

32. Colonial studies grew initially as a reaction to the older imperial history, in part out of the influence of anthropological work on colonial societies, and in part from movements in literary and critical theory; it has also been the focus of historical projects such as those represented by "subaltern studies," a historical collective initially directed by Ranajit Guha. For representative works, see Edward Said, *Orientalism* (New York: Random House, 1978); Bernard Cohn, *An Anthropologist among the Historians and Other Essays* (Delhi: Oxford University Press, 1987); Nicholas Dirks, ed., *Colonialism and Culture* (Ann Arbor: University of Michigan Press, 1992); Gyan Prakash, ed., *After Colonialism: Imperial Histories and Postcolonial Displacements* (Princeton, N.J.: Princeton University Press, 1995); Frederick Cooper and Ann Laura Stoler, eds., *Tensions of Empire: Colonial Cultures in a Bourgeois World* (Berkeley: University of California Press, 1997); Partha Chatterjee, *Nationalist Thought and the Colonial World: A Derivative Discourse?* (London: Zed Books, 1986); Gayatri Chakravorty Spivak, *A Critique of Postcolonial Reason: Toward a History of the Vanishing Present* (Cambridge, Mass.: Harvard University Press, 1999); Ranajit Guha, *Elementary Aspects of Peasant Insurgency in Colonial India* (Delhi: Oxford University Press, 1983); and Ranajit Guha, ed., *Subaltern Studies* (Delhi: Oxford University Press, 1982–).

33. See, for example, Partha Chatterjee, *The Nation and Its Fragments:*

Colonial and Postcolonial Histories (Princeton, N.J.: Princeton University Press, 1993).

34. See Edward Said, *Culture and Imperialism* (New York: Knopf, 1993); Bernard Porter, *The Absent-Minded Imperialists: Empire, Society, and Culture in Britain* (Oxford: Oxford University Press, 2004); and Thomas R. Metcalf, *Ideologies of the Raj* (Cambridge: Cambridge University Press, 1995).

35. See, for example, Ranajit Guha, *Dominance without Hegemony: History and Power in Colonial India* (Cambridge, Mass.: Harvard University Press, 1997).

36. Empire has increasingly been seen as a "laboratory of modernity." The colonial encounter was made up of a set of histories that have helped produce not only many of the commodities that have become so critical to the modern world, but also fundamental ideas of citizenship, political rights, culture, race, sexuality, health, urban planning, and state discipline. See Bernard S. Cohn, *Colonialism and Its Forms of Knowledge* (Princeton, N.J.: Princeton University Press, 1996); Paul Rabinow, *French Modern: Norms and Forms of the Social Environment* (Cambridge, Mass.: MIT Press, 1989); Richard Helgerson, *Forms of Nationhood: The Elizabethan Writing of England* (Chicago: University of Chicago Press, 1992); Ann Stoler, *Race and the Education of Desire: Foucault's History of Sexuality and the Colonial Order of Things* (Durham, N.C.: Duke University Press, 1995); Jean Comaroff and John Comaroff, *Of Revelation and Revolution* (Chicago: University of Chicago Press, 1991); and Catherine Hall, *Civilising Subjects: Metropole and Colony in the English Imagination, 1830–1867* (Chicago: University of Chicago Press, 2002). In the field of the historical anthropology of empire, most studies so far have focused on periods beginning only in the mid nineteenth century, and even the studies that take on earlier periods have not sufficiently worked through the radical potential of Fanon's critical insight that Europe is the creation of the third world. If "Europe" (as we understand it in the conceptual terms familiar to those who teach and study "western" civilization) emerged in its modern form as the precipitate of its multiple, and fundamental, encounters with the "non-west," it is imperative that we begin to chart the historical conditions of western modernity from the seventeenth and eighteenth centuries.

37. For a recent study of scandal in eighteenth- and nineteenth-century British politics that was published just as I was completing the main draft of this manuscript, see Anna Clark, *Scandal: The Sexual Politics of the British Constitution* (Princeton, N.J.: Princeton University Press, 2004). Clark writes primarily about sexual scandals, but argues that they are about a lot more than sex. As she notes, "The secret becomes a scandal when it triggers a widespread public controversy . . . Scandals raise the

question of what politics is really about . . . in fact, scandal opened up politics by revealing corruption and by making political debate accessible to a wider audience" (pp. 2–3). In retelling the way in which Burke used sexual scandal to paint Hastings in the most critical light, as one of her chief examples, Clark anticipates and supports one of my major contentions here, namely that Burke used the trial to create "new justifications for empire" (p. 17).

38. Cited in Robin Blackburn, *The Overthrow of Colonial Slavery, 1776–1848* (London: Verso Books, 1988), p. 148.

39. Eric Williams, *Capitalism and Slavery* (Chapel Hill: University of North Carolina Press, 1944).

40. David Brion Davis, *The Problem of Slavery in the Age of Revolution, 1776–1823* (Ithaca, N.Y.: Cornell University Press, 1975); see also David Brion Davis, *The Problem of Slavery in Western Culture* (New York: Oxford University Press, 1966).

41. Christopher L. Brown, "Empire without Slaves: British Concepts of Emancipation in the Age of the American Revolution," in *William and Mary Quarterly*, 3d ser., vol. 56, no. 2 (April 1999): 273–306, quotation on p. 306.

42. For a view on this issue that combines utopian political thought with a sustained critique of imperial history, see Michael Hardt and Antonio Negri, *Empire* (Cambridge, Mass.: Harvard University Press, 1999). But for a more realistic assessment of the problems of globalization, see Joseph E. Stiglitz, *Globalization and Its Discontents* (New York: W. W. Norton, 2002).

2. Corruption

1. "Commission of Appointment from the Court of Directors to Streynsham Master," Master Diary, vol. 1, p. 213, paras. 41–42, quoted in Brijen Gupta's *Sirajuddaullah and the East India Company, 1756–1757: Background to the Foundation of British Power in India* (London: E. J. Brill, 1966), p. 11.

2. Quoted in Gupta, *Sirajuddaullah and the East India Company*, p. 13.

3. K. N. Chaudhuri, *The Trading World of Asia and the East India Company, 1660–1760* (Cambridge: Cambridge University Press, 1978), p. 507.

4. Stocks in the East India Company, the Bank of England, and the ill-fated South Sea Company were the only ones always quoted on the market. See Lucy Sutherland, *The East India Company in Eighteenth Century Politics* (Oxford: Clarendon Press, 1952), pp. 24–25. Sutherland's book is in fact an extraordinarily detailed excavation of the political reach of the Company in domestic politics throughout the eighteenth century; despite her acceptance of the "values" of the time, which works to undermine her critique, her skeptical history—the result in part of her

Namierite training—makes for an unusually critical account of the role of empire, if not exactly in those terms.

5. Peter Marshall, *East India Fortunes: The British in Bengal in the Eighteenth Century* (Oxford: Clarendon Press, 1976), p. 229.
6. Thomas Macaulay, *Prose and Poetry*, ed. G. M. Young (Cambridge, Mass.: Harvard University Press), p. 308. Macaulay's heroic view of Clive has continued, in Britain even to the present day. As the historian Tapan Raychaudhuri has wryly noted, "The British school child who reads in his history text book of Lord Clive's wonderful achievements should also be told that the man was a criminal by any definition." Raychaudhuri, *Perceptions, Emotions, Sensibilities: Essays on India's Colonial and Post-Colonial Experiences* (New Delhi: Oxford University Press, 1999), pp. x–xi.
7. Despite the plethora of documents available about Clive's life, it is difficult to assess many parts of his career because of the extent to which the archive itself, beginning with the extensive histories of Robert Orme, is so embedded within the natural assumptions of imperial expansionism. Biographies, of which there are many, are even less helpful, since the biographical tradition has been so uniformly hagiographical. Even critical comments about Clive's excesses, his intemperance or greed, his military shortcomings or his political failures, tend to be used to balance accounts that are generally awed by his extraordinary life and its accomplishments. I shall return to Clive in Chapter 7, where I will comment further about the historiographical tradition concerning empire and its "founders."
8. The first authority for Clive's early career was Robert Orme's narrative *History of the War in Indostan*, published in 1764. Orme's account was especially responsible for making the Arcot siege a mythic account of Clive's precocious military genius and significance. Orme follows Clive's story up to 1757, but in his later accounts makes clear his growing disapproval of the methods and manners of his young hero. In the end, Orme never finished his promised grand history of Clive's full career, nor indeed of the final conquest of Bengal. For more on Orme, see Chapter 7.
9. Macaulay, *Prose and Poetry*, p. 322.
10. On indications of Clive's military incompetence, see Percival Spear, *Master of Bengal: Clive and His India* (London: Thames and Hudson, 1975), pp. 76–79.
11. Sutherland, *East India Company*, p. 64.
12. Marshall, *East Indian Fortunes*, p. 165.
13. Ibid., p. 166.
14. Quoted in Spear, *Master of Bengal*, p. 111.

15. See Sudipta Sen's *Empire of Free Trade: The East India Company and The Making of the Colonial Marketplace* (Philadelphia: University of Pennsylvania Press, 1998), a fascinating description of the cultural economy of trade and exchange in late-eighteenth-century Bengal. Sen makes the compelling argument that the Company servants used the political meanings of trade in these commodities to further their own political aspirations, a history that gets lost in the rhetoric of free trade and the naturalization of a colonial archive of economic "exchanges" that succumbed to the opacity of imperial history by the early nineteenth century.

16. The phrase "empire of free trade" is Sudipta Sen's. See ibid.

17. Quoted in ibid., p. 86.

18. Appendix to G. Forrest's *The Life of Lord Clive*, vol. 2, (London: Cassell & Co., 1978), pp. 412–414, marked Calcutta, January 7, 1759.

19. Quoted in Spear, *Master of Bengal*, p. 119.

20. Quoted in Marshall, *East Indian Fortunes*, p. 156.

21. Rajat Kanta Ray, "Indian Society and British Supremacy," in Peter J. Marshall, ed., *Oxford History of the British Empire*, vol. 2: *The Eighteenth Century* (Oxford: Oxford University Press, 1998), p. 514.

22. Alexander Dow, "An Enquiry into the State of Bengal, with a Plan for Restoring that Province to Its Former Prosperity and Splendor," preface to vol. 3 of *The History of Hindostan* (Dublin: Luke White, 1792); William Bolts, *Considerations on India Affairs, Particularly Respecting the Present State of Bengal Dependencies* (London: n.p., 1772).

23. See the account of the passing of the Regulating Act in Sutherland, *East India Company*, pp. 240–268.

24. The quotations are from Clive Papers, Eur. Mss. G37, box 4 (India Office Records, British Library).

25. "The nabob, Macaulay tells us, was in the popular conception of the late eighteenth century a gentleman with a tawny complexion, a bad liver, and a worse heart. Clive might describe him in the House of Commons as a hospitable friend, a humane master, and a benevolent citizen, and claim that none was flagitious enough for Mr. Foote to mimic at the Haymarket. But he spoke too soon. In a little while that actor was presenting Sir Matthew Mite, surrounded by all the pomp of Asia, profusely scattering the spoils of conquered provinces, committing to memory the latest oaths, and learning to flourish the dice-box with a fashionable air. The caricature was intended to represent the hero of Plassey himself." William Dodwell, *The Nabobs of Madras* (London: Williams and Norgate, 1926), p. ix.

26. See, for example, Spear, *Master of Bengal*.

27. Quoted in Sutherland, *East India Company*, p. 54.

28. Quotations are from Clive Papers, Eur. Mss. G37, box 15.

29. Ibid.
30. Quoted in Sutherland, *East India Company*, p. 256.
31. Spear, *Master of Bengal*, p. 192; H. V. Bowen, *Revenue and Reform: The Indian Problem in British Politics, 1757–1773* (Cambridge: Cambridge University Press, 1991), p. 173. George III was upset at the about-face, writing to North, "I own I am amazed that private interest could make so many forget what they owe to their country." Quoted in Sutherland, *East India Company*, p. 258.
32. *The Correspondence of Edmund Burke* (Cambridge: Cambridge University Press, 1960), vol. 2, p. 434.
33. Sutherland, *East India Company*, p. 262.
34. Bowen, *Revenue and Reform*, pp. 187–189.
35. I am grateful to Philip Stern for noting the scandalousness of suicide during that era.
36. Quoted in Peter Marshall, *The Impeachment of Warren Hastings* (London: Oxford University Press, 1965), p. 1.
37. Consisting of 231 villages to the south and west of Madras, the tract around Poonamalee encompassed some 330 square miles.
38. Quoted in J. D. Gurney, "The Debts of the Nawab of Arcot, 1763–1776," Ph.D. thesis, Oxford University, 1968, p. 79.
39. Ibid., p. 83. See also the Madras Despatches, March 17, 1769, pp. 678–680 (India Office Records, British Library).
40. When Dupre left Madras a few years later, he was said to be worth £360,000.
41. John Macpherson was the brother of James Macpherson, Scottish man of letters and compiler, or forger, of the Gaelic epic *Fingal*, first published in 1763. A well-connected man, friend of such figures as Adam Fergusson, John claimed to have succeeded in persuading the *darbar* of his potential usefulness. John Gurney writes, "He was in his training and background different from most of the adventurers and bankrupts who attached themselves to the darbar at Chepauk. Impressed by his knowledge of English politics and his plausible, confident manner, the nawab, according to Macpherson's account, gave him a letter for Lord Chatham, 1,000 pagodas in cash, 3,000 pounds in jewels, and a promise of 1,200 pounds more, and sent him to England to represent his grievances before the king and the ministry." Gurney, "Debts of the Nawab of Arcot," p. 87. Macpherson served in Parliament, ostensibly bankrolled by the nawab, for many years, and went on to succeed Warren Hastings as governor-general of India in 1785.
42. *The Letters of George Dempster to Sir Adam Fergusson*, ed. James Fergusson (London: n.p., 1934) , pp. 87–88, quoted in ibid., p. 331.
43. Paterson Diary, vol. 5, fol. 157 (India Office Records, British Library).

44. Quoted in Pamila Nightingale's *Fortune and Integrity: A Study of Moral Attitudes in the Indian Diary of George Paterson, 1769–1774* (New Delhi: Oxford University Press, 1985), p. 85.
45. Just before leaving Madras Paterson wrote, "Mr. Benfield's desire is more money, which I never thought of before, for he always had endeavored to appear to me as wanting nothing of the Nabob but his accounts settled and his present debts paid off . . . B's mind is full of suspicions. He bribes thro' everything himself. He is anxious to be in every man's secrets. He suspects all mankind and is ready to believe everyone is as bad as himself." Paterson Diary, vol. 9, p. 111.
46. See the extraordinary account of Paterson in Nightingale's *Fortune and Integrity*. Nightingale largely accepts Paterson's self-representation as a man of integrity committed above all to the good of the nawab, whose interest in his own fortune was strictly tied to his own sense of rendering the nawab an invaluable service. Nightingale's book not only defends Paterson's personal reputation but also largely discounts the criticisms made of the Madras nabobs, whose corruption and self-interest in the end paled before that of the nawab. Even J. D. Gurney, who is less critical of the Company than I have been, has demonstrated beyond doubt that the corruption of the Company and its servants more than matched the managerial ineptitude and failure of the nawab. Gurney writes, "The high hopes of a general reorganization of the nawab's financial administration had been ruined, first by his reluctance to let any European take a direct part in the 'country business' and then by the intervention of Macleane in durbar politics," and concludes: "Inconstancy, incompetence and wilful advice denied him, and his creditors, of the fruits of his victory." Gurney, "Debts of the Nawab of Arcot," pp. 266, 210. We still await a more detailed and complete account of the court, administration, and general historical context of the nawab of Arcot, who was certainly one of the most colorful, and influential, characters of the eighteenth-century Anglo-Indian world.
47. Nightingale, *Fortune and Integrity*, p. 211.
48. Pigot's *dubash* (agent) had fallen out with the nawab, and his inam, a village granted him by Tuljaji, the raja of Tanjore, was confiscated in 1773. Pigot had clearly received some of the proceeds of this village.
49. Gurney, "Debts of the Nawab of Arcot," p. 287.
50. Macpherson returned to London where he appealed unsuccessfully to the directors for reinstatement. He returned to India in 1781 as a member of the Bengal Council.
51. H. D. Love, *Vestiges of Old Madras* (1913; New Delhi: K. M. Rai Mittal, 1988), vol. 4, p. 85.
52. Quoted in Jim Phillips, "Parliament and Southern India, 1781–83: The

Secret Committee of Inquiry and the Prosecution of Sir Thomas Rumbold," *Parliamentary History* 7, pt. 1 (1988): 84.

53. Ibid., p. 87.

54. Phillips, "Parliament and Southern India," pp. 81–97.

55. *The Works of the Right Honorable Edmund Burke*, 8th ed., vol. 11 (Boston: Little, Brown, 1884). The quotations are from pp. 87, 23, 24, 28–29, 39, and 49. Dundas's word carried particular weight because he had been a great supporter of Paul Benfield. Burke also quoted from John Clavering, a member of the Bengal Council, to describe one mode of contracting debt: "One mode of amassing money at the Nabob's cost is curious. He is generally in arrears to the Company. Here the Governor, being cash-keeper, is generally on good terms with the banker, who manages matters thus. The Governor presses the Nabob for the balance due from him; the Nabob flies to his banker for relief; the banker engages to pay the money, and grants his notes accordingly, which he puts in the cash-book as ready money; the Nabob pays him an interest for it at two and three per cent per mensem, till the tunkaws [assignment of revenue of particular localities to individuals] he grants on the particular districts for it are paid. Matters in the mean time are so managed that there is not call for this money for the Company's service till the tunkaws become due. By the means not a cash is advanced by the banker, though he receives a heavy interest from the Nabob, which is divided as lawful spoil" (pp. 44–45).

56. Ibid., pp. 101, 99, 97, and 102.

57. Ibid., p. 100.

58. Edmund Burke, *A Philosophical Enquiry into the Origin of Our Ideas of the Sublime and Beautiful* (1757; New York: Oxford University Press, 1990).

59. Sara Suleri alone has captured this sense of ambivalence in her analysis of Burke's relationship to the Indian sublime. She writes, "When Burke invokes the sublimity of India, therefore, he seeks less to contain the irrational within a rational structure than to construct inventories of obscurity through which the potential empowerment of the sublime is equally on the verge of emptying into negation . . . India as a historical reality evokes the horror of sublimity." See Suleri, *The Rhetoric of English India* (Chicago: University of Chicago Press, 1992), p. 28.

60. Edmund Burke, "Speech on Mr. Fox's East India Bill," in Peter Marshall, ed., *The Writings and Speeches of Edmund Burke*, vol. 5 (Oxford: Clarendon Press, 1981), p. 464.

61. As we shall see in a later chapter, drawing a veil across the oppressions of history was necessary in order to sustain the legitimacy of government as well as of civil society.

62. For the general context of Burke's view, see J. G. A. Pocock, *The Machiavellian Moment: Florentine Political Thought and the Atlantic Republican Tradition* (Princeton, N.J.: Princeton University Press, 1975).

63. The quotation is from Philip Harling, *The Waning of Old Corruption: The Politics of Economical Reform in Britain, 1779–1846* (Oxford: Clarendon Press, 1996), p. 1.

64. It was not difficult for Hastings to secure many letters of praise and support from Indians to buttress his defense in the trial. And it is not insignificant that Ghulam Hussain, author of the *Seir Mutaqherin*, dedicated his book to Hastings. See Seid-Ghulam-Hussain-Khan, *Seir Mutaqherin; or, Review of Modern Times: Being an History of India, as Far Down as the Year 1783* (London: R. Cambray, 1789).

3. Spectacle

1. Thomas Macaulay, *Poetry and Prose* (Cambridge, Mass.: Harvard University Press, 1967), p. 454.

2. Quoted in Sara Suleri, *The Rhetoric of English India* (Chicago: University of Chicago Press, 1992), p. 53.

3. *The History of the Trial of Warren Hastings, . .* (London: Printed for J. Debrett, 1796), p. 1.

4. *Diary and Letters of Madame D'Arblay*, ed. Charlotte Barrett (London: Swan Sonnenschein & Co., 1893), p. 481.

5. Peter Marshall, ed., *The Writings and Speeches of Edmund Burke*, vol. 6 (Oxford: Clarendon Press, 1981), pp. 275–276 (February 15, 1788).

6. Hastings had been dubbed the "savior of India" by Henry Dundas in a speech in the House of Commons in June 1786. See Peter Marshall, *The Impeachment of Warren Hastings* (London: Oxford University Press, 1965), p. 46.

7. Macaulay, *Poetry and Prose*, p. 457.

8. Ibid., p. 458.

9. *Diary and Letters of Madame D'Arblay*, p. 509.

10. It seems to have been the general view that Burke frequently overdid his oratory. Conor Cruise O'Brien writes that the impeachment speech was one of his weaker speeches, in large part because he was speaking on behalf of the managers rather than as an independent Member of Parliament, but O'Brien is peculiarly attuned to Burke's excess. See O'Brien, *The Great Melody: A Thematic Biography of Edmund Burke* (Chicago: University of Chicago Press, 1992), pp. 364–365.

11. Burke to T. O'Beirne, September 29, 1786, in *The Correspondence of Edmund Burke* (Cambridge: Cambridge University Press, 1960), vol. 5, p. 281.

12. Macaulay, *Poetry and Prose*, p. 457.

13. Quoted in Marshall, *Writings and Speeches of Edmund Burke*, vol. 6, p. 276 (February 15, 1788).
14. For "illegal, unjust, and impolitick," see Burke to C. O'Hara, August 20, 1773, in *Correspondence of Edmund Burke*, vol. 2, p. 452.
15. Conor Cruise O'Brien has disputed the possibility that Burke was influenced in any way by financial or family considerations, expostulating that "one should not spend too much time on swatting these pullulating insects of trivializing calumny." O'Brien, *Great Melody*, p. 306, fn. 1; Marshall, *Impeachment of Warren Hastings*, p. 4.
16. Burke was never especially well off, and given the society he kept in Britain, his lack of means must have marked his life in significant ways. He lost any chance for a significant fortune when his investments in East India Company stock lost most of their value in the great crash of 1769. While O'Brien sees this as a further sign of Burke's greatness, many other commentators have noted the constant stress, and contradictions, of Burke's financial position.
17. Macaulay, who wrote his ringing denunciation of Bengali character as part of his own characterization of Nandakumar, still assumed that Hastings was behind the prosecution: "The crime imputed to him was that six years before he had forged a bond. The ostensible prosecutor was a native. But it was then, and still is, the opinion of every body, idiots and biographers excepted, that Hastings was the real mover in the business." Macaulay, *Poetry and Prose*, p. 402. For a detailed critical account of the affair, see Chapter 6.
18. On Francis's determination that Hastings would not consult him, see Sophia Weitzman, *Warren Hastings and Philip Francis* (Manchester, Eng.: Manchester University Press, 1929), p. 26.
19. For excoriating reviews of the war, see James Mill, *History of British India*, vol. 5 (London: Chelsea House Publishers, 1968), pp. 361–409; Macaulay, *Poetry and Prose*, p. 449. For commentary more generous to Hastings and the Company, see Sir John Strachey, *Hastings and the Rohilla War* (Oxford: Clarendon Press, 1892).
20. See Richard Barnett, *North India between Empires: Awadh, the Mughals, and the British, 1720–1801* (Berkeley: University of California Press, 1980), pp. 67–95.
21. For more details about the running conflicts between Francis and Hastings, see Weitzman, *Warren Hastings and Philip Francis*.
22. "To be a chef de Parti and not to succeed is everything that can be called damnable," Francis wrote in one of his letters. Ibid., p. 133. For a detailed account of the scandal with the Frenchwoman, see H. E. Busteed, *Echoes from Old Calcutta, Being Chiefly Reminiscences of the Days of Warren Hastings, Francis, and Impey* (Calcutta: Thacker, Spink and Co.,

1897). When the young woman (she was but fifteen at the time of the affair) returned to Europe, she married Talleyrand.

23. See Francis Papers, Eur. Mss. E. 16 (India Office Records, British Library).
24. See David Nokes, *Jane Austen: A Life* (Berkeley: University of California Press, 1997), p. 31. Also see the account in Jeremy Bernstein, *Dawning of the Raj: The Life and Trials of Warren Hastings* (Chicago: Ivan R. Dee, 2000), pp. 49–52.
25. Francis Papers, Eur. Mss. D. 19 (India Office Records, British Library).
26. Ibid.
27. Before departing, Francis wrote to many of his friends and correspondents that although he was leaving the scene of conflict, he did not mean to abandon the struggle: "Be assured, the house is on fire, and I really think the mischief will begin in Oudh . . . we are on the eve of some great calamity, in the consequences of which both the guilty and the innocent will probably be involved together . . . The moment I shall have made my exit, enter desolation." Quoted in Weitzman, *Warren Hastings and Philip Francis*, p. 133.
28. Marshall, *Writings and Speeches of Edmund Burke*, vol. 5, p. 18.
29. Ibid., p. 39.
30. Francis wrote to Mackenzie, in India, that "Wonders have already been done by the perseverance of two individuals, against the whole kingdom and against every power and influence in it." Francis Letters, vol. 2, p. 363. Burke sent Francis the rough draft of the first article of charges they had planned together in December 1785 (Burke to Francis, December 10, 1785, quoted in Weitzman, *Warren Hastings and Philip Francis*, p. 176).
31. Burke to Francis, December 23, 1785, in *Correspondence of Edmund Burke*, vol. 5, p. 245.
32. James Mill, who criticized Burke for his willful neglect of the legal issues in impeachment, wrote, "Edmund Burke lived upon applause—upon the applause of the men who were able to set a fashion; and the applause of such men was not to be hoped for by him who should expose to the foundation the iniquities of the juridical system." Mill, *History of British India*, vol. 5, p. 232.
33. Burke was severely taken to task for this resistance by James Mill in his *History*, though Mill's more fervent critique was against the "professors" of English law who used what seemed an unlimited power of obstructing justice. See his chapter on the trial in ibid., chapter 2, for his discussion of the legal issues raised by the trial. For a rhetorical analysis that suggests Burke's conscious advocacy of a general, and classical, rhetoric of denunciation, see Elizabeth Samet, "A Prosecutor and a Gentleman: Edmund

Burke's Idiom of Impeachment," in *ELH* 68, no. 2 (2001): 397–418. Also see Sara Suleri's reading of the trial, in which she argues that Burke's "rhetoric is most crucially self-disempowering, escaping the confines of a criminality that can be attached to specific acts." Suleri, *Rhetoric of English India*, p. 63. She further notes on p. 56: "Burke converted the legal space of the trial into a rhetorical arena that was designed to implicate each member of its audience in its catalog of the Indian sublime."

34. *History of the Trial of Warren Hastings, . . .*, p. 9. For a more accurate transcript, see Marshall, *Writings and Speeches of Edmund Burke*, p. 459.

35. Ibid., vol. 6, p. 271.

36. Ibid., quotations on pp. 275, 277.

37. Ibid., p. 278.

38. Ibid., p. 350.

39. Ibid., p. 366.

40. *The Works of the Right Honorable Edmund Burke*, 8th ed. (Boston: Little, Brown, 1884), vol. 11, p. 219.

41. Ibid.

42. Marshall, *Writings and Speeches of Edmund Burke*, vol. 6, pp. 294–298.

43. Even by the standards of eighteenth-century knowledge about India in Britain, these statements reveal serious confusion about the social position of the men who stood as agents, translators, and brokers for Company servants.

44. Marshall, *Writings and Speeches of Edmund Burke*, vol. 6, quotations on p. 294.

45. Ibid., pp. 420–421.

46. *History of the Trial of Warren Hastings, . . .*, pp. 7–8. Given that Debrett's account is favorable throughout to Hastings, this praise of Burke's rhetoric—not unlike that of Fanny Burney—suggests the theatrical character of the performance, pleasure derived even from the eloquence of the enemy.

47. *The Speeches of Mr. Sheridan, Mr. Fax, Mr. Burke, Mr. Pitt, Major Scott, Mr. Beaufoy, . . . on the Charges Brought Against Mr. Hastings, and on the Commercial Treaty* (London: Printed for John Stockdale, 1787), p. 110.

48. Edward Gibbon, who witnessed the performance, wrote, "Sheridan, on the close of his speech, sunk into Burke's arms, but I called this morning, he is perfectly well. A good actor." Quoted in Keith Feiling, *Warren Hastings* (London: Macmillan, 1954), p. 357.

49. Two years later, Burke was reported to have said, "The most brilliant day of my life, and that which I would wish most to live over again, was the day I appeared at the bar of the House of Lords with the censure of the Commons in my hand. I had but an hour to prepare myself; the resolution of the other managers to proceed in the business had only just been

taken. Mr. Fox strongly urged me to relinquish the prosecution at that time:—Mr. Pitt as anxiously hoped that I should; but had there been no higher motive, no moral principle at work to induce me to persevere, the disgrace of such a retreat, on account of such a provocation, and the weakness of mind it would have indicated, must have proved fatal to any public character." Marshall, *Writings and Speeches of Edmund Burke*, vol. 7, p. 71.

50. On Francis's support of the French Revolution, see Ranajit Guha, *A Rule of Property for Bengal: An Essay on the Idea of Permanent Settlement* (Durham, N.C.: Duke University Press, 1996), pp. 81–104.

51. All trial quotations by Hastings that follow are from Debrett's account, dated June 2, 1791, and published in *History of the Trial of Warren Hastings*, . . ., pp. 81–104.

52. Quotations are from *The Speeches of Richard Brinley Sheridan* (London: n.p., 1842), vol. 1, p. 374.

53. Ibid.

54. While suggesting that the managers deserved to lose their case, Marshall confessed that he believed the charges against Hastings "were not without foundation." Marshall takes a dim view of Hastings's treatment of both Chait Singh and the begums, on the grounds that they all deserved greater justice from the very Company that had made them guarantees and assurances, however ambiguous the terms and precedents. And Marshall feels sure that Hastings had awarded contracts to friends that were extravagant, without benefit of open and competitive bids. At the same time, Marshall laments that Hastings ruled during a time of rapidly changing standards, making any lapses of judgment the products in part of the historical moment. See Marshall, *Impeachment of Warren Hastings*.

55. Conor Cruise O'Brien is notably of a different mindset. He writes that the trial was a tribute to Burke's unshakeable idealism and anti-imperialist convictions, for which he has been vindicated in full by history.

56. Of all those who have written about the trial, Sara Suleri was one of the first to note that both the legal defeat and the general loss of interest in India that attended the trial did not, necessarily, spell failure. She writes, "That the impeachment failed on a literal level does not preclude the possibility of its wider symbolic success." Suleri, *Rhetoric of English India*, p. 56. At the end of her analysis, however, she too saw Burke's efforts squandered, the trial ending with the repression of all ambivalence around the colonial guilt that gave rise to the trial in the first place. For Suleri, the trial only returned in the muted space of theater, around Sheridan's 1799 play *Pizarro*.

57. John Seeley, *The Expansion of England* (Chicago: University of Chicago Press), p. 13.

58. Burke to French Laurence, July 28, 1796, in *Correspondence of Edmund Burke*, vol. 9, pp. 62–63.

59. Dundas himself was brought up on charges of impeachment in 1806. His was the last impeachment in Britain. See Cyril Matheson, *The Life of Henry Dundas: First Viscount Melville* (London: Constable & Co., 1933).

60. Rev. G. R. Gleig, *Memoirs of the Life of the Right Honorable Warren Hastings, First Governor General of Bengal*, vol. 3 (London: Richard Bentley, 1841), p. 460.

61. Keith Feiling, *Warren Hastings* (London: Macmillan, 1954), p. 390.

62. Quoted in Peter Marshall, "The Making of an Imperial Icon: The Case of Warren Hastings," *Journal of Imperial and Commonwealth History* 27, no. 3 (September 1999): 2.

63. I repeat, only moderately chastened. See the recent assessment of the respected historian, Peter Marshall: "The conventional wisdom of the later nineteenth century was not seriously mistaken . . . Hastings deserved his place in an imperial pantheon." Ibid.

4. Economy

1. Much of Burke's analysis here, as elsewhere, derives in fact from writings of Philip Francis, as Ranajit Guha has demonstrated. In letters and manuscripts dating from 1777, Francis had adumbrated four "articles of tribute" that constituted the drain of wealth from Bengal. The first was the "investment," which was described as a "clear acknowledged Tribute from Bengal to India"; the second was the remittances made to other Presidencies, another "direct Tribute"; the third was the transfer of private income to England; and the fourth was the transfer of income. Ranajit Guha, *A Rule of Property for Bengal: An Essay on the Idea of Permanent Settlement* (Durham, N.C.: Duke University Press, 1996), pp. 138–140.

2. *Ninth Report of the Select Committee*, June 25, 1783, in Peter Marshall, ed., *The Writings and Speeches of Edmund Burke*, vol. 5 (Oxford: Clarendon Press, 1981), pp. 223–224.

3. See Guha, *A Rule of Property for Bengal*, pp. 137–139.

4. Quoted in Adam Smith, *An Inquiry into the Nature and Causes of the Wealth of Nations* (1776; Chicago: University of Chicago Press, 1976), book 4, quotations on p. 154.

5. Ibid., quotations on pp. 155 and 153.

6. Ibid., quotations on pp. 155–157.

7. See Uday Mehta's *Liberalism and Empire* (Chicago: University of Chicago Press, 1999). Mehta has argued persuasively that British liberalism accommodated itself to empire with little sense of strain. As we shall see

throughout this book, however, this hardly sets liberalism apart from other political tendencies, all of which accept the legitimacy of imperial formations.

8. The term "state of exception" is Carl Schmitt's. See his *Political Theology*, trans. George Schwab (Cambridge, Mass.: MIT Press, 1985).

9. Sidney W. Mintz, *Sweetness and Power: The Place of Sugar in Modern History* (New York: Viking Penguin, 1985), p. 114.

10. Quoted in ibid., p. 119.

11. See Om Prakash, "Opium Monopoly in India and Indonesia in the Eighteenth Century," *Indian Economic and Social History Review* 24, no. 1 (1987): 63–80; and J. F. Richards, "The Indian Empire and Peasant Production of Opium in the Nineteenth Century," *Modern Asian Studies* 15, no. 1 (February 1981): 59–82.

12. Alexander Dow, *The History of Hindostan, from the Death of Akbar to the Complete Settlement of the Empire under Aurangzebe* . . . (Dublin: Luke White, 1792), pp. liii, lxviii, and lxxviii.

13. H. Verelst, *View of the Rise etc., of the English Government in Bengal* (London: J. Nourse, 1776), appendix, p. 117.

14. Verelst to unknown recipient, April 5, 1769, quoted in Romesh C. Dutt, *The Economic History of India* (London: Keegan Paul, 1908), p. 31.

15. Dutt neglected to mention, however, that the argument was made rarely if at all since the ascension to power of Cornwallis and Wellesley, and that both the earlier reforms and the later demise of the Company monopoly were used by many to suggest that the principle of free trade had become fully operational.

16. For an example of a historical work that downplays the negative role of the British, see Holden Furber, *John Company at Work* (New York: Octagon Press, 1970).

17. Irfan Habib, *Essays in Indian History: Towards a Marxist Perception* (New Delhi: Tulika Publishers, 1995), p. 304.

18. Ibid., p. 304.

19. Furber, *John Company at Work*, quotations and calculations on pp. 306, 310, and 305.

20. Habib, *Essays in Indian History*, p. 112.

21. Ibid., p. 113.

22. Peter Marshall, *East India Fortunes: The British in Bengal in the Eighteenth Century* (Oxford: Clarendon Press, 1976), p. 271.

23. Furber, *John Company at Work*, quotations on pp. 313 and 317.

24. Ibid., quotations on pp. 320, 321, 323, 324.

25. "The ideal historian for modern India should doubtless be neither a European nor an Asian, but that ideal historian does not exist. Yet I have felt that a work on this period should be written by an American. Though

fully aware of a European heritage from which I cannot divest myself, I have done my best to present a narrative which is unaffected by any sort of bias." Ibid., p. viii.

26. Ibid., p. 311.
27. Marshall, *East Indian Fortunes*, p. 256.
28. Rudrangshu Mukherjee, "Early British Imperialism in India: A Rejoinder," *Past and Present* 106 (February 1985): 169–173.
29. Javier Cuenca Esteban, "The British Balance of Payments, 1772–1820: India Transfers and War Finance," *Economic History Review* 54, no. 1 (2001): 69.
30. J. R. Ward, "The Industrial Revolution and British Imperialism, 1750–1850," *Economic History Review*, n.s. 47, no. 1 (February 1994): 60.
31. Ibid., p. 61.
32. Peter Marshall, "Debate: Early British Imperialism in India," *Past and Present* 106 (February 1985): 167–168.
33. The political basis for Wellesley's imperialism is readily acknowledged by Mukherjee as well.
34. H. Wellesley to S. Swinton, Commercial Resident at Etawah, September 24, 1802, Home Miscellaneous Series, vol. 583, p. 254 (India Office Records, British Library).
35. Wellesley to Scott, January 22, 1801, Correspondence of Wellesley, vol. 2, p. 427; Wellesley to the Hon'able Mr. Petrie at Madras, 2 July 1802: Correspondence of Wellesley, vol. 5, Oude Supplement, p. 81 (India Office Records, British Library).
36. See Blair Kling, *Blue Mutiny: The Indigo Disturbances in Bengal, 1859–1862* (Philadelphia: University of Pennsylvania Press, 1966).
37. See the powerful argument of Sudipta Sen, *Empire of Free Trade: The East India Company and the Making of the Colonial Marketplace* (Philadelphia: University of Pennsylvania Press, 1998).
38. Ibid., p. 18.
39. Marshall, *Writings and Speeches of Edmund Burke*, vol. 5, p. 277 (February 15, 1788).
40. Philip Lawson, *The East India Company: A History* (New York: Longman, 1993), p. 141.
41. Ibid., p. 142.

5. Sovereignty

1. "Speech, on Mr. Fox's East India Bill, December 1, 1783," in Peter Marshall, ed., *The Works of the Right Honorable Edmund Burke* (Boston: Little, Brown, 1884), vol. 2, p. 442.
2. Ibid., p. 448.
3. Thomas Macaulay, "Essay on Warren Hastings," in Macaulay, *Prose and*

Poetry, ed. G. M. Young (Cambridge, Mass.: Harvard University Press), p. 384.

4. Despatch book, June 9, 1686, vol. 91, pp. 142, 145 (India Office Records, British Library), cited in K. N. Chaudhuri, *The Trading World of Asia and the English East India Company, 1600–1760* (Cambridge: Cambridge University Press, 1978), p. 454.

5. C. A. Bayly, "The British Military-Fiscal State and Indigenous Resistance: India, 1750–1820," in Patrick Tuck, *The East India Company: 1600–1858*, vol. 5 (London: Routledge, 1998), p. 205.

6. Chaudhuri, *Trading World of Asia*, p. 112.

7. H. H. Dodwell, ed., *The Cambridge History of India, British India*, vol. 5 (Delhi: S. Chand & Co., 1968), p. 591.

8. For my own analysis of shared sovereignty and notions of proprietary rights in precolonial India, see Nicholas Dirks, *The Hollow Crown: Ethnohistory of an Indian Kingdom* (Cambridge: Cambridge University Press, 1987).

9. Bayly, "British Military-Fiscal State," p. 206.

10. Clive to Pitt, January 7, 1759, quoted in Sir George Forrest, *The Life of Lord Clive* (London: Cassell and Co., 1918), vol. 2, p. 412.

11. Home Miscellaneous, vol. 211, speech dated November 24, 1772 (India Office Records, British Library).

12. Clive to William Pitt, January 7, 1759, quoted in Forrest, *Life of Lord Clive*, vol. 2, p. 413.

13. Quoted in Percival Spear, *Master of Bengal: Clive and His India* (London: Thames and Hudson, 1975), p. 145.

14. Quoted in Forrest, *Life of Lord Clive*, vol. 2, pp. 256–258.

15. Richard Barnett, *North India between Empires: Awadh, the Mughals, and the British, 1720–1801* (Berkeley: University of California Press, 1980), p. 74.

16. As Percival Spear approvingly put it, "The dominion of Bengal was not desired in itself, but only as a safeguard for peaceful commercial operations . . . Rule by legal fiction and by deputy was both safer and cheaper in the conditions of the time." Spear, *Master of Bengal*, p. 156.

17. Quoted in Bernard Cohn, *Colonialism and Its Forms of Knowledge* (Princeton, N.J.: Princeton University Press, 1996), p. 59.

18. Quoted in H. V. Bowen, *Revenue and Reform: The Indian Problem in British Politics, 1757–1773* (Cambridge: Cambridge University Press, 1991), p. 10.

19. "Speech on the Second Day of the Impeachment of Warren Hastings, Saturday, February 16, 1788," in Marshall, *Works of the Right Honorable Edmund Burke*, vol. 9, p. 441.

20. James Mill, *History of British India*, vol. 5 (London: Chelsea House Publishers, 1968), vol. 3, p. 286.
21. Clive Manuscripts, vol. 218, ff. 149–151 (India Office Records, British Library).
22. Quoted in Bowen, *Revenue and Reform*, pp. 9–10.
23. T. Pownall, *The Right, Interest, and Duty of Government, as Concerned in the Affairs of the East Indies* (n.p., 1773).
24. Quoted in Bowen, *Revenue and Reform*, p. 12.
25. Ibid., p. 62.
26. Quoted in J. W. Kaye, *The Administration of the East India Company: A History of Indian Progress* (London: Riley, 1853), p. 134.
27. Lucy Sutherland, *The East India Company in Eighteenth Century Politics* (Oxford: Clarendon Press, 1952), p. 256.
28. Quoted in Bowen, *Revenue and Reform*, p. 171.
29. Quoted in ibid., p. 173. George III was upset at the about-face, writing to North, "I own I am amazed that private interest could make so many forget what they owe to their country." Quoted in Sutherland, *East India Company in Eighteenth Century Politics*, p. 258.
30. See George Rous, *The Restoration of Tanjore, Considered*, printed in 1777, private collection (British Library), as well as "Policy of Making Conquests for the Mahometans," in Peter Marshall, ed., *The Writings and Speeches of Edmund Burke*, (Oxford: Clarendon Press, 1981), vol. 5, pp. 41–124.
31. "Speech on the Debts of the Nawab of Arcot," in Marshall, *Works of the Right Honorable Edmund Burke*, vol. 3, p. 90.
32. Quoted in Bowen, *Revenue and Reform*, p. 113.
33. Rev. G. R. Gleig, *Memoirs of the Life of the Right Honorable Warren Hastings, First Governor General of Bengal* (London: Richard Bentley, 1841), vol. 1, pp. 534–544.
34. Ibid., vol. 2, p. 50.
35. Ibid., vol. 1, p. 401.
36. Ibid.
37. Hastings to George Colebrooke, March 7, 1773, quoted in ibid., vol. 1, p. 290.
38. Ibid., p. 293.
39. Quoted in Ranajit Guha, *A Rule of Property for Bengal: An Essay on the Idea of Permanent Settlement* (Durham, N.C.: Duke University Press, 1996), p. 147.
40. Quoted in Philip Lawson, *The East India Company: A History* (New York: Longman, 1993), p. 128.
41. "Fox's Indian Bill Speech," in Marshall, *Writings and Speeches of Edmund Burke*, vol. 5, p. 385.

42. Speech of February 15, 1788, quoted in Marshall, *Writings and Speeches of Edmund Burke*, vol. 6, p. 271.
43. Bernard S. Cohn, "Representing Authority in Victorian India," in Eric Hobsbawm and Terence Ranger, eds., *The Invention of Tradition* (Cambridge: Cambridge University Press, 1983).
44. Michael Hardt and Antonio Negri, *Empire* (Cambridge, Mass.: Harvard University Press, 2000), p. 70.
45. Ibid., pp. 105–109.
46. Ibid., p. 70.
47. "Speech on a Motion Made in the House of Commons, May 7, 1782, for a Committee to Inquire into the State of the Representation of the Commons in Parliament," in Marshall, *Works of the Right Honorable Edmund Burke*, vol. 7, pp. 94–95.
48. Ibid., quotations on p. 95.
49. See J. G. A. Pocock, "Burke and the Ancient Constitution," in Pocock, *Politics, Language and Time: Essays on Political Thought and History* (New York: Atheneum, 1971), pp. 202–232.
50. Burke's speech of February 16, 1788, in Marshall, *Writings and Speeches of Edmund Burke*, vol. 6, p. 341.
51. Ibid., pp. 345–346.
52. Ibid., quotations on pp. 346, 350–351.
53. Carl Schmitt, *Political Theology*, trans. George Schwab (Cambridge, Mass.: MIT Press, 1985). Also see Giorgio Agamben, *State of Exception*, trans. Kevin Attell (Chicago: University of Chicago Press, 2005).
54. The term "immemorial" is Pocock's; see Pocock, "Burke and the Ancient Constitution," p. 227.
55. Marshall, *Writings and Speeches of Edmund Burke*, vol. 6, pp. 348–349.
56. Quoted in Pocock, "Burke and the Ancient Constitution," p. 227.
57. Marshall, *Writings and Speeches of Edmund Burke*, vol. 6, p. 351.
58. Ibid., p. 367.
59. In a recent and penetrating analysis, Uday Mehta has emphasized Burke's commitment to the importance of place, or territory. Mehta shows how Burke was always careful to set up the mise-en-scène by emphasizing territorial and geographical markers, as a way to frame his call to respect India's historical and political integrity. He reads Burke's treatment of Muslim law as a belief in Indian equivalence. Thus he sees Burke's defense of Indian sovereignty as a tacit acceptance of Indian nationality. And he suggests that Burke's emphasis on location or territory, combined with his use of territory to provide the experiential basis for collective or political identity, anticipates the anti-imperial nationalism of the next century (p. 149). He goes on to suggest that "Burke's defense of Indian history vindicates a social order in which freedom would not be

'solitary, unconnected, individual, selfish liberty, as if every man was to regulate the whole of his conduct by his own will.' It vindicates what subsequent nationalists might have called the conditions appropriate for the right of self-determination" (p. 186). But in making this argument, Mehta not only underplays the complementary emphasis Burke puts on the theistic universality of the law; he also glosses over Burke's own belief in the possibility of legitimate imperial rule. Far from seeing in India an incipient nationhood that could compromise Britain's own nationhood (p. 189), Burke saw in British conduct in India a challenge to two different but allied forms of sovereignty that put at risk the sacredness of sovereignty itself. India's sovereignty did not constitute the basis of a claim for liberty so much as a second argument against the "absolute power," or despotism, of Hastings. And the French Revolution only brought more urgency, and proximity, to the danger. In missing the defensiveness, as well as the reflexive character, of Burke's rhetoric about India, Mehta undermines his own compelling argument that English political theory was significantly shaped by imperial connections. See Uday Singh Mehta, *Liberalism and Empire* (Chicago: University of Chicago Press, 1999).

60. C. B. Macpherson, *The Political Theory of Possessive Individualism: Hobbes to Locke* (Oxford: Clarendon Press, 1962); on the limits of wealth and gender, see Carole Pateman, *The Sexual Contract* (Stanford, Calif.: Stanford University Press, 1988).

61. Richard Helgerson, *Forms of Nationhood: The Elizabethan Writing of England* (Chicago: University of Chicago Press, 1992).

62. See the argument of David Armitage, *The Ideological Origins of the British Empire* (Cambridge: Cambridge University Press, 2000).

63. For a larger argument about the formation of British identity in an imperial context, see Kathleen Wilson, *The Island Race: Englishness, Empire, and Gender in Eighteenth Century England* (New York: Routledge, 2003).

64. Armitage, *Ideological Origins of the British Empire*, p. 3.

65. On the importance of empire for the consolidation of British identity, see Linda Colley, *Britons: Forging the Nation, 1707–1837* (New Haven, Conn.: Yale University Press, 1992), p. 156.

66. I do not mean to exonerate the liberal political tradition, for Mehta and other critics are clearly correct to note the ways in which liberal theory depends on exclusions to its universal claims. But this does not mean that Burke's peculiar commitments to universalism and particularity escape the very same anthropological conundrum.

6. State

1. Here I refer to the project of the colonial state, not the ways in which the Company had been a state masquerading as a merchant body since at

least the late seventeenth century. For the best account of the Company as an early state form, see Philip Stern, "'One Body Corporate and Politick': The Growth of the East India Company State in the Later Seventeenth Century," Ph.D. diss., Department of History, Columbia University, 2004. Also see Stern, "Statemaking and Sovereignty and the English East India Company-State in the Late Seventeenth Century," unpublished paper, 2003, in author's possession.

2. Philip Lawson, *The East India Company: A History* (New York: Longman, 1993), p. 122.

3. Michel Foucault, "Governmentality," in Graham Burchell, Colin Gordon, and Peter Miller, eds., *The Foucault Effect: Studies in Governmentality* (Chicago: University of Chicago Press, 1991), p. 91.

4. For a discussion of some of these state forms, see Philip Corrigan and Derek Sayer, *The Great Arch* (New York: Blackwell, 1985); and Benedict Anderson, *Imagined Communities: Reflections on the Origin and Spread of Nationalism* (London: Verso, 1991). For debates over the difference between metropolitan and colonial governmentality, see David Scott, "Colonial Governmentality," *Social Text* 43 (Fall 1995): 191–200; Gyan Prakash, *Another Reason: Science and the Imagination of Modern India* (Princeton, N.J.: Princeton University Press, 1999); and Partha Chatterjee, *The Nation and Its Fragments: Colonial and Postcolonial Histories* (Princeton, N.J.: Princeton University Press, 1993).

5. I take the term "rule of property" from Ranajit Guha's book, *A Rule of Property for Bengal* (1963; Durham, N.C.: Duke University Press, 1996).

6. For commentary both on the rule of law in a colonial context, and on the necessary relationship between law and property, see my "From Little King to Landlord: Colonial Discourse and Colonial Rule," in Dirks, ed., *Colonialism and Culture* (Ann Arbor: University of Michigan Press, 1992). For "arbitrary power," see Peter Marshall, ed., *The Writings and Speeches of Edmund Burke* (Oxford: Clarendon Press, 1981), vol. 6, pp. 348–349.

7. John Brewer, *The Sinews of Power: War, Money, and the English State, 1688–1783* (Cambridge, Mass.: Harvard University Press, 1990), pp. 250–251.

8. For Francis's physiocratic philosophy, see Guha, *Rule of Property for Bengal.*

9. Peter J. Marshall, *Bengal: The British Bridgehead* (Cambridge: Cambridge University Press, 1987), p. 120.

10. Revenue Consultations, March 26, 1777 quoted in ibid., p. 121.

11. Francis to Lord North, February 24, 1775, quoted in Guha, *Rule of Property for Bengal*, p. 152.

12. Francis to Lord North, November 21, 1775, quoted in Guha, *Rule of Property for Bengal*, p. 152.

13. G. W. Forrest, *Selections from the Letters, Despatches, and Other State Papers Preserved in the Foreign Department of the Government of India, 1772–1785*, vol. 2 (Calcutta: Superintendent of Government Printing, 1890), p. 456.

14. See John McLane, *Land and Local Kingship in Eighteenth Century Bengal* (Cambridge: Cambridge University Press, 1992). See also Nicholas B. Dirks, *The Hollow Crown: Ethnohistory of an Indian Kingdom* (Ann Arbor: University of Michigan Press, 1993).

15. Rosanne Rocher, *Orientalism, Poetry, and the Millennium: The Checkered Life of Nathaniel Brassey Halhed, 1751–1830* (Delhi: Motilal Banarasidass, 1983), p. 48.

16. G. R. Gleig, ed., *Memoirs of the Life of the Right Hon. Warren Hastings, First Governor-General of Bengal* (London: Richard Bentley, 1841), vol. 1, p. 272.

17. Committee of Circuit to Council at Fort William, August 15, 1772, in J. E. Colebrooke, *Supplement to the Digest of Regulations Additions and Corrections, and Completing the Several Articles to Close of 1806*, vol. 1 (Calcutta, 1807): 8. As Hastings explained, "The only material changes we have made in the ancient constitution of the country are in dividing the jurisdiction in civil and criminal cases by clearer lines than were formerly drawn between them, and in removing the supreme courts of justice to Calcutta. There are other trivial innovations, which will appear in comparing the ancient forms of judicature as they are described in the letter to the Board with the regulations; but the spirit of the constitution we have preserved entire" (Hastings to J. Dupre, October 8, 1772, quoted in ibid., p. 263). Hastings went on to note that his regulations were, in general, "little more than a renewal of the laws and forms established of old in the country, with no other variation than such as was necessary to give them their due effect, and such as the people understood and were likely to be pleased with." He argued that in his new judicial establishment, "no essential change was made in the ancient constitution of the province. It was only brought back to its original principles, and the line prescribed for the jurisdiction of each Court, which the looseness of the Mogul government for some years past had suffered to encroach upon each other" (Hastings to Lord Mansfield, March 21, 1774, quoted in ibid., p. 400).

18. Both quotations are from Letter from Warren Hastings, July 10, 1773, recorded in the *Proceedings of Council*, August 3, 1773, supplement, pp. 114–119, quoted in Radhika Singha, *A Despotism of Law: Crime and Justice in Early Colonial India* (Delhi: Oxford University Press, 1998).

19. As Radhika Singha has argued, "The Company's early regulations began to extend the punitive jurisdiction of the state against the punitive and

restitutive claims of its subjects." This was especially true for its enhancement of the domain of "public justice." See Singha, *Despotism of Law*, pp. 3–4.

20. Quoted in G. R. Gleig, *Memoirs of the Life of Warren Hastings*, vol. 1 (London: n.p., 1841), p. 402.

21. Rocher, *Orientalism, Poetry and Millennium*, p. 51.

22. Warren Hastings to Court of Directors, March 24, 1774, quoted in ibid., p. 53.

23. William Jones to Lord Cornwallis, March 19, 1788, quoted in Rocher, *Orientalism, Poetry and Millennium*, p. 51.

24. Henry Thomas Colebrooke, *A Digest of Hindu Law on Contracts and Successions*, 4 vols. (Calcutta: n.p., 1797–1798).

25. Rocher, *Orientalism, Poetry and Millennium*, p. 62.

26. Charles Grant, "Observations on the State of Society among the Asiatic Subjects of Great Britain . . . ," *Parliamentary Papers* 10, no. 282 (1812–1813): 39–75.

27. Gleig, *Memoirs of the Life of Warren Hastings*, vol. 1, p. 222.

28. Peter J. Marshall, *The Impeachment of Warren Hastings* (London: Oxford University Press, 1965) p. 136.

29. Quoted in ibid., p. 140.

30. Quoted in Clavering to Francis, May 7, 1775, Additional MSS., 34287, fol. 81 (India Office Records, British Library).

31. See the account in Marshall, *Impeachment of Warren Hastings*, p. 142. Also see Lucy Sutherland, "New Evidence on the Nandakumar Trial," *English Historical Review* 72, no. 284 (July 1957): 438–465. On p. 465 she writes: "Hastings spoke truly, it would seem, when he said, 'I have carefully avoided every circumstance which might appear to be an interference in that prosecution,' but, even if we assume that the decision to prosecute was taken without his sanction, he spoke with an economy of truth."

32. Thomas Metcalf, *Ideologies of the Raj* (Cambridge: Cambridge University Press, 1994), p. 24.

33. See Elizabeth Denise Kolsky, "The Body Evidencing the Crime: Gender, Law and Medicine in Colonial India," Ph.D. diss., Department of History, Columbia University, 2003.

34. Singha, *Despotism of Law*, pp. 215, 246.

35. The summation was later used in the aborted impeachment effort against Impey.

36. Henry Beveridge, *The Trial of Maharaja Nanda Kumar, a Narrative of a Judicial Murder* (Calcutta: Thacker, Spink and Co., 1886). Beveridge avers three main points: that the forgery was not proved, that the prosecution was "got up" by Hastings, and that Impey hanged Nandakumar from "corrupt motives" (pp. 336–337).

37. Elizabeth Kolsky, "Codification and the Rule of Colonial Difference: Criminal Procedure in British India," *Law and History Review* 23, no. 3 (Fall 2005): 631–684.

38. Quoted in Marshall, *Writings and Speeches of Edmund Burke*, vol. 6, p. 108.

39. Foreign Department, Select Consultations, October 4, 1773, file no. 1 (India Office Records, British Library).

40. Rudrangshu Mukherjee has argued that "in Awadh in the 1770s, gradual economic penetration moved hand in hand with growing political control." See Mukherjee, "Trade and Empire in Awadh, 1765–1804," *Past and Present* 94 (February 1982): 94.

41. Sudipta Sen noted, "In spite of the task of reform the Company had set for itself, it succeeded in supplanting older webs of trade and prestation prevalent in the Nawabi realm with short-term gains. In the closing decades of the eighteenth century, monopolies both lawful and questionable continued to exist side by side with the movement toward a more responsible government favoring the freeing of trade." See Sen, *Empire of Free Trade*, p. 87.

42. Lawson, *East India Company*, pp. 118–119.

43. Ibid., p. 119.

44. Ibid., p. 124.

45. For more details, see Edward Ingram, introduction to *Two Views of British India: The Private Correspondence of Mr. Dundas and Lord Wellesley: 1798–1801* (Bath: Adams and Dart, 1970), pp. 3–14.

46. See Mildred Archer, *Tippoo's Tiger*, Victoria and Albert Museum monograph, no. 10 (London: H.M. Stationery Office, 1959).

47. For a brilliant account of this group of men, read Eric Stokes, *The English Utilitarians and India* (Oxford: Clarendon Press, 1959).

7. History

1. There is uncertainty as to whether the title "official historiographer" was ever formally bestowed on Orme, though this is how he referred to himself. See "Life," preface to Robert Orme, *Historical Fragments of the Mugol Empire, of the Morattoes, and of the English Concerns from the year MDCLIX* (London: C. Nourse, 1782), p. lxiv.

2. See S. C. Hill, ed., *Catalogue of Manuscripts in European Languages Belonging to the Library of the India Office*, vol. 2, pt. 1: *The Orme Collection* (London: Oxford University Press, 1916).

3. On Mackenzie, see my *Castes of Mind: Colonialism and the Making of Modern India* (Princeton, N.J.: Princeton University Press, 2001), pp. 81–106.

4. The term is Orme's own. See *Catalogue*, preface, p. xxi.

5. Thomas B. Macaulay, "Lord Clive," in his *Poetry and Prose* (Cambridge, Mass.: Harvard University Press, 1967), p. 307.

6. Orme to Richard Smith, February 1, 1766, vol. 222, p. 121, Orme Collection (India Office Records, British Library).

7. Orme to Richard Smith, November 18, 1767, vol. 222, Orme Collection, p. 189.

8. Alexander Dow, *The History of Hindostan . . .* (Dublin: Luke White, 1792), vol. 3, p. v.

9. Ibid., p. xxii.

10. Quotations are in ibid., pp. xxix, xlix, liii, lxviii, and lxxviii.

11. Quoted in Patrick Tuck, ed., *The East India Company, 1600–1858* (London: Routledge, 1998), vol. 3, p. xiii.

12. William Bolts, *Considerations on India Affairs* (London: Printed for J. Almon, 1772), p. x.

13. Ibid., pp. 36–37.

14. Harry Verelst, *A View of the Rise, Progress and Present State of the English Government in Bengal* (London: n.p., 1772), pp. 42, 31.

15. Quotations are from Mackenzie Manuscripts, uncatalogued, box 4, no. 77 (India Office Records, British Library).

16. Quotations are from Mackenzie Manuscripts, box 4, no. 77.

17. Ibid.

18. Ibid.

19. James Macpherson, *History and Management of the East India Company, from Its Origin in 1600 to the Present Times* (London: Printed for T. Cadell in the Strand, 1792), p. 58.

20. Ibid., p. 61.

21. Ibid., pp. 234, 237–238.

22. Ibid., pp. 237–238.

23. Ibid., p. 250.

24. Ibid.

25. Edmund Burke, "Policy of Making Conquests for the Mahometans," in Peter J. Marshall, ed., *The Writings and Speeches of Edmund Burke*, vol. 5 (Oxford: Clarendon Press, 1981).

26. Ibid., quotations on p. 63.

27. Ibid., p. 113.

28. Ibid., quotations on pp. 92, 62, and 86.

29. Ibid., pp. 117–118.

30. Ibid., pp. 113–114.

31. See ibid. Here Burke expressed stronger views than most other pamphleteers writing on behalf of Tanjore. See as another example George Rous, a Company man who supported the Tanjore raja and defended the inviolability of the Company's 1762 treaty with the raja as well as the upright-

ness of the deposed Governor Pigot. In his tract he wrote, "The conquest of the Mahommedans in India produced a revolution singular in the history of mankind. The whole government of the territories subdued passed into the hands of men, who bore no resemblance to the original inhabitants. Adventurers from Tartary, Persia, and Arabia, have been constantly entertained, and an uniform preference given by Mahammedan Princes to men of their own religion, and of hardy robust constitutions. These men, during the course of more than eight centuries, have gradually formed in India a mighty nation . . . the milder manners and delicate frame of the natives, rendered them unable to resist these fierce invaders; yet the singular institutions of their religion have fixed insuperable barriers to an union with their conquerors; and the Hindoos at this day continue a perfectly distinct race, even in the countries under a Mahammedan Government" (Rous, *The Restoration of Tanjore, Considered*, printed in 1777, private publication, British Library). Arguing thus that the raja of Tanjore's sovereignty was at least in part justified by his being Hindu rather than Muslim, Rous also attacked the nawab for his ill treatment of the raja, including his efforts to block the waters of the River Cauvery to devastate Tanjore's harvest.

32. Macaulay, "Lord Clive," pp. 315–316.
33. Nicholas Dirks, *The Hollow Crown: Ethnohistory of an Indian Kingdom* (Cambridge: Cambridge University Press, 1987).
34. J. G. A. Pocock, *Barbarism and Religion*, vol. 2: *Narratives of Civil Government* (Cambridge: Cambridge University Press, 1999), p. 204.
35. Edward Gibbon, *The Decline and Fall of the Roman Empire*, ed. J. B. Bury (New York: Heritage Press, 1946), p. 1219.
36. J. G. A. Pocock, "Gibbon and the Late Enlightenment," in Pocock, *Virtue, Commerce, History: Essays on Political Thought and History, Chiefly in the Eighteenth Century* (Cambridge: Cambridge University Press, 1985), p. 146.
37. Ibid., p. 155.
38. Ibid., p. 156.

8. Tradition

1. See Frederick G. Whelan, *Edmund Burke and India: Political Morality and Empire* (Pittsburgh: University of Pittsburgh Press, 1996). Whelan writes: "References to Burke as a traditionalist conservative may initially stumble on Michael Freeman's claim that Burke does not actually use the word 'tradition,' and that tradition should therefore not be taken to be a category of his thought. If correct, this omission is odd, since the literal meaning of the word—a 'handing down' from past to present—connotes a social process that Burke often invokes approvingly" (p. 262). Noting

that Burke uses many terms that are synonyms for tradition, Whelan argues that J. G. A. Pocock, the most forceful exponent of Burke's belief in tradition, is indeed correct in his reading of Burke.

2. David Bromwich, *A Choice of Inheritance: Self and Community from Edmund Burke to Robert Frost* (Cambridge, Mass.: Harvard University Press, 1989), p. 58.

3. Edmund Burke, "Speech on the Opening of the Impeachment," in Peter J. Marshall, ed., *The Writings and Speeches of Edmund Burke* (Oxford: Clarendon Press, 1981), vol. 7, quotations from pp. 280–283.

4. Edmund Burke, "Speech in Reply, II," in Marshall, *Writings and Speeches of Edmund Burke*, vol. 7, p. 230.

5. Edmund Burke, "Speech on Fox's India Bill," in Marshall, *Writings and Speeches of Edmund Burke*, vol. 5, p. 425.

6. Burke, "Speech on the Opening of the Impeachment," quotation on pp. 345–346.

7. Edmund Burke, "Speech in Reply," in *The Works of the Right Honorable Edmund Burke*, 8th ed., vol. 11 (Boston: Little, Brown, 1884), p. 225.

8. Hastings to Court of Directors, March 24, 1774, European Manuscripts, H/115/3, pp. 433–435 (India Office Records, British Library).

9. Letter printed as part of the introduction to Charles Wilkins, ed., *The Bhagvet-Geeta; or, Dialogues of Kreeshna and Arjoon* (London: n.p., 1785), p. 13.

10. Quotations are from Burke, "Speech on the Opening of the Impeachment," pp. 302–303.

11. Seid-Ghulam-Hussain-Khan, *Seir Mutaqherin; or, Review of Modern Times: Being an History of India, as Far Down as the Year 1783* (London: R. Cambray & Co., 1789), pp. 161–163.

12. Ibid., p. 194.

13. Ibid., p. 188.

14. Ibid., p. 189.

15. Ibid., p. 190.

16. Quoted in Kate Brittlebank, *Tipu Sultan's Search for Legitimacy: Islam and Kingship in a Hindu Domain* (Delhi: Oxford University Press, 1997), pp. 11–12.

17. Quoted in Ainslee Embree, *Charles Grant and British Rule in India* (New York: Columbia University Press, 1962), p. 152.

18. Quotations are from Charles Grant, *Observations on the State of Society among the Asiatic Subjects of Great Britain, Particularly with Respect to Morals; and on the Means of Improving It—Written Chiefly in the Year 1792* (London: House of Commons, 1813), pp. 66–67, 60–61, 66–67.

19. Speech by William Wilberforce, June 22, 1813, *Parliamentary Debates*, vol. 26 (London: R. Bagshaw), pp. 831–872.

20. William Wilberforce to J. Butterworth, February 15, 1812, quoted in Embree, *Charles Grant and British Rule in India*, p. 273.
21. Lata Mani, *Contentious Traditions: The Debate on Sati in Colonial India* (Berkeley: University of California Press, 1998), p. 136.
22. See ibid, pp. 134–151.
23. Quoted in ibid., p. 142.
24. Quoted in ibid., p. 149.
25. Lata Mani has demonstrated that early colonial efforts to monitor the performance of sati worked in fact to increase the visibility and prestige of the practice, and by implication the actual number of documented burnings. Even early efforts at neutrality served to constitute a form of colonial intervention.
26. Lord William Cavendish Bentinck, Minute on Sati, November 8, 1829, reprinted in C. H. Philips, ed., *The Correspondence of Lord William Cavendish Bentinck*, vol. 1: 1828–1831 (Oxford: Oxford University Press, 1977).
27. In some cases the Company defined sati only as "voluntary culpable homicide by consent." See Mani, *Contentious Traditions*, p. 25.
28. [William Henry Sleeman], *Calcutta Literary Gazette*, October 3, 1830.
29. William Henry Sleeman, *The Thugs or Phansigars of India . . .*, 2 vols. (Philadelphia: Carey & Hart, 1839).
30. Ibid.
31. Ibid.
32. The *thuggee* campaign served as the basis for the development of various policies concerning "criminal castes and tribes." Also see Radhika Singha, *Despotism of Law: Crime and Justice in Early Colonial India* (Delhi: Oxford University Press, 1998); and my *Castes of Mind: Colonialism and the Making of Modern India* (Princeton, N.J.: Princeton University Press, 2001).
33. Singha, *Despotism of Law*, pp. 192–193.
34. Dirks, *Castes of Mind*.

9. Empire

1. J. R. Seeley, *The Expansion of England* (Chicago: University of Chicago Press, 1971), p. 196.
2. Ibid., p. 198.
3. Ibid., p. 169.
4. Ibid., p. 13.
5. Ibid.
6. Ibid., p. 12.
7. Ibid., p. 143.
8. Ibid., p. 165.

9. Ibid., pp. 169–170.
10. This continues to be a worry even in the most critically informed imperial history. Thus the imperative for revisionist work in imperial history to recognize the need to link even an expanded metropolitan history with work in colonial history (with all that is implied for work in colonial archives and languages), at the same time that it takes newly critical views both of nation and of national history. For two excellent examples of how this objective can be achieved, see Sudipta Sen, *Distant Sovereignty: National Imperialism and the Origins of British India* (New York: Routledge, 2002); and Catherine Hall, *Civilising Subjects: Metropole and Colony in the English Imagination, 1830–1867* (Chicago: University of Chicago Press, 2002). Sen's recent book anticipates a number of the critical issues and questions I have raised in this book. Also see Kathleen Wilson, ed., *A New Imperial History: Culture, Identity and Modernity in Britain and the Empire, 1660–1840* (Cambridge: Cambridge University Press, 2004).
11. James Mill, *The History of British India* (1817; New Delhi: Atlantic Publishers and Distributor, 1990), vol. 2, pp. 482–483.
12. For "crooked artifice," see ibid., p. 418.
13. Ibid., pp. 415–416.
14. Ibid.
15. Thomas Macaulay, "Lord Clive," in his *Poetry and Prose* (Cambridge, Mass.: Harvard University Press, 1967), quotations on p. 307.
16. See Elizabeth Kolsky, "The Body Evidencing the Crime," Ph.D. diss., Department of History, Columbia University, 2002.
17. Macaulay, "Lord Clive," quotations on pp. 313–314.
18. Quoted in ibid., p. 316.
19. Ibid., p. 319.
20. "Had the entire direction of the war been entrusted to Clive, it would probably have been brought to a speedy close," Ibid., p. 322.
21. Ibid., p. 331.
22. Ibid.
23. Ibid., quotations on p. 334.
24. Ibid., p. 370.
25. Thomas Macaulay, "Warren Hastings," in Macaulay, *Poetry and Prose*, pp. 373–469.
26. Ibid., quotations on pp. 447 and 445.
27. Mill, *History of British India*, 1817 ed., vol. 2, p. 510.
28. Quotations are from Mill, *History of British India*, revised ed. with notes by Horace Hayman Wilson (1858; New York: Chelsea House Publishers, 1968), book 6, chapter 2, pp. 198–199.
29. Ibid., p. 199.

30. G. R. Gleig, *Memoirs of the Right Hon. Warren Hastings*, 3 vols. (London: Richard Bentley, 1841).

31. Fitzjames Stephen, *The Story of Nuncomar and the Impeachment of Sir Elijah Immpey*, 2 vols. (London: Macmillan & Co., 1885).

32. Sir John Strachey, *Hastings and the Rohilla War* (Oxford: Clarendon Press, 1892).

33. P. J. Marshall, "The Making of an Imperial Icon: The Case of Warren Hastings," *Journal of Imperial and Commonwealth History* 27, no. 3 (September 1999): 1–16.

34. H. H. Dodwell, ed., *Cambridge History of India*, vol. 5: *British India* (1922–1929; Delhi: S. Chand & Co., 1968), pp. 141–180.

35. Ibid., p. 309.

36. Ibid.

37. Ibid., p. 310.

38. Ibid., p. 312.

39. For a view similar to Dodwell's, if also one more popular and florid, see Philip Woodruff's widely read two-volume history, *The Men Who Ruled India*, vol. 1: *The Founders of Modern India*, and vol. 2: *The Guardians* (New York: St. Martin's, 1954). Woodruff is a pseudonym, his real name being Philip Mason, and he has written a number of books, among them a serious history of the Indian army.

40. Seeley, *Expansion of England*, p. 154.

41. William Roger Louis, Introduction to *Oxford History of the British Empire*, vol. 5: *Historiography* (Oxford: Oxford University Press, 1999), pp. 8, 10.

42. Ibid., p. 3.

43. See my discussion of some of this literature in my *Castes of Mind: Colonialism and the Making of Modern India* (Princeton, N.J.: Princeton University Press, 2001), pp. 303–315.

44. This is not at all to say that empire meant the same thing to colonizer and colonized, as is convincingly portrayed in Bernard Porter's recent account *The Absent-Minded Imperialists: Empire, Society, and Culture in Britain* (Oxford: Oxford University Press, 2004). But colonial self-representations can no more be taken at face value than any other ones.

45. This idea is implied in David Cannadine's *Ornamentalism: How the British Saw Their Empire* (New York: Oxford University Press, 2001), pp. xix–xx.

46. This is not, of course, to argue that the history of empire has no room for victimization or subordination when the tables were turned between "colonizers" and "colonized." For a recent study of "captivity" narratives in imperial contexts, see Linda Colley, *Captives: Britain, Empire, and the World, 1600–1850* (New York: Random House, 2004).

47. Such "frozen paradigms" can be seen, for example, not just in the framing of the *Oxford History of the British Empire*, but in some of the specific contributed chapters as well. The essay on the historiography of India before 1858 by Robert Frykenberg exemplifies my point; Frykenberg complains that all the recent work influenced by Edward Said is both dogmatic and Orientalist, in certain cases the ironic—and flawed—outcome of the thinking of Westernized Indians. See Robert E. Frykenberg, "India to 1858," chapter 11 of Robin W. Winks, ed., *Historiography*, vol. 5 of the *Oxford History of the British Empire* (Oxford: Oxford University Press, 1999), pp. 211–212.

48. Niall Ferguson, *Empire: The Rise and Demise of the British World Order and the Lessons for Global Power* (New York: Basic Books, 2002).

49. Ibid., p. 27.

50. Ibid., p. 358.

51. Ibid., p. 359.

52. Ibid., p. 360.

53. Ibid., p. 370.

⊰ *Illustration Credits* ⊱

Map: James Rennell, "A General View of the Principal Roads and Divisions of Hindoostan, 1792." From *Memoir of a Map of Hindoostan: or, The Mogul Empire . . .* (Calcutta: Editions Indian, 1976 [1793]).

1. Scandal: Anonymous (perhaps J. Doughty), *Such Things May Be a Tale for Future Times*. March 1, 1788, for J. Doughty & Co. British Museum 7279, private collection. © Copyright the Trustees of The British Museum.

2. Corruption: *The India Directors in the Suds*. The Trustees of the British Museum, Department of Prints and Drawings (Political Satires no. 5102). © Copyright the Trustees of The British Museum.

3. Spectacle: R. G. Pollard, *The Trial of Warren Hastings before the Court of Peers in Westminster Hall, 13 February 1788*. 1789, after E. Day. India Office Library and Records, P2376.

4. Economy: [James Gillray,] *The Political-Banditti Assailing the Saviour of India*. May 11, 1786, by William Holland. British Museum 6955, private collection. © Copyright the Trustees of The British Museum.

5. Sovereignty: Mughal, unknown artist, *Warren Hastings in European Court Dress*. Ca. 1782. The British Library Board (Or. 6633, fol. 67a). By permission of the British Library.

6. State: Francis Hayman, *Lord Clive Meeting Mir Jafar, Nawab of Murshidabad, after the Battle of Plassey*. Ca. 1761–1762. National Portrait Gallery, London (5263).

7. History: George Willison, *Muhammed Ali Khan, Nawab of the Carnatic (1717–95)*. Ca. 1774. India Office Library and Records (F12). By permission of the British Library.

8. Tradition: Studio of Sir Joshua Reynolds, *Edmund Burke (1729–97)*. Ca. 1771. National Portrait Gallery, London (655).

9. Empire: Sir Joshua Reynolds, *Warren Hastings (1732–1818)*. Ca. 1768–1769. National Portrait Gallery, London (4445).

⊰ *Index* ⊱

Index

Walpole, Horace, 15, 143, 181
Ward, William, 303, 304
Warehouse system, 140–141
Wealth, 81, 82, 84, 125. *See also* Bengal:
    drain of wealth from; India: drain of
    wealth from
Wealth of Nations (Smith), 133, 136–139
Wellesley, Arthur ("Iron Duke"), 22, 125,
    157–159, 162, 189, 191, 297, 298, 357n15;
    British nationalism and, 239; College,

129; financial irresponsibility, 238, 240–
241; military and political ambition, 238,
239–241
Whig politics, 39, 114, 187
Wilberforce, William, 23, 32, 33, 34, 239,
297, 301–302

Zamindari (landlords), 103, 115, 119, 161,
172, 173, 218, 222, 266, 272, 277